Off With His Head

ALSO BY SEAN PATRICK GREENE

The Purple Elephant Artist

OFF WITH HIS HEAD

A Guide to Spiritual Awakening in a
Polarized, Radicalized and Digitized Society

SEAN PATRICK GREENE

For You, the Self behind the self

ACKNOWLEDGMENTS

This book would not have been possible without the help of Sveta Wunnenberg and Steve Greene. Both contributed in their unique way, the former creating art and the latter serving as de facto editor. Besides the tangible contributions each of them made to this book, it has been their willingness to read or listen with an open mind, give useful feedback and, at times, serve as the devil's advocate that has allowed the book to reach its polished form. I am grateful for each of them as well as all the others who took time to read the manuscript prior to book's release.

CONTENTS

Preface i

Introduction: Who Are You? 1

ESSAYS

CHAPTER 1: Growing Pains: How to Loosen the Stranglehold of
"Personal Identity" 21

CHAPTER 2: Memento Mori: Unmasking the Fear of Death 35

CHAPTER 3: Enlightened Self-Expression: Abandon the Wild Goose
Chase for Your Life's Purpose 42

CHAPTER 4: Political Polarization: Where to Find Wholeness in Our
Society of Division 56

CHAPTER 5: Social Justice Activism: When Moral Virtue Fuels Fear,
Hate and Vengeance. 77

CHAPTER 6: Q&A: On the Insidiousness of the Ego. 117

CHAPTER 7: The Infinite Narrative: From Unwitting Actor to
Conscious Participant. 139

POETRY

THE BOY: POETRY SERIES
The Boy, Introduction 162
*Boy Wonder 164
Bugging Me 167

The Blue Balloon 167
Big Tall Tree 168
Rage/Timidness 168
The Boy Who Picked The Sun 170
A Bird Fell 171
Fontanini, The Frog 171
Barbarian 174
Tamed Barbarian 175
Released Barbarian 176
Knight Me 177
Father to Son 178
Old Man & The Young Traveler 179

THE VOID: POETRY SERIES
The Void, Introduction 182
A Ghost From The Void 184
The Great Big Stump 185
"Sean Patrick Greene" Explains Enlightenment 186
The Meaning Of Life 188
Mental Noise 190
Kill The Wolf 191
*Fire *192
Death 193
Mediocre Individual 194
Thick Green Fog 194
#27 195
The Thinker 196
That Familiar Thing 197

THE MAN: POETRY SERIES
The Man, Introduction 198
The Jester's Many Kings 200
War On Religion 201
*Man In The Middle 203
Numbers Game 207
Intellectualism 208
Scapegoat 211
News Cycle 212
Mob Mentality 214
Hedonistic 216

All Praise The Science 218
Self-Mastery 219

THE MUSE: POETRY SERIES
The Muse, Introduction 222
*L'uomo Universale 224
Fire Ablaze 226
Jazz In The Air 228
Nature's Orchestra 231
She Is 231
The Hunter & The Doe 232
The Swan 233
Land Locked 234
L'amore Che Non Distingue 235
Beggar 238
Jasmine Green Tea 239
Become What You Are 240

Afterword 241

Endnotes 250

*Denotes the author's favorite poem from each section.

PREFACE

This book explores and seeks to open the reader's eyes to the *sickness of ideology* as it stands in our culture today. Sickness may be too visceral a word, so "collective hallucination" will also suffice. The thesis, which the majority of the poems and essays center around, is a proposed process of how an individual may break away from any collective ideological groups he or she has attached to (political, religious, etc.) in an authentic way by cultivating Self-knowledge. I use "authentic" deliberately, despite such a cliched word tasting like soap in my mouth, because for the individual to break away from a certain collective group because someone—some writer or speaker—told them to is inherently a phony act. *A reaction is not an authentic act.* This breakaway requires a revolt which stands outside the collective's call for more revolution.

It is clear to me that American society, which serves as a microcosm for divisiveness in geopolitics, is caught in the accelerating spins of both technological and moral progress, which has been intensified to the nth degree because of social media and, as will become clarified after this book is released, AI technologies.

We are in dire need of seeing *what is*—unobstructed by abstraction.

Concepts and theories have so overtaken the psyche that the vast majority of human beings cannot see what is right in front of them except through many layers of opinionated thought. Yes, I am speaking about political views—liberal and conservative equally—but in a much wider sense than who one votes for. I am making the claim that moral-political sects are substituting religion (in the social institution sense of the word) and that the ideal of heaven/salvation has been replaced by the ideal of total equality (liberal) or the ideal of returning to the good ol' days (conservative).

The danger in such ideals is often clear from the opposition's perspective (just ask a conservative what's wrong with the liberal's agenda and vice versa), but almost everyone is blind to their own flaws. This willful blindness to the flaws of one's own opinions and ideas for "a better tomorrow" are the crux of the insane behaviors we are witnessing in, and of, the media—both on television and social platforms—on each side of the political aisle. Not only does it hurt our fellow human beings, who have been cast to the rank of "other" because of your opinion about their opinion, but this resistance to what we don't "vibe with" is poisoning our own mind and body.

Depression, anxiety, lack of self-esteem, binge eating, anorexia, social media dependency, drug or alcohol addiction, social isolation, chronic stress, unquenchable greed or lust, uncontrollable rage, seeking historical retribution—all of these are symptoms; expressions of a resistance to *what is* (both in one's inner and outer environment).

Though who am I, to stand on my high horse, and claim that everyone with a political leaning is flawed in their thinking? Read this closely: *The flaw is not in whichever opinion one holds, but the very nature of thought and self-identity as a whole.*

"Off With His Head" is a preemptive declaration, an anticipation of the reader's response to the author of this book; a book which will so alter one's awareness of his or her own mental noise that no mind will come away unscathed.

I lost my head writing this book; by that I mean I lost all fear of preserving my self-identity. I wish the same freedom for you.

Nothing of my background explains why this book came to be. I am no expert. I am no professor. I am no intellectual (and I reference very few of them). The beauty, though, is that the message seeded throughout the book doesn't need a qualified voice to make it stick. It is entirely based on the "fertility of the soil" in the reader's mind whether this book will read as life-altering or nonsensical babble. My status as a nobody allows the words to be read without another filter of abstraction layered over it.

At times, I will touch on certain religions or philosophies to make a point, but this is not a book *about* Christianity, Taoism, Buddhism, Hinduism, stoicism, postmodernism, etc. This book is nothing but an antonym to all "-isms." With that said, I am attempting to fight fire with fire (i.e., using concept-heavy essays and poetry to assist the reader in seeing such concepts as merely a shadow of *what is*), so you will be required at times to make leaps *off the page*. If I write, "poke your head out of this book and take notice of where you are," I mean that. That is a leap off the page. If your nose stays in the book for its entirety, then the message will be lost on you.

It has been a great joy and honor to write this book. This has been the most important project I have undertaken in my life so far. While it may not move mountains in the culture, as long as it alters *your* awareness of the thoughts swimming in *your* mind—however subtle that shift may be—it has succeeded in its mission.

— Sean Patrick Greene
St. Louis, Missouri
January 2024

Introduction:
Who Are You?

I believe that I have cosmic religious feelings. I never could grasp how one could satisfy these feelings by praying to limited objects. The tree outside is life, a statue is dead. The whole of nature is life, and life, as I observe it, rejects a God resembling man. I like to experience the universe as one harmonious whole. Every cell has life. Matter, too, has life; it is energy solidified.

— Albert Einstein

This book is not for everyone, nor even for most people. What began as a chance to write a collection of poetry with no constraints has transformed into something much deeper. This is a spiritual book written for the rational, secular thinker. It is also a philosophical book written for the dogmatic, theistic thinker.

It appears paradoxical that a single book could be written for two groups so different from each other. Their connection is not in the specific contents of their beliefs, but their fundamental assertion that *they* have *the* correct framework for which to interpret the world. In simple terms, they assume their beliefs make them superior to all others.

Together they stand: United in their arrogance.

I am, of course, speaking in generalities, and there are large segments of people with the kind of humility described throughout the book's essays. In one sense, what is meant by the title "Off With His Head," is to live with a self-selected humility in the face of the Great Mystery (i.e., one's own existence), which most people in developed countries arrogantly, or ignorantly, presume has been demystified with the scientific method many times over.

There is a cosmic irony in this demystification process whereby the more one learns about the universe, the more branching questions arise out of one's supposed knowledge. To pick just one example, it was Democritus, the Grecian philosopher, who philosophized the existence of the atom. The original Greek word, *atomos*, could be translated as "indivisible." Yet, the question soon became, what makes up the atom? And of the things that make up the atom, what makes up those particles? And so, and so, *ad infinitim*.

The thinking mind, as will be shown, is ignorant of its own arising thought processes. Not necessarily in retrospect, but in the moment when emotion-sparking situations arise. As the late spiritual teacher Ram Dass used to say, "If you think you're so enlightened, go spend a week with your parents." How often does one feel competent and in control of their life before some person or event flips it all upside down? In these "All is Lost" moments, most would hold a clenched fist to the sky and curse their Creator (or some secular equivalent like "Society"), but what if such moments were treated as part of the adventure? As opportunities for growth? As the fullness of life?

If such shifts in perspective sound foolish or unrealistic, then it is clear that the rational mind has overstepped and is creating more suffering than it relieves. **As one reads this book with an open mind, leaving presuppositions at the door, they will see not an attack on secular rationality, but a critique of its limitations and a chance to go beyond them.**

Just as an art critique is designed to make the future work better and not belittle the artist, this critique on the thinking mind is designed to turn thought into a work of art and return the metaphorical paint brush back to the Self. Thus, the most important question for the reader to ask, as the critique of rational thought (and theistic thought) is presented, is *who am I?*

If one feels offended in reading anything in this book, *who is it that feels offended?* If one doubts the experiential truth that the words point to, *who is it that doubts the truth?* Such questions are not meant to be answered in words, but by being aware of who (or what) exists as the observer of the arising thoughts and emotions in the mind and body.

WHO AM I?

In asking "Who am I?" from a Western perspective, it is assumed—at least when sitting across from a therapist—that there is a mask of outward personality and a *single*, fearful, insecure self lying behind it. The latter being who one "truly" is. Something like a ghost in the shell, but not a "soul"—something more secular and scientific-sounding.

We might call it "ego," as Sigmund Freud presented it: That abstract mass of the human psyche caught between the *id* (i.e., animalistic desire) and the *superego* (i.e., moral standards and social acceptability). Yet, even in common speech the average person says, "I *have* an ego," or "That's *my* ego talking."

Who, then, *has* the ego?

We cannot say it is mind or body because both terms are used in a similar fashion: "I *have* a body," or "*My* mind keeps on ..." Nor is it enough to throw up one's hands and claim that "Who am I?" is too complex a question or too inconsequential to daily life. The implications of understanding who one is, in their essence, can shift the entire outlook of one's life, and thereby, end the fear and suffering once foundational to one's existence (i.e., the so-called human condition).

It sounds like a lofty, near-utopian promise. It is not. Only from a state of ignorance does the end of suffering read as hyperbole.

Conversely, only with Self-knowledge is the end of suffering self-evident.

The idea that one's identity *is* the content of one's thoughts, no matter how starkly they change from day to day, has its philosophical foundation in René Descartes' work. Along with his famed quote, "I think, therefore I am," he is also popular for his philosophy of mind-body dualism. This idea supposes that mind (i.e., thoughts) and body (i.e., physical matter) are of two distinct substances; the former being non-material.

I believe this generalized understanding of mind-body dualism *alone* underlies the conception of self for most, if not *all*, secular/areligious individuals.

Thus, "mind," in this sense, encompasses id, ego and superego as they arise as thoughts. When I previously mentioned "*my* mind keeps on... ," (implying an entity which supersedes the mind), to keep with Descartes' philosophy, this thought is a product of language, which *still* originates from the non-material substance called "mind."

In simple terms, who the average person *thinks* he or she is a self-conditioning bundle of thought patterns that begin with the body's birth and ends with its death. A person is not the body, per se, but the collection of thoughts and memories that occur *while* one is alive.

Although most people would not answer "I am my thoughts!" upon sincere inquiry into one's self, all specific and idiosyncratic answers to "Who am I?" (e.g., I am a young writer who grew up in ... who wants to ... who likes to ...) are products of thought that stem from "mind."

The problem with the rational sentiment, "I think, therefore I am," is that someone can "think" while remaining totally ignorant to the real-world consequences of those thoughts. Those consequences, often originating from idealist sentiments like, "We must rid the world of evil oppressors," can in themselves lead to tyrannical genocides and a baffling denial of common sense.

On an individual level, **when the thinking mind runs unchecked, a sense of helplessness—of being bound to a stream of self-guilting, self-sabotaging and self-loathing thoughts—can arise.**

Therefore, to accept that the mind is *who you are* despite its corrosive and counterproductive nature, is like watching a horror movie convinced that you trapped in the film!

This naive clinging to Descartes' rationalism (i.e., that self-aware thought is foundational to one's existence) prevents a human being from observing reality beyond the level of thought and mind; beyond the level of fear and suffering.

FROM DESCARTES TO FREUD

Such an assumption (of equating one's "self" with one's thoughts) does have strong ties to modern psychology. The goal is often to change one's perception of self by altering one's thought patterns and changing (or coping with) the undesirable personality traits—like anxious or depressive tendencies—by "getting to the root of it."

It comes back to Sigmund Freud, who emphasized the "unconscious mind" as the driver behind undesirable thoughts and emotional patterns. Although based on clinical experience, this observation simply provided new language for Descartes' original insight: The body influences the mind and vice versa.[1] In contemporary terms, one might phrase it as "the body keeps score."

---

1   In combining mind-body dualism (in philosophy) with the unconscious-conscious split (in psychology), we might say "mind" relates to the conscious and "body" relates to the unconscious. Although laypeople have a vague understanding that their unconscious is "a piece of them," it is only ever known directly when it rises to the level of thought. Said another way, someone can understand that he is both his conscious and unconscious self, but he only *identifies* with his conscious side. It is this direct experience of identification that matters—not the conceptual knowledge of psychological buzzwords—when talking about disidentifying from one's thoughts and outgrowing mental suffering.

So, coming into the 20th century, the role of childhood trauma in present day neuroses was popularized, "repression" became a buzz-word, and sex, Freud claimed, was always on the brain. Over time, his theories and interventions were overshadowed by new, contemporary schools of psychology, but many of his foundational concepts endure.

The most notable of which—at least notable to this book—is that one's "self" is formed by one's collection of thoughts that bubble up from the unconscious mind, which all get masked behind an out-ward-facing personality (that takes on a consistent, habitual quality).

I believed that for most of this life.

Thus, the people who knew that adolescent named Sean Greene knew only the shallow surface of him, or so I believed. This belief that I was hiding a piece of me from the world was accompanied by a heavy, trembling sense of fear. *If the people only knew!* Or so the inner-mono-logue often cried in its melodramatic pitch. Knew what? I know not, except that this fear had a shadowy, world-ending quality to it.[2]

THE SHIFT

It is difficult to point to exactly what shifted, but sometime in col-lege, and more deeply in the midst of writing this book, the melo-drama of mind became easier to spot as such: Drama. Drama is not reality. Drama is acting. Drama is emotion played out for cathartic viewing—except that implies seeing the drama of mind *as* a drama. For the young Sean Greene, this mind drama was never given such a perspective. I presume most readers have not given their thoughts this perspective either.

This "mind drama" will only grow more severe as generative AI models like ChatGPT become increasingly entwined in people's lives. In the turmoil of this technological revolution, many human beings will wake up to the realization that they are (or will soon be) inferior to these AI systems in every way once deemed unique to human beings. That makes this time in history especially ripe for a shift in conscious-

---

2   In one instance that seems trivial now, in high school, I was mortally ter-rified of my peers discovering that I played the video game Minecraft in my spare time (because it was known as a childish game) and being ridiculed for it. It's clear the fear coincided with, and was likely influenced by, pubescent growth, but the fear was intensified by the illusion of *total identification* with the thoughts. I could not escape the fear because, I presumed, I *was* the sense of fear (and corresponding thoughts) in the moment they arose.

ness: to escape the trap of compulsive thinking and to identify with something much more expansive, yet ineffable in comparison to one's stream of thoughts.

This is not an abstract, conceptual idea, but rather something quite real that can only be known directly—in this moment now. As an analogy, it is the difference between a *picture* of a tree and the *actual* tree.

We can acknowledge that language and thought (i.e., the picture of …) can *approximate* what is happening, but the trap is in believing thought and language are *equivalent* to what is happening. The photo is *not* the actual thing—yet, the thinking mind is blind to the difference because it *is* the photo! This fundamental mistake of how we relate to the world, as will be shown throughout the book, can allow ideals and ideologies, which always originate as thoughts, to take precedence over the actual-ness of the present moment. On the surface, it seems like aiming for a better future is "the right thing to do," but there have been enough violent revolutions, fascist dictatorships and genocides to prove that the ends *do not* justify the means.

I consider it willful ignorance when an individual acknowledges a history of past injustices based on ideology, yet sees their own ideological-based ambitions (political or otherwise) as something uniquely pure. However, when the game feels like life or death (as when one's egoic identity is at stake), I can understand why this blindness occurs on such a massive scale.

In a way, this book points to the drama of mind directly within the reader so as to inspire joy and peace in observing the spectacle of existence from this "here and now" rather than being swept into the drama as an unwitting actor. Too many people are caught in their acting role as it stands today.

All the more dangerous are the people who *think* they're rebelling against such mind drama; who believe they have seen behind the curtain of "brainwashing" institutions and now see the *real* truth. These conspiratorial types often believe a reactive, convoluted ideology to the one that the mainstream world presents. While I do believe some mainstream ideologies are becoming an impediment to objective science and cultural open-mindedness, I do not presume that it is merely a handful of billionaires pulling all the strings. As the adage goes:

> "Never attribute to malice that which is adequately explained by stupidity."

So it is both groups, the mainstream and the fringe (which encompasses a range of viewpoints), who believe they have discovered "absolute truth" and thereby close themselves off to opposing evidence and people with different opinions.

This kind of ideological tribalism stems from a lack of Self-knowledge. So long as the reader assumes she is the controller of her thoughts, she will have no choice but to believe her mental monologue that vilifies, belittles and demeans anyone with a different perspective. Only by *being aware* of one's thoughts—rather than identified purely with the *contents* of thought—can this tribal tendency be superseded.

To point to the sky on a cloudy day and proclaim, "It will rain," is not to control the weather. By the same token, to say, "I think these thoughts! I choose my beliefs! I make up my mind!" is not to be the controller of arising thoughts (since those claims *are* arising thoughts too).

The question may then arise, *if you say I don't think my own thoughts, then who does?* You do, of course, but this "You" whom I refer to is not the limited, conditioned egoic self (i.e., who you *think* you are), but something more expansive. You are Awareness—the witness of all experience. I can say this, and know it as self-evident, but it will not be understood by the reader until it is experienced directly. Although the experience cannot be put into words, this book seeks to point to It for you to access this Self-knowledge.

What the hell is this guy talking about? Has he lost his mind?

Has a judgement arisen in the reader's mind yet? To some, this book may read as "spiritual," in the degrading and disregarding connotation of the word. God will be mentioned more than once (in ways that are sure to offend *someone*). If certain terms—whether of Christian, Hindu, Buddhist or of a contemporary origin—create enough resistance in the reader as to prevent them from finishing an essay or poem, then it is quite certain such a reader is not ready to hear its message. Perhaps there is not enough curiosity, nor enough suffering, to read with an open mind.

I say that like a gadfly (i.e., someone who intentionally provokes) because resistance to *any* kind of language, and a firm clutching to *some* language, is a trap. The same trap that ensnares you in your vices and addictions. The same trap that ensnares you in perpetual seeking and unease with this moment. The same trap that ensnares You to you: the Unconditioned Consciousness to the fearful, egoic self.

In surrendering to the mind drama, which requires only a small shift in perspective, an immense sense of freedom, peace and child-like joy opens up to the individual. This is not hypothetical or abstract, and any thoughts that "this must be hyperbole" exists only in the reader's mind.

These innate qualities of joy, which arise when you become aware of who you are (beyond name and form), do not require the reader to buy-in to a certain religious doctrine or understand a certain psychological theory or be blessed by some supernatural figure.

It requires surrendering to this moment now.

THE PURPOSE OF THIS BOOK

The prelude of this book expressed the work's central premise: *Ideology has blinded us from reality*. Concepts and theories and philosophies of all sorts, and on all [political] sides, have filtered the way we perceive the world to a dizzying degree. These conceptions of the world are now so ingrained in the psyche that, like a pair of forgotten contact lenses, we consider dry and irritated eyes (i.e., an agitated, fearful, self-centered worldview) to be the way things must be.

I write so the reader may remember. Remember what, exactly? That who you *think* you are—the little ol' egoic you—is not the thinker of thoughts but the byproduct *of* thought patterns. The real You, on the other hand, is the observer of that which occurs Now. You are Unconditioned Awareness; the thinking mind is only a small aspect of that.

As a simple way to verify this, close the book for a brief moment and listen for the faintest or most distant sound that can be heard. This exercise is most effective in a quiet place.

☼☼☼

What was heard is irrelevant. All that matters (assuming the reader did the exercise) is that there was listening without labeling the sounds with thoughts. How can one *be aware* that there is a quiet electric buzzing or a faint hum from an air vent in the other room or a trickling sound from the faucet or a bird chirping on the tree in the backyard? It surely was not the thinking mind that *knew* how to hear these sounds or "willed" them into clarity.

"Enter Zen from there," says the master to the pupil who listens for the faint sound of the babbling brook, in a classic Zen anecdote. This is to walk the razor's edge of Now. This is the immeasurable suchness of reality before thought-forms pull one's focus into its drama and incessant labeling of what is.

For any reader familiar with the story of Buddha's flower sermon, that is what it points to—the suchness. For those who do not know, the Buddha was said to have held a white flower before his disciples without saying a word. No one understood the message—except one person, who smiled. *This* is the suchness; not the summarized story a line ago, but the hands that hold this book and the eyes that see this ink. The total, *unspeakable* perception. If the book has a smell when you leaf through the pages—that too is real.[3]

With a phenomenon like smell, it is obviously sensory. One is aware when they are smelling something—especially something pungent like a rose—but thinking is not required to confirm this awareness. To think, *I smelled this rose and it smells quite nice,* occurs retrospectively and as a way for the egoic mind to maintain the illusion of control over the world.

So, just like the sense of smell, there is the sensation of thinking. You are sensing thought (i.e., being aware of thought) but not willfully squeezing it into existence. I understand that, on the surface, it's not so revelatory an insight. Most people understand that thoughts aren't *always* in their control. Modern cognitive behavioral therapists have coined the term ANTs (Automatic Negative Thoughts) for those pesky things.[4] It's almost cute; let's just squish them out of mind. How wonderful …

Except what's missed is the obvious truth that *the thoughts that theorized the concept are just as "automatic" as the ANTs.*[5] A single idea sprung to mind out of the near infinite possibilities. Even in brainstorming multiple ideas (in this example, to coin a certain theory),

---

3   I am hesitant to use the word "real," especially after reading *The Nature of Consciousness* by Rupert Spira, but for most people who have never separated awareness from thinking, it is fair to say unlabeled perception (i.e., pure, silent awareness) is "more real" than the thinking mind which, as an example, labels every distinct and unique tree in the forest with a catch-all term called "tree."

4   The term appears to have its origins with Dr. Aaron T. Beck, one of the fathers of cognitive behavioral therapy.

5   The word "automatic" has a connotation of being mechanical. The arising of thoughts is closer to the growth of a flower, so organic growth may be a closer description. However, even the term "organic" seems to be confined to plant growth. *I find "self-so" to be the label that best embodies the middle ground of automatic/mechanical and organic growth.* It will be used quite a bit throughout the book and has its origins in Taoist and Buddhist philosophies.

each answer arises "self-so." To claim, as I imagine a neuroscientist would, that these creative ideas arise while "such and such part of the brain" is active and it is called the "*such and such* activation system" is again placing abstract concepts *retrospectively* on what is.

This is not a point to gloss over: To realize that the contents of thought are being observed by You is to realize that *all* of one's assumed-to-be identity is being sensed (i.e., being made aware of). Most people I presume, without further inspection, would disagree with me:

> *Of course I'm my thoughts! I'm thinking right now, aren't I? How can you say something so stupid!*

This total identification with one's thoughts is what is called "ego," in the spiritual sense. It is that unconscious identification with thoughts that *is* the root of violence and divisiveness in any society. You do not need to believe all thoughts, and with alertness, patience and discernment, you can begin to distinguish fearful or anger-inducing *thought patterns* from creative, responding-to-the-present-situation thoughts.

In this, the thinking mind becomes a tool rather than a trap. The paintbrush is thereby returned to the Painter.

To get to that point, it requires a foundation of something deeper to identify with in moments where no thought is required. Without this, one will continue to be swept into the ever-shifting drama of the thinking mind, which will continue to feel uncontrollable and create mental suffering.

✿✿✿

Many thoughts, potentially fearful ones, may arise when the above paragraph is meditated on for a few extra moments, but it will ultimately boil down to:

> *Even if I believe what you're saying, what am supposed to do with this realization? Am I meant to feel something new or be compelled to take some kind of action?*

Not at all. There is no special emotional state that is felt because You realize that, in your essence, you are Pure Awareness—the eternal subject to all passing objects (including inner-objects like thoughts and emotions). It is like resting in the deep part of the ocean while all the surface-level waves of emotion, memory, external perception and thoughts flow through the body. It is a bedrock of peace; an understanding, beyond language, that *this* is all okay.

So, although this book *is* information and one could hypothetically do a book report summarizing the main points, I seek to write in a way that makes you quite conscious that you are reading a book in this present moment. You have already arrived; you are in the Now! In fact, *You* are indistinguishable from the Now (but this will be explained later on).

If such a message when communicated through language would inspire and enlighten upon impact, then I would not be writing this book for there would be no need for it. So I see this book as one bucket of water in the pool of spiritual books that ultimately point to the same spacious, formless, empty, nothing-ness. *Śūnyatā, Tao, Para Brahman*—these words, too, point the same way, from their respective Eastern traditions.

I add a splash of artfulness in the poems, but at its core, this book is written to wake up the reader to their true Self. Who you are beyond name and form. I did not know that from the outset, but as I near the end of writing, that has become clear.

It must be understood though that the ego can convince itself that it has "gotten it." To *think* that you understand what this book points to, "Oh, yes, that makes sense. I agree, I agree," is to allow the ego to enter through the back door, per se.

There is no need to agree with the thoughts that arise in the mind as you read. The answer is experienced, not conceptually understood. Let stillness of mind be the measure of understanding.

A NOTE ABOUT THE ESSAYS

In the essay portion, I switch between referring to myself as "I" and "the author" on an essay-by-essay basis. The three essays where "I" is used consistently is because of one of three reasons:

- To signify a personal opinion, not a spiritual truth.
- To reflect on a personal memory, not a universal insight.
- To add a level of humility to the work.

The ultimate goal has been to minimize my personality as much as possible in order to create a book that shares spiritual truth without the baggage of me, the ego, Sean Patrick Greene (especially if the reader knows the author on a personal level). It is not *my* spiritual truth. I did not invent it, but rather realize it, as many others have, and do my best to point to it.

One other thing the reader may notice is the many words capitalized in a grammatically incorrect context: "Self," "You," "Consciousness," "Awareness," "Presence," "It," etc. This is a symbolic way of differentiating between the egoic self and the essential Self.

Since the words are merely pointer sticks, not absolute in their own right, I mix terms often. Sometimes ego is referred to as the "egoic self," the "conditioned personality" or the "thinking mind." Sometimes Self is referred to as "Pure Awareness," "Silent Awareness," "Unconditioned Consciousness" or "the Witness." *Be aware of the distinction, but do not get caught up on any specific term.* The difference will become intuitive as you read on.

A NOTE ABOUT THE POETRY

This book closes with a variety of poems. I am sure, if the book is read in order, that many readers will feel compelled to skip or gloss over them. Poetry is not for everyone—including myself. Yes, as ironic as it reads, I have written more poems than I have read over the past five years, and most of that writing appears in this book. It is for this reason that I believe the poetry here will be more enjoyable to the layperson than the creative writing scholar (for the poems' contents took priority over the precision of poetic form).

Read the poems with a sense of ease. Let the realizations, if any arise while reading, come naturally. The themes of the poetry will overlap with the essay, and this is by design. The hope is that, if the essays are read first, then the poetry will read like flowing water. They provide rhythm, rhyme and visual metaphors to crystallize the points emphasized in the essays.

Since there are more than 50 poems included, I have decided to organize them up into four sections: The Boy, The Void, The Man and The Muse. The order is representative of my personal evolution from boyhood to now. I will touch on each of them briefly.

The Boy

The poems in this section represent a childish stage of mind. Although they vary in content and mood, the overarching point is an archetypal disillusionment with the adult world. Not everyone is helpful. Adults no longer bend to a child's will, as they may have when the kid was a wailing infant. In some poems, the subject craves validation (as seen in *Knight Me* or *Boy Wonder*). Other poems, like *The Boy Who Picked the Sun* and *Rage/Timidness*, are written as if giving advice to the reader still navigating their own youth.

I cannot imagine a young child reading this book, but it is one I may have read myself around the age of 16 or 17. Rather than alter one's current childhood, this section speaks to the adult or teenager (man or woman) who has become aware of certain childish elements in their own behavior as it stands today (e.g., validation seeking, holding grudges, acting like a know-it-all, etc.).

Not all the poems are written from a young child's point of view. The most clear example of an "aging" perspective is the trilogy poems of "Barbarian," "Tamed Barbarian" and "Released Barbarian."

Those three poems stand for the arc of my own experience in K-12 schooling. My rambunctiousness was quickly curbed in elementary school, and I spent the majority of my adolescence as a quiet, well-behaved student. This behavior was not out of goodwill, but out of fear.

These learned morals, taught by other tamed ones,
Clogged the nozzle from which the barbarian's spirit flows.

This line in "Released Barbarian" stands for the tipping point and a true "waking up" from the conformity of this character's schooling. I believe my experience of stifled creativity in school is common. I hope any reader still caught in this stifled, insecure state will become aware of it through these poems so as to grow beyond it.

THE VOID

Although the previous section had hints of disillusionment regarding the behavior of adults, "The Void" takes this disillusionment even deeper: The disillusionment of the nature of reality. Although word "void" rightly embodies the mental image of nothingness (or black, empty space), this section *avoids* what could become a nihilistic or hopeless-sounding worldview. Although death is mentioned more than once in this section, the optimistic message underscoring this section is expressed at the end of "The Great Big Stump":

No, I will not resist the heaviness in my heart
When death strikes down too soon,
But Nature has taught me to keep
A keen ear for the ever-longer tune.

The point is not to dwell in the hopelessness that initially arises in facing one's mortality, but to keep on listening to Nature—which includes the natural, like plants and animals, and the artificial, like human-made systems. Hopelessness comes as a wave, not an eternal feeling.

I expect the poem "'Sean Patrick Greene' Explains Enlightenment" to be one which stands out in this section. It represents an insight of peace in the realization that there is no "jackpot" emotional state of mind called enlightenment. There is a touch of irony, of course, for explaining enlightenment or claiming to be enlightened misses the point. No ego can be enlightened. I am aware of this even if "Sean Patrick Greene" is sometimes swept into the allure of praise.

THE MAN

This section, I sense, is most bound for misinterpretation. "All Praise the Science" and "War on Religion" both have the potential to polarize the audience. Yet, it all boils down to the same theme: **Belief in any theory, creed, ideology or ideal can lead to insanity and divisiveness in the unexamined mind.** Said another way, without a clear understanding of *who* the believer of beliefs *is*, there can be no acceptance of the "other" (i.e., people who think differently) and no humility about one's own opinions.

Many attempts have been made in this book to avoid one-sidenessness, and the measure of success in this task will ultimately be: *Does everyone feel, at least, a little bit offended?*

Yes, offense may be taken. Take it or leave it. Just be aware of any double standards you impose. Blind belief in "the Science" is the same blindness as blind belief in a religious dogma. The only difference is language, justification and fervor (which is more closely tied with dogmatic religious belief).

The note about blind belief in science, synonymous with scientism, is not to be confused with true, impartial, non-politicized science. This will be detailed in length in a later essay *because* it is something that requires careful phrasing. I am endlessly curious about the advances of science, but I take issue with individuals who hold a morally superior stature because of their knowledge of politically justifying scientific facts. Statistics-based sociological, psychological and economic studies are what come to mind when I think of this kind of scientism (i.e., using weak, unscrutinized statistical evidence to justify moral beliefs). This point is far removed from physics, engineering or any other hard science.

There is also no shying away from politics either. "Man in the Middle" perhaps most embodies my [limited] perspective regarding the modern political landscape. In the work, the allusion to Emmanuel Goldstein from George Orwell's *1984* (the scapegoat to the Big Brother government) feels particularly relevant to today's political discourse:

> *Die, Emmanuel Goldstein! Die!*
> *(In the name of justice, we seek the villain).*
> *Die, Emmanuel Goldstein! Die!*
> *(In the name of virtue, we seek the villain).*
> *Die, Emmanuel Goldstein! Die!*
> *(In the name of peace, we seek the villain).*
> *Die, Emmanuel Goldstein! Die!*
> *(In the name of purpose, we seek the villain).*

Substitute "Emmanuel Goldstein" with Donald Trump or Joe Biden or even an abstract word like "racism" and voilà, the stanza holds true to a number of Americans' attitudes. Liberal or conservative, there has been a crescendo of villains to point out as "our enemy."

This kind of vilification is a mental filter that keeps one at a distance from the states of mind they claim to be "fighting" for. This is how insane the mind can be when an individual derives their sense of self from ideology and idealism![6]

If such claims were dropped, even if only in the reader's mind, then the foundation of ideology one "fights for" would have to be dropped as well. That means, one's sense of self would *have to* dissolve in the process. Said another way, if there is peace in this moment, then no

---

6   In regards to idealism in particular, there is nothing wrong with holding an ideal (e.g., be humble, give charitably, love thy neighbor, etc.), but the problems arise when such ideals are imposed on the whole population: Suddenly, non-humble people are being killed in the name of humility. The point is that ideals become poisonous when a person decides that the imperfect world we all live in must be made perfect according to *their* conception of perfection. Ego is at the root of this impulse.

clash for the sake of future peace is required[7]—no "social activist" identity needs to be clung to.

Like the point about science vs. scientism, there is a line to walk. There can be the pursuit of justice *without* vilifying the political opposition. The essay titled "Political Polarization: Where to Find Wholeness in Our Society of Division" will explore this in more depth.

THE MUSE

In a way, the topics covered in the Man are more bleak than those in the Void section (and more pressing to modern culture). Thus, the poems in The Muse attempt to wrestle with the question: *What does one do if they're not fighting for some future idealistic goal?* One can make art, of course, as I am doing here. Though, I am not so arrogant as to think *everyone* is destined to spend a lifetime as an artist.

The pursuit of justice or scientific knowledge or certain political policies can still be pursued, but the vilification of the other *must* be released in the process if one is to end suffering in their own mind.[8] It requires coming to terms with one's own capability for evil, or one's "shadow," as the late analytical psychologist Carl Jung put it. To let go of the compulsion to identify more enemies requires a deep dive into the nature of one's self as the silent awareness that underlies all thought.

I find "Fire Ablaze" to be the response to the incessant search for a perfect theory to explain the nature of things:

> *Between the untenable void, between the spinning galaxies,*
> *Between the sun and the moon,*
> *There is us. There is I. There is You.*
> *Small is our glint, rhythmic is our tune.*

---

7   The reader must understand that this is not a grand and sweeping call for pacifism on a geopolitical level, but rather for you, the individual who reads this now. Be cautious of taking the words in this book and making them ideological. This work is not a plea to change the fabric of "society," only to raise the consciousness of the present reader.

8   *But I can't be at peace until the last hungry child is fed! But I can't be happy until I have made my first million dollars! But I can't _____ until _____!* And who came up with these thoughts? Must you believe such insane thoughts, which keep you perpetually dissatisfied and tense? Of course you must, to the extent you believe it's good for "you."

We are the loud. We are the quiet. We are the real.
    Feel, in every porous sense, our true and mighty repose.
Untold, but always shown,
    Indefatigable *is the chant by which all life grows.*

I must give a nod to Pablo Neruda; his work inspired the repetitious quality of the poem.

Other poems in this section point to "The Muse" as a symbol of that which compels effortless action. There is an element of faith involved (strip the word of its religious connotation, please) because no cut-and-dried answer of what one ought to do with their life can ever be given with absolute certainty.

Even if an answer were provided by some authority figure, would there not be doubt as to whether they are correct in their advice?

This "seeking of certainty" is not exclusive to the realm of career-based purpose; it also relates to intimate love. "L'Amore Che Non Distingue (The Love Which Does Not Distinguish)" explores how "true love," as an ideal of perfection, is a contrived aim that ultimately misses the point of love. From the poem:

Ten-thousand more metaphors,
    Spoken until blue in the face.
Ten-thousand more expressions,
    Spoken until hollow to the ear.

This stanza points not only to overused love lines (more often in Hallmark cards than said aloud), but encompasses an overuse of *all* "tried and true" information. We, as in all of humanity, are not needing a new combination of words for a certain message, one of world peace or total equality, to click. We are in need of silence and stillness. No amount of words will ever give us that. This ever-increasing "sea of information" is, in fact, the impediment.

A NOTE ABOUT THE TITLE

I feel it is only right to conclude with the intention of the violent-sounding title. Of course, the obvious reference is to the Middle Ages capital punishment of beheading. The not-so-difficult leap to the present day regards the digital beheading of certain influential figures (i.e., canceling someone). These modern day beheadings are often less related to someone breaking the law and more related to someone breaking one of the ever-changing cultural morals. Even in the midst of writing this book, I have observed a general pendulum shift away from a distaste for the all-too-eager canceling "woke mob" to a distaste for the all-too-eager complainers of "cancel culture."

When individuals, especially those in their 20s and younger, are building their morals and virtues on foundations of sand, an existential insecurity can arise. "Sand" in this case represents the plentiful and ever-evolving narratives of "how to live rightly" found on all social media platforms.

Without a deeper foundation of meaning and understanding of one's identity, which is ultimately infinite and ineffable, individuals are incredibly susceptible to propaganda, unquestionable ideology and feelings of hate toward those with an oppositional belief system.[9]

It is no surprise that the rise of social media has correlated with the rise of divisive politics in America; when attention is the commodity, on platforms with no gatekeepers, extremism and sensationalism are more fundamental than dignity and integrity. Winning is more important than winning fair-and-square because the rules (as in, collective moral principles) are always changing and splitting *within* the game.

> As an analogy, it is as absurd as a football game in which the running back declares a one-minute, no-tackle rule *while* he runs down field with the ball. And it is as nonsensical as someone on the other team simultaneously declaring a 15-yard penalty because they don't approve of the other team's no-tackle rule. This is not to say "referees" are the solution, as in a top-down regulatory approach. It goes much deeper: There must be a collective understanding of the game [of modern life] and its rules of play.

Although disputes are inevitable in every sport, any of them can be played by a group of strangers in a scrimmage fashion regardless of the presence of a referee. It's only because the fundamental rules

---

9   I will not be surprised if someone completely disagrees with the book's central theme; I would have no feelings of hate or resistance because I am secure in my knowing. It requires no external proof and cannot be swayed by any external counter proof. It sounds closed off until one understands that this "closed off point of view" is in defense of an openness toward, and awareness of, all points of view.

are understood. These rules are synonyms with "how to play." The structure *makes* the game; only in a state of ignorance would someone believe these mutually understood rules ruin the game or make it unfair for one side.

It is also true that when someone believes the game is life and death, rules fly out the window. This is what we are witnessing in the media with sensationalized politics. *If this man or woman wins the election, then life as you know it is over! We must do everything in our power to stop them!*

In its more subtle manifestation, we miss the influence it has on how we see our fellow human beings. Vaccinations, trans rights, racism—these words, these mental concepts, mere *vibrations of air* when spoken aloud, can turn an open-minded person into a brick wall of belief:

> *But we must stand for (or against) these things! It is the right thing to do! We must help (or tear down) this ignorant person so they see how wrong they are! It's for their own good!*

No, too often, the vehement defense of certain, vaguely described ideals and ideologies is the means by which one feels superior to another. It's how the ego feeds itself. I ask that the reader remain open-minded enough throughout this book to explore if there's any truth to that idea.

But I digress. Yes, the book's title nods to this cancel/post-cancel culture we are living in (depending where one gets their news). However, the title has a much more intimate meaning. "Off With His Head" refers to my own, to Sean Patrick Greene's head: The man, the myth, the ego; the collection of past experiences, present-day beliefs, and ambitions aimed out in the future. I use my own limited, egoic identity as a way to spot your own.

This "egoic identity" is not exclusive to one's selfish or arrogant behaviors as the term "ego" has come to mean in modern times. Yes, it is true that anyone who "has a big head," in reference to an inflated opinion of one's self, will one day have his worldview broken because it does not align with the reality of the world at large. However, I am claiming that, in our modern techo-centric culture on the brink of an AI revolution, selfish and arrogant behavior is baked into the system (namely, social media platforms).

So, whether you consider yourself humble or cocky, cautious or courageous, modest or unabashed, the nature of our social technologies are pushing us toward solipsism (i.e., the philosophical view that the world *literally* revolves around you) and tribalism simultaneously. In essence, social media makes us self-centered, overconfident in our opinions, and sheltered in echo chambers of like-minds.

We need an antidote, something to offset the social pull to engage in egoic tendencies, but what? This does not require a religious conversion or a change in philosophy, but an awareness of what underlies all existence, in general, and all language, in particular. To know this, to experience it, not merely as a concept or bundle of words, is to know who you are in your essence.

So let us both, the reader and the writer of this book, begin the search for a sense of self that is not reliant on *any* set of beliefs or opinions. This search is dissimilar to finding a buried treasure—we need not travel to distant lands. In fact, all that is required to discover who we are is to remove all the filters of belief, judgement and opinion that have so blinded us from the suchness of life.

Who are you, if you cannot bring in the past or future? Who are you, if you cannot stand atop your foundation of meaning any longer? Who are you, if you cannot use even a single word for your description?

Do not fall into despair,
For the greatest joy of all
Is to observe the world with
A mind that is empty and bare.

CHAPTER 1

GROWING PAINS: HOW TO LOOSEN THE STRANGLEHOLD OF "PERSONAL IDENTITY"

The foregoing generations beheld God and nature face to face; we, through their eyes. Why should not we have a poetry and philosophy of insight and not of tradtition, and a religion by revelation to us, and not the history of theirs?

— Ralph Waldo Emerson

Personal identity solidifies quickly for an adolescent. Invariably it is tied to one's clique, or lack thereof, in K-12 education. By sixth or seventh grade, most kids can point out, from their group of peers, "the brainiacs," "the artistic ones," "the bookworms," "the jocks (of each respective sport)," "the theatre crowd," "the geeks," "the mathletes," "the anime lovers," "the goths," "the stoners," "the loner," "the bullies," "the normals," "the mean girls," "the populars," "Mr. and Ms. Student Government," etc.

These labels may look as if they are clichés pulled from a high school sitcom, but they are, in fact, based in truth. At least to the extent that research has shown the existence of social hierarchies and thematic peer crowds regardless of the high school.[1] The reader can verify the existence of such cliques and personality types from their own time in school. Perhaps one's own peer group and its place on the abstract social hierarchy flashes to mind now: scenes of loud lunchrooms and crowded hallways.

This piece, however, is not about social groups, but rather the individuals within them. It is about identity in the sense of external

---

1   Carey, Jacqueline. "UIC Study Details How Today's High School Cliques Compare to Yesterday's." *UIC Today*, University of Illinois Chicago, 2019, today.uic.edu/uic-study-details-how-todays-high-school-cliques-compare-to-yesterdays/.

personality traits and internal emotions; one's self-perceived "home base." All individuals—regardless of their upbringing—will gravitate toward certain behaviors, emotions and patterns of thought that coalesce into stereotypical personal identities such as the ones mentioned before. This is not good or bad, but it is inevitable. Even if someone chooses to avoid such a cut-and-dried label like "goth," the categorization will occur in the minds of all who observe the person (with the expectation, perhaps, of close friends and family).

Ignorance of one's personal identity—at least, as it is generalized by their peers—is not bliss; **in this instance, a lack of self-awareness reveals an unconscious identification with a certain set of attitudes and behaviors.** Without awareness of one's behaviors and general outlook on life (whether in school, work or extracurricular activities) one is caught in a kind of riptide of thought patterns with no way to keep distorted thoughts in check.

On the "popular" end of the social hierarchy, this can lead to sadistic bullying behavior (cyberbullying, in particular) and a suppression of genuine self-expression.[2] On the "outcast" end of the spectrum, this lack of awareness can allow nihilistic, cynical patterns of thought to flourish, which, in severe cases, can lead to suicide or mass violence.

So, although the reader is unlikely to fall into either extreme, it must be made clear that the "stranglehold of personal identity" can have serious consequences. Even at a lesser extreme, this identity stranglehold can encourage self-loathing, self-hate and fatalistic despair. Therefore, it is imperative that one learns how to "loosen the hold" of personality—first for themselves and later to teach others—so that one is no longer trapped and isolated by the thought patterns spinning in their mind.

This process is, in fact, the beginning of spiritual awakening.

✵✵✵

Coming back to identity development in high school, whether an adolescent has any control over how they are generalized by their peers is up for debate. To the extent one is willing to contort their own morals and interests to fit a certain mold, they do; but this contortion is just as much a part of identity development as pursuing one's interests

---

2   In this case, self-expression refers to any activity done for its own sake, which is driven by an intuitive desire to pursue it, without concern for how it will be judged by one's peers.

unabashedly. Said another way, a football player who also loves chess will make a choice of which to signal to his peers as "his identity," but this choice is based on an immeasurable number of factors out of his control to the point that it will not *feel like* a choice.[3]

Therefore, I argue, it is *not* in one's control how they are generalized by their peers. Besides the handful of people who make a concerted effort to change their social status in the transitional years (i.e., entering high school or college), most accept their peer-imposed identity as inevitable. It is possible an adolescent doesn't *like* such a label, as some are more prone to ridicule and social ostracization than others, but it is nearly impossible to be oblivious to it.

Every reader knows if, in high school, they rolled with the smart crowd, with the outcasts, with the athletes, with the popular kids, with the drama students, or some other subset. And it is from these cliques that one's identity is gleaned by their peers.

In something of a self-fulfilling feedback loop, this peer-based identity influences one's perception of self, which influences their attitudes and behaviors and *reinforces* their peer-based identity, *ad infinitum*.[4] This feedback loop is usually harmless. In fact, most people pursuing their interests unabashedly are unlikely to care how they are perceived by their peers. For example, if someone enjoys anime and hangs out with a group of like-minded peers, then whether others see the activity as "lame" or "cool" is a non-factor to their love of the genre. The problem, though, is that most people are *not* pursuing their interests unabashedly.

Most people constrain some or all aspects of their personality in order to "fit in," which creates a cognitive dissonance—however slight—between outward behavior and internal feelings. Their

---

3   Does the football player get attention from girls that others on the chess team do not? Invited to exclusive parties? Gain a bigger circle of friends? Assuming the individual enjoys chess and football equally, then incentives such as these skew the decision in favor of pursuing football. So if chess club and football practice overlap in time, then the social benefits will make the choice all but predestined. Take any two mutually exclusive activities and the one with greater incentives and less constraints will be picked—those factors, of perceived benefits and constraints, are what make the choice *feel like* a non-choice.

4   Imagine, even if you have no desire to be popular yourself, there is an intimidation factor if a popular person starts up a conversation with you. Assuming the "popular" person perceives this change of attitude, her status is further cemented in her own mind.

outward behavior becomes a Venetian masquerade mask, a mask of "standard behavior," to be worn around all but the closest of friends and family. It is from this dissonance that something like "smiling" depression can arise.[5] Less severely, it can prevent positive risk-taking (e.g., taking a challenging or unpopular class, asking questions in class, making new friends, pursuing new hobbies, etc.).

THE CHICKEN OR THE EGG: AN ORIGIN STORY

Boxing someone in, or pinning an individual to a specific identity, can have profound effects on their life, but this is not to blame the community for imposing an undesirable identity on the individual. As I will attempt to make clear, there is no single origin to how someone's identity develops in adolescence.

I ask the reader to consider their own personal identity and life situation as they read on. This essay is not meant to persuade the reader to agree with the ideas presented, but to offer a chance to reflect on one's own self-identity at this moment.

If high school is taken as the microcosm of where personal identity develops and solidifies, then what does it take for the aforementioned "peer-imposed identities" to truly stick (e.g., at what point does someone become known as "smart" or "stupid")? How early in one's life do they take hold? How often do they change? What is required for the school population to change their perception of a peer? How much effort is required for the adolescent to "break out of the box"? What might spark the change?

I will use my own experience as an example—and the reader must know this is how I *thought* people perceived me:

> I was intensely shy. I was smart, though not in an outstanding way. I played hockey, though I was not often associated with the sport at school. I had one of the worst cases of cystic acne at the school. I overthought nearly everything. I had a strong interest in entrepreneurship, which shifted to marketing (as such, all my elective classes were business related). I was the question-asker in most classes. I went to parties on occasion—almost always indirectly

---

5   Although not a clinical form of depression, this refers to someone with symptoms of depression who hides them from others using a cheerful demeanor.

invited—and I was no straight arrow. I had a handful of close friends and two handfuls of semi-close friends; all of whom were guys. I had no romantic relationships. I was not one for attending football or basketball games. I was friendly, but often in a surface-level way.

I don't know which of these details would have stood out to my peers, but at the time, I often perceived myself as "the shy friend of a friend." I often felt buried in the crowd with a conflicting desire to stand out. My "mask" identity of being shy was as much a crutch as it was a hindrance. Perhaps the reader can relate. I find this particular trait influenced the majority of my behaviors at the time, so I would like to investigate its origins.

Was it my genetics that influenced my shy personality or the cultural conditioning of my early years? Nature or nurture? The chicken or the egg? Put another way, was it my peers who influenced my view of my "self" or was it *I* who influenced *their view* of my "self"?

By "self" I am referring to the ego. I would like to clarify how I am using the word because it is often misinterpreted in the context of personality:

I often hear *ego* used as a catchall term for selfish behavior. I am using the word in a more encompassing way. Ego, in this context, is all thoughts and behaviors with a link (or rationalization) to the past or future. *I did this because I ... in the past. I did this because I'm trying to reach ... in the future.* Ego is one's selfish behavior plus the thoughts and attitudes *about* the selfish behavior. Ego is the thinking *about* thinking as well as the original thought. Ego is one's self-image and all thoughts *about* one's self-image and the thoughts about those thoughts, *ad infinitum*. Imagine the ego as a shadow of one's true "Self" and with a sun always shining behind them. No matter how quick one spins their head, the shadow remains the only thing in sight.

When shadows speak and shake hands with other shadows, it is no wonder most human beings believe they *are* the shadow. (I am intentionally avoiding possessive terms like their, his or her shadow). To say "*I* have an ego," is the water calling itself wet. It is the ego that makes judgements; it is the ego that desires self-improvement. Therefore, acknowledging "Yes, *I* am selfish. *I* need to quiet my ego. *I* concede. *I* will be a good person from here on out," is the ego maintaining its existence in another mask. **It is like a captured enemy in war saying anything and everything to prove its allegiance to the other side to prevent its own death.** (In truth, there is no other side—no opposing moral point of view to switch over to—but this will be discussed in a later essay).

In its most insidious fashion, the ego uses lofty ideals and aspirations of making a better world, of a life of service to others, of a life pursuing the spiritual path, in order to strengthen its sense of self again. Why? The ego wants to keep existing, and it only exists when each one of us believes we are it—the conditioned personality, that is. The Watcher of the thoughts becomes so identified with thoughts that the Watcher believes it *is* the thoughts, and by extension, the limited ego identity.[6]

So, the shy kid, the optimistic one, the gifted student, the bookworm, the football player, the soccer star, the idiot, the bully, the goth, etc.— all these labels are forms of ego attachment. Do not get caught up in the haphazard categorization of these labels (some are emotion based, some are intelligence based, some are physical based, etc.). The common link is that *an adolescent individual falls into the hypnosis that they* are *whichever label has been imposed on them by their community of peers.* When the label, or set of labels, is accepted as their own (even reluctantly or subconsciously), then the individual's thoughts, feelings and behaviors all fall in line with that identity.[7]

Again, to use my high school sense of self as an example because it serves as a model that any reader can use to reflect upon their own personal identity:

My intensely shy personality evolved into a negative feedback loop. A few early social events in high school where I was struck with intense anxiety (and no method or insight to relieve it) created a pain-association with having conversations with acquain-

6   Be cautious not to personify the watcher into yet another "I." That is the ego's attempt at creating yet another identity to buy into. "The Watcher" is formless and selfless; it is Awareness. This is discussed in more detail in later essays.

7   In rejecting, say, the identity that one is shy, even if confidence-building becomes a focused practice, it is still that "shyness" that acts as the foundation of self for that person to push away from.

tances. Rather than creating stronger friendships with new people, I shirked from the chances and clung tighter to my initial group of friends.

As acne developed, around 15 years old, this heightened my feelings of insecurity in social settings—leading to more anxiety and more resistance to attend social settings in the future (although social lubricants were introduced, my anxious and insecure thinking-patterns could not be reversed, only temporarily numbed). Toward the end of my schooling, I avoided almost all social events, avoided almost all friendship-producing conversation with acquaintances, and avoided almost all behaviors that would produce even the slightest anxiety (e.g., talking to a member of the opposite sex—one-on-one—outside of school conversation).

I point the finger at no one for this turtle-like behavior: not my upbringing, not my close friends, not even my "self." At the time, I harbored feelings of anger and resentment for that sense of shyness (and I'm sure I blamed *someone* for being who I was), but *now it is laughably clear how counterproductive any and all blame was.* There was no chicken and there was no egg. It all happened self-so (i.e., arising spontaneously). I cannot blame my genetics any more than I can blame my peers for ostracizing me. Neither *caused* my shyness, and in the latter case, my distorted perception of the world (from an anxious lens) meant that I interpreted, for example, a non-invite to a party to mean someone *intentionally* didn't want me there at all.

For the reader still caught in adolescent distortions (and that is not to call it "childish," only to point to their origins), I wish not to keep you dwelling in the past. The way out of a miserable personal identity is not hidden in the depths of one's subconscious mind. Even awareness of the events that first produced profound social anxiety/feelings of inadequacy do not make it any easier to dive head-first into a similar situation now. The fear response still exists and it is still uncomfortable.

Clarity is not power in this instance.[8] In truth, clarity of past per-

---

8   I have no doubt that uncovering a forgotten memory of inadequacy *can* spark spontaneous change in a patient lying on their therapist's couch. I would posit that such discovery did not *cause* the change. Surface-level awareness using the "rational" mind does not alter emotional patterns. Those patterns couldn't care less if John Doe knows the origins of his fear of clowns or not.

sonal sufferings is one of the primary ways your mind validates ego (i.e., the limited, habituated personality) as one's true and only self. As the reader imagines her or his own high school experience throughout this essay, *you* remain exactly where you are. The body does not teleport to the past but rather holds this book (or e-reader) and looks at these words. The lungs breathe in the air. The ears take in the sounds bouncing around the room. It is fantastic and requires no thought you to be aware of these processes

The way out of one's identity is here. It is always here. It is *only* here.

LOOSENING THE STRANGLEHOLD

It appears too simple and at the same time too "new age-y." Invariably, the mind of the reader will run through all its memories, which symbolize, signify or explain its current neuroses and undesirable personality traits. *I can't just* stop *being shy/anxious/insecure! It's not a switch I can just turn off at will,* says the mind. Of course, the unexamined mind (i.e., the ego) cannot stop being shy because the illusory sense of self has been conditioned to *be* shy.[9] This influences all thoughts, feelings, reactions and behaviors. It cannot be flipped off like a switch, *but* once Awareness is unclouded and no longer identifies with the thought patterns, then those identity-aligning thoughts are not given the focal energy that perpetuate and validate them.

Put another way, it was my dissatisfaction with my shyness that *kept* me shy. All the internal reactions I had in high school toward my shyness (e.g., *I hate feeling like this; no one else feels this shy; why me?*) upheld the identity that *I am shy*. Those examples were reactions to thought-patterns, which sounded like, "Everyone's looking at me and thinking I'm ugly. My skin looks so bad. They'll laugh at me if I try talking to her."

The reader *must* distinguish insecure thoughts, which arise from external stimuli, from *resistance to* those thoughts, which arises as a

---

9   Although I have been writing about identity in all forms, it would be wise for the reader to consider his or her most prominent *emotional* identity as they read on (e.g., angry, goofy, serious, depressed, anxious, shy, arrogant, inferior, insecure, lonely, stressed, optimistic, etc.). If it is not immediately obvious to the reader what is their "emotional home base," then consider how you *cope* when things do not go the way you expected: What is the emotional charge of the thoughts in such a situation?

reaction to the original thoughts. For clarity, I will call the original, arising thoughts "A" thoughts and the resistant, suppressing thoughts "B" thoughts.

"A" thoughts arise *without your willful control*. No one consciously chooses to think about how inferior or ugly they are. In a poor attempt to take control of the "A" thoughts, a person may willfully think "B" thoughts. This is like fighting fire with more fire; though, without a higher level of awareness, those "B" thoughts *appear* to be the water that will subdue the blazing "A" thoughts.[10]

For a time "B" thoughts might manage to suppress "A" thoughts. A person may ignore or reject their fearful thoughts of talking to a girl or boy they like and ask for their phone number (or Snapchat, I suppose). The fear has been overcome! Or so it seems. But even if the goal has been achieved, the emotional "home base"—of insecurity, in this case—will return with a vengeance: *She only gave you her number because she felt bad and didn't want to embarrass you. She still thinks you're a loser.*

I have been using examples from adolescence, but the cycle of "A" thoughts and "B" thoughts perpetually fighting for dominance are just as apparent in adulthood, as in the workplace:

> **"A" thought:** *She critiqued my report because she thinks I'm stupid and don't know what I'm doing.*

> **"B" thought:** *No, I'm actually good at my job, and she was just trying to be helpful.*

> **"A" thought:** *Yeah, she's helpful, but I'm such a burden to her, and I'm keeping her from doing her job.*

Only in witnessing the mind's activity—as a silent observer would—can one *be aware* that this is an unwinnable war. The white flag of surrender is the only way out. But what exactly *is* surrender? It runs the risk of be misinterpreted to mean, "Pile on the insecurity and negative

---

10   It appears complex when written out so blatantly, but this process is happening *all the time* in most people's heads. I am pointing out the times when "A" thoughts are negative and fear provoking, but "A" thoughts can be as trite as walking into the living room and thinking "Oh, what am I going to watch on TV tonight? I've got the show I'm binging, but I want to watch a movie too … ."

already swirling in one's mind; use willful "B" thoughts to feel even more insecure, angry, shy or anxious." **This is not true surrender**. Any such willful "B" thoughts still imply an attempt at controlling one's stream of thinking. The sense of control over mind *is* the illusion of ego. Following still?

Any willful "B" thoughts that attempt to suppress, resist, or even support "A" thoughts arise just as spontaneously as the latter. The only difference is that *"A" thoughts arise as reactions to the external world* and *"B" thoughts arise as reactions to the internal world (i.e., the psyche).*

☼☼☼

But if "surrender" does not mean using "B" thoughts to get rid of "A" thoughts, then what is it? If, as I seem to imply, one has no control over his or her thoughts, then what could surrendering do to change things?

Surrender means to let the thoughts *be as they are.* It is a constant letting go process: First by letting go of "B" thoughts (i.e., judgemental thoughts about one's internal world) and soon, without willful effort, it becomes possible to let go of "A" thoughts (judgemental thoughts about the external world).

This may sound like "mindfulness" meditation, and letting go of reaction is the "mental muscle" that is trained in the practice, but what I am speaking of is capable of occurring every waking moment, regardless of whether someone is cross-legged and thinking "breathe in, breathe out" or not. I also see that mindfulness meditation has been captured by the collective Western ego as something to do "to be more productive." Even if someone is wise enough to see the irony of such a claim, the mind may latch onto the opposite/original purpose of mindfulness meditation as a spiritual practice to *pursue nirvana*. The irony is equivalent.

Being aware of the mind when "A" thoughts, rooted in negativity or self-judgement, arise and surrendering to them (i.e., letting them be) is *neither a practice nor a skill.* It's nothing. It only *is.* I cannot put it into words because it reads like a paradox if I write, "Let the thought be without *trying* to stop it and without *trying not* to try to stop it."

You just watch. You just watch the thoughts as you would the passing cars on a highway from an overhead view. When you get tangled in the "A-B-A" thought-pattern, you watch from there, too. Whenever you realize the thought is *only* a thought, with less substance than a shadow, in this moment now, then you have returned to Awareness.

The reader's nose may be too close to the book to know what I am pointing to. That is okay. For now, realizing that "B" (willful) thoughts are *just as reactive* as "A" (instinctive) thoughts can loosen the grip of one's personality identity enough to slow the unconscious tug-of-war between self-judgement and self-affirmation. This has the added benefit of releasing some mental energy that had been previously wasted on self-criticism.

IDENTITY AND POLITICS

I have omitted talk of identity in the modern, politicized sense (e.g., race, gender and sexuality) because such topics refer to collective rather than personal identities. The heart of this essay is about the reader's core emotional states and personality traits. With this focus, the conversation becomes universal. Yet, how often is the conversation shifted back to these collective identities—some of whom are historical victims, others historical oppressors—in a way guaranteed to divide individuals? The current identity politics movement in America unwittingly ostracizes and divides rather than unites the people, though I find the division is not along lines of race or gender, but between those who embrace a certain political ideology and those who do not.

This will be detailed in a later essay, but for now, I will say this: **We, as a collective of individual human beings, are <u>not</u> responsible for making everyone feel included at all times.** We are not responsible for making sure everyone feels happy—or at least diagnosed as unhappy and given happy pills. There has been a collective repression of "feeling bad," in the mundane, non-clinical sense, in recent years, and though I can only speak from my own experience in school, I observed the greatest push *away* from "discomfort," synonymous with feeling "offended," toward my final high school years.[11]

Inevitably, in the school system, there are people who resist these protective trends as not for them. There is no point in dwelling on *why* certain people do not feel included despite the greater push for diversity and inclusion—I have saved the topic of political divisiveness and idealism for later on—but there must be an acceptance of those people without vilifying them as the "evil" or "morally flawed." As I have sought to show through my own example, the negative feedback loop

---

11   It was also apparent in my experience in college, but because attending such an institution is optional, it will remain outside the scope of this essay.

that solidifies someone's personal identity has no pointable cause. It happens self-so.

ESCAPING THE CAGE OF IDENTITY

The development of personal identity may be out of one's conscious control, but anyone is capable of escaping the cage of identity they find themselves locked in. That said, it requires a dissolution of the ego, which is so aptly called "ego death" as a nod to its fear factor. Although it only provokes fear to the degree You identify as the egoic self.

In truth, ego dissolution is an untangling of one's mental faculties so that the mind (and thought-forms) become a subservient tool for You, the Watcher of thought, rather than a cage that keeps one in the trap of perpetual seeking and dissatisfaction. I do not need you to believe me, or agree or disagree; I only wish for You to be aware of any reactive thought patterns spinning in the mind now. Be the space that surrounds the thought-forms. Rest in the stillness between the words.

Internal suffering is a part of the growing pains of adolescence. Rather than suppress or avoid the pain (for example, with a top-down policy approach, as I have observed in my own schooling), it must be faced, head-on, with courage and clarity. In cases where anxiety or insecurity are most intense, remember this: *suffering cannot exist when Conscious Awareness is aware of Itself.*

THE ILLUSION OF SOLIDNESS

In school, social roles appear to solidify and leave little to no wiggle room for drastic change after the dust cloud of freshman year finally settles. Whether a person makes the field hockey team or gets cut in her first year will profoundly affect her external world, which will affect her internal world, which will affect her external world, *ad infinitum.* That is the case for every event in one's life: significant or insignificant. The reader may choose a handful of significant, emotionally driven moments in their life that had more pivotal alterations to their identity compared to the days before or after the event, but all that does is *solidify the illusion of personal identity.*

As an illustrative metaphor, imagine each individual's identity as a ball of clay getting slightly molded each time it hits a wall. Sometime in adolescence, the kiln is fired up (call it "the heat of social pressures") and the ball of clay becomes much more stiff and dry. The individual may deceive themselves into believing that "they like the shape of their clay and don't want to change it." Now when the brittle clay hits walls it begins to chip rather than mold to the impact. Fear develops. The clay ball must be protected from further damage. Routines are established. Moments that may chip the ego are avoided. Monotony arises. Life dulls. Conceptual knowledge replaces true discovery. An existential bleakness sets in.

"What happened to the good ol' days?" asks the clay. "When I was fresh and moldable? I miss my innocence." Drugs and alcohol provide a moment of that childish moldability, but when it fades, the clay dries more stiffly than before. "All hope is lost!" cries the clay. "I am stuck! I see no way out!" This is the greatest moment of pain. The hairline cracks in the clay have deepened. The clay is bound to split open. Death is on its way! "Goodbye, cruel world," the clay whispers and begins to cry. It cries all night long, and with every tear, with every drop of letting go of self-preservation, it is hydrated to its youthful stage.

It wakes in the morning, feeling refreshed. Not only have all the cracks and chips melded back into the soft ball of clay, but the clay is *aware of its infinite moldability*. The kiln heat still exists, but the ball of clay is *aware that it can soften itself at any moment*. Now, that clay can be as it was in its youth, but with an added element of appreciation and confidence.

That allegory of the little ball of clay represents one's mental facilities. I am not saying the physical body is as infinitely durable as Conscious Awareness. A level of self-preservation of the physical body remains even upon realizing that You are not the ego. In fact, the self-destructive behaviors, which are common when ego runs the mind (e.g., drinking to excess, over-eating, under-eating, any destructive act for the sake of *trying to become like someone else*, the physical ailments of chronic stress, etc.), fall away. The egoic thoughts that drive craving for the vice—often used as a way to suppress "mental noise"—are no longer identified with, and are therefore unmasked as the desperate, withering ego. Something to watch, but not believe.

The noise fades away when You learn how to observe the mind without reacting to its antics.

☼☼☼

Even though I write with clarity, my daily experience is not immune to the fog of habituated emotional reactions. I fall into the trap of ego identification every day. I wish for the reader to see the author's experience not as some kind of lofty, unattainable mental state called "enlightenment." The dissolution of ego is gradual (unless it is not). This "Sean Patrick Greene" personality is quite a sticky thing.

I am, of course, having fun in the process of letting go of processes. I feel like that moldable ball of clay once again, despite the many times I "stiffen" back into old patterns of thought. It is no easy task, but it is a simple one. This process is much like shifting the focus of one's eyes: Many distractable things may come into view from outside, but remember to focus on the window glass from which all is seen—without it, nothing else could be.

Although, who is it that watches from behind the window?

CHAPTER 2

MEMENTO MORI: UNMASKING THE FEAR OF DEATH

Nothing real can be threatened. Nothing unreal exists. Herein lies the peace of God.

— Helen Schucman, A Course in Miracles

What is it about death that scares most people to their core? Religious or not, it is rare to find someone unafraid of their own death: Why is this so?

Of course, for the Christians, the fear is inspired by the vivid depictions of an infernal Hell awaiting the damned. Although there is a catch-22 built into this belief of a tortuous afterlife: The more likely one is to believe in the reality of Hell as the consequence of misbehavior, the more likely they are to act in a way that avoids misbehavior. Any of the Hell-bound crooks in this society likely don't believe in Hell as a place or, in a masochistic way, revel in the idea of it.

Put short, Hell only scares the people who choose to be scared by it.

So what is it then? For the religiously unaffiliated, an increasing group in modern times[1], plus the religious individuals who don't cower at the thought of Hell—there remains a palpable fear of one's death in the psyche. What creates such a fear? A fear unique to humans with our pattern-finding abilities and self-aware thoughts. An existential fear so universal and powerful that, in the West especially, it is too taboo to speak of so directly.

---

1 The number of religiously unaffiliated U.S. adults has increased from 16% to 29% from 2007 to 2021; those who identify as Christian have fallen from 78% to 63% in the same span. Put another way, Christians outnumbered non-religious people around 5 to 1 in 2007. It was down to 2 to 1 in 2021.[38]

Language is used to soften the blow (e.g., to pass away, to kick the bucket, to no longer be with us, to depart this world, etc.), but this serves the grieving; not the person facing their own demise. How may an essay, a mere bundle of words, serve the individual paralyzed by the fear of his or her *own* death?

Such individuals are not limited to those taking their final breaths in a hospital bed at this moment; the fear of death can strike anyone, at any age, in any life situation. Thus, in writing about a universal subject, a paradox arises in which the simplicity of the message must reach 10,000 unique sets of ears.

Have the Heaven-bound Christians already set this work aside? Have these words already begun to stink of heresy? The author seeks to limit any offending statements of one's beliefs so that all readers may remain open-minded enough to finish the essay. That said, there is no guarantee that everything will fall in line with one's current worldview; the same is true of life in general. **The author commends any reader willing to confront the fear of death by choice rather than waiting for the Grim Reaper's untimely knock at the door.**

Opinions may form while reading—anger may boil in the blood, fear may tremble in the body—read on regardless. The reward for such courage is peace. The peace which passeth all [rational] understanding.

A BATTLE AGAINST FEAR

Why someone might fear death is quite a multifaceted thing, is it not? To rattle off 10 reasons *why* the fear arises would only point the reader's mind to the 11th cause.[2] It becomes like battling the Grecian monster Hydra: Cut off one head and two more grow in its place.

So if that head-sprouting monster stands as a symbol for one's fear of death, then—to follow the myth to its conclusion—a person must be like Hercules and set fire to the headless necks before they grow again.[3] Though, what does that mean in terms of facing the fear of death? It means to face the very entity that invents, legitimizes and rationalizes the existential fear of death.

---

2   This is another way of saying the mind can't outreason the fear of death.

3   In the actual myth, Hercules continued clubbing off the heads of Hydra with no clear end in sight. It was his nephew, Iolaus, who had joined him on the quest, who discovered that burning the stumps would prevent the regrowth. Both assisted the other in defeating the monster.

The reader must face their own psyche—in its unconscious inner-workings—and demand that the thinker of such unwelcome thoughts *be revealed*.

It is, of course, the ego (i.e., the conditioned personality) who devises such terrible imaginings for what lies in the Great Beyond. But who is the ego? Or rather, *what* is the ego? Moreover, how does the one distinguish their "true self" from this illusory entity?

FREUDIAN EGO VS. SPIRITUAL EGO

Ego, as the word is used by most people, is often in reference to Sigmund Freud's definition: According to him, ego is one of the three parts of the personality—the id (which symbolizes one's primitive instincts) and the superego (which symbolizes one's moral views internalized by their cultural upbringing) being the other two.

In being the mediator between the id and the superego—between instinct and morals/ideals—the ego allows an individual to fulfill their primitive instincts in a socially acceptable way. Thus, according to Freud, ego is the deal broker between carnal pleasures and higher aims.

This, however, is not what the author is referencing. Nor is the author referring to the pseudo-psychology use of "ego" as someone who is quite selfish.

Ego, in the author's use of the word, refers to a more spiritual/ Eastern philosophical view.[4] It is also less rigid than Freud's theorization of the mind, and therefore, more difficult to put, in its entirety, into words. Put simply, [spiritual] ego is the illusion of a sense of self embedded in continuous thought. It is the same kind of illusion that gives a chair its solid feeling when it is mostly empty space.[5]

The historical sense of self, the ego, the conditioned personality— all are akin to the solid-feeling chair, which is mostly emptiness. One cannot *see* the empty space, for from the perspective of one's human eyes it looks all put together; but one can be *aware* that the empty

---

4   Although Eckhart Tolle's book, *The Power of Now,* has shaped the author's view of "ego" and the "egoic mind," it would be meaningless to call it *his* theory. This essay is not accepting or refuting Tolle's words; just as one writing about nature would not feel compelled to claim that Ralph Waldo Emerson's writing on the theme must be correct or incorrect by comparison. There is only the subject with no one to claim it.

5   This is not completely accurate because "empty space" still contains wave functions and quantum fields, but it is meant only as a metaphor.

space encompasses all the solidness.

The same is true of the mind and the thought-forms it produces. When one is so caught up in the river of never-ending thought—never taking a moment to lift one's head out of the water—the egoic personality develops through a mix of social influences and superficial observations of one's thoughts and behaviors.

It requires a hard-pressed intention to "know thyself" in order to fixate one's awareness on one's mind in order to uncover how ephemeral and ungraspable the personality truly is. This is not a theory. The author is not claiming anything is true or false. The point is only being made to the reader to take a brief moment to ask *"Who am I?"* and to listen for the next thought to arise. No effort or willpower is needed; only silent and focused attention.

Ask yourself now, "Who am I?"

✫✫✫

What was discovered? How long was it before a verbalized thought "popped up" in the mind? It is likely there was a long gap of mental stillness before something arose.

If, however, a superficial answer came to mind without any gap of stillness, such as "I'm a mother," or "I'm an athlete," (likely due to having been asked the question before), the authors asks for the reader to follow up on the superficial identity, with a genuine curiosity and an openness to discovery, with "Yes, but who was I before that?" or "Yes, but who am I in this moment now?" for no external identity is permanent or ever-present. To hold so tightly to a superficial label invites only suffering when that identity is stripped away.

This simple exercise is a form of focusing awareness on ego. To bring the hazy (or ignored) understanding of one's identity to the focal point of this moment now.

"I think, therefore I am," as the philosopher Descartes so proudly claimed, expresses the greatest fallacy that the "civilized" mind is capable of making. To equate the process of thinking with one's sense of self. **Self-aware thought is an incredible and distinguishing factor between humans and other animals, but it is not who one *is*.**

In rising *above* the level of thought (as the reader just experienced while patiently awaiting a mental response to "Who am I?"), sense perceptions still perceive the external world. It is likely that the reader heard, saw, felt, tasted and smelled in more clarity than when caught in a state of continuous thought.

Again, the author asks the reader to do the exercise before—asking "Who am I?" and waiting for a *unique* thought response—but to do so with a newfound alertness to the five senses. There is no effort or willpower required; only silent focused attention.

Ask yourself again, "Who am I, in this moment now?"

☼☼☼

There is no correct or incorrect way to practice the exercise: no right or wrong discoveries. That said, a good rule of thumb to see if one has "gotten it" is by how little they feel compelled to confirm their realization.

For the time being, it may be simpler for the reader to see what they are not—namely, the ego, in the spiritual sense (encompassing all three parts of Freud's personality theory), which is nothing more than a fleeting bundle of thought-forms seen out of the corner of one's mental eye.[6]

> The author would like to take a moment to address the Awareness within the reader for a moment. There may be opinions—agreements and disagreements—floating around as thoughts, but those thoughts are not the Being hearing or reading this now. You are the Being *aware of* the thoughts. You are both the stillness between … and the thoughts; the silence between … and the sounds; the formless between … and the forms. In the intuitive understanding of this truth, You may, in essence, expand your identity to include the silence between thoughts rather than be confined to total belief in the contents of thought. You no longer have to identify with every thought that begins with "I …"

> You are able to detach from any thought pattern once you realize that You, Unconditioned Consciousness, are not the thinking mind. By resting in mental stillness, you can remain fully conscious and present without the compulsion to *think about it*. The author is not saying you must do anything with this information

---

6   The author is not claiming that one must have *no* personality or live without *any* identity in order to be at peace with the shortness of life. Rather, one can be "in the world, but not of the world"—play the game of being a human, but without the existential dread of being "little, ol' me" and nothing else. The next essay will focus on the positive side of the coin—namely, what to do while one exists in form.

or become someone new or change anything at all. The words are only to point to a space that the ego—the hazy, self-aware bundle of thoughts—cannot understand or rationalize. The space that You, Unconditioned Consciousness, truly are. It is a know-ing-feeling; the personality who agrees or disagrees with these words is incapable of knowing, much less *being*, You.

SETTING FIRE TO THE HEADS OF HYDRA

So, in uncovering the ego—one's mentally constructed sense of self—as an illusion of solidness in mostly empty space, the author takes for granted that the average reader will instantly "get it." Even to under-stand the point conceptually is not true understanding.

No amount of words will ever touch the space being pointed to. No amount of agreement in the mind of the reader will ever allow one to *experientially* know the blissful, peaceful emptiness that blankets the world; the Silent Awareness that You are—beyond name and form. Nor will meditating alone in a cave for 30 years promise a detachment from the afflicted ego (i.e., the thought-forms that conjure and validate the *fear* of death).

The author must trek on, despite the potential to be misunderstood through filtered concepts in the reader's mind. In a way, this essay is the fire and you—the reader who has yet to realize what is being pointed to—are the head-sprouting Hydra. No, the reader is not being called evil or a monster (no matter how cunningly the mind might attempt to make an enemy of the writer). Rather, the author is pointing to the Hydra and the Hercules *both* within the reader.

It is not a fight—except in the storytelling conventions of ancient myth—but rather like a detective in search of a slithering crook. It is a game in the most joyous sense of the word. When you interrogate the ego/conditioned personality with questions like, "Who am I?" and "Who thinks this thought now?" you can observe the mind make a dazzling, roaring display that *thinks* all it can to convince Awareness, You, that the contents of thought—the narrative of conditioned iden-tity—contain the "real" you.

The more focus placed on this moment-to-moment introspective awareness of thought, the more likely you are to realize that thought is only a small piece of You. In this realization, ego begins to dissolve. The heads of Hydra can no longer spout two-fold because You have set fire to their origins (with conscious awareness). All thoughts with origins in the past or future, with concerns of "I, me and mine," are unmasked as *ego*.

That total identification with thought *is* the root of existential fear. It is at the core of the fear of death. It is the trap that binds You to an egoic identity, which leads you to cling to the known and crave certainty even when it is not in your best interest.

So whether one believes self-awareness is a gift or a curse to humanity, it exists. It is how the author and the reader have become connected through the words on this page. There is no point wishing for anything different. Each human will make the choice whether to sink below (with drugs and alcohol) or rise above the level of thought (by resting in the space of no-thought), but, when the going gets tough, it's really no choice at all, is it? When life becomes difficult—when the body is sluggish and drained—one will unconsciously return to vices that numb the mind until you realize you are not forced to believe, or identify with, the thoughts that provoke fear, suffering and anguish.[7]

There exists—above or behind or deeper than—the level of self-aware thinking in which human beings are capable of simply Being. This is the space of inner peace. This is the space of no-mind. This is the peace of God. This is the arising of Unconditioned Consciousness. This is the beginning of spiritual awakening. This is to "be here now."

They all point to the same unspeakable no-thing.

The author asks not for the reader to believe or disbelieve the words, but to be the Awareness that observes the mental monologue from here on. The ego may instantly attempt to reassert the necessity of fear-provoking thoughts ... Just watch. Just be aware. The ruse lasts only as long as You cling to the stream of thought as "who you are."

---

7   Cultivating good physical health and caring for the body makes this natural disidentification process easier.

CHAPTER 3

ENLIGHTENED SELF-EXPRESSION: ABANDON THE WILD GOOSE CHASE FOR YOUR LIFE'S PURPOSE

Beauty is in the heart of the beholder.

— *H. G. Wells*

Uniqueness, as distinct from conformity or phoniness, strikes the author as something admirable to most people in this modern era;[1] at least it is something often sought after. This in no way denies the importance and impulse for social connection. For the sake of the essay, let the reader see "uniqueness" as equivalent to "self-expression."

This pull toward self-expression is not exclusive to the domains of art, acting and writing. Such a term encompasses any number of domains: From gardening to golfing to cooking to business creation to monastic living to child rearing and on and on. It is, as so often idealized, the activity that an individual feels "they were born to do." The key word is "do," for this is not merely a passive act, nor is it a means to an end; the action is its own reward.

The purpose of this essay is not to confuse or impose specific activities on any reader who already feels they've clarified their medium of expression to themselves (e.g., the artist already working on her next

---

[1] Such desire "to be unique" correlates with an individual having enough excess time and wealth (beyond satisfying their basic needs) to ponder such lofty questions as "What is my purpose in life?" In the author's view, self-expression is only one flavor of many potential answers to the question of one's *unique* life purpose. Of course, asking the question does not mean it needs to be answered in clear terms, but more on that later.

exhibit). Rather it seeks to inspire the readers who feel they have *not* understood or clarified their "born-to-do" activity, but wish to. For those who already know their self-expressive activity of choice, this essay will serve to add a level of faith and openness to the content that flows onto "the blank page" as one creates.[2]

It should be noted that for any reader who, for whatever reason, feels they have no urge or desire to express themselves (the author imagines some parents and retirees will fall into this category) by reading this essay, a latent calling may arise. The fact that you are reading this essay now is no accident. Read on with an open mind and a quiet ear turned inward. Who knows what will come of it.

Whether one's adolescence transpires in a way in which they come out labeled "an artist" or just the opposite—as shown in a previous essay—there is little to be done about the box that their experience has placed them in. Socially-imposed identity has only a faint correlation with one's natural, unencumbered form of self-expression. The engineering student can have just as much of an urge to write fiction as the creative writing major; even if every outward indicator has them labeled as "uncreative and logical." Said another way, **who you *think* you are influences what you do only *to the extent you allow it.***

There is no point in dwelling on the past to explain the riptide of higher aims the reader finds him or herself caught in: To seek to write a novel, to create a business, to make an album of music, to illustrate a children's book, to film a feature, to paint abstract art, etc. There is no point in justifying any of it. Only the egoic mind cares *why* the urge exists.

THE IDEALIZATION OF SELF-EXPRESSION

If you remain open for the length of the essay, you might discover a peculiar truth: *What was assumed to be your highest calling has actually been muddled and deadened by an ideal.* That ideal often, if not always, boils down to, "do X thing … and make a living doing

---

2   From this phrasing, it appears that the author could only be referring to writers and artists. Let "the blank page" stand as a metaphor for the starting point of any activity or endeavor and "faith and openness" to mean performing the activity with no-mind: To act without self-conscious thought. This ought to apply as deeply to the painter as it does to the golfer.

so." It is a delusional and uniquely modern privilege. Older generations would be hard-pressed to find individuals who hold, from the
get-go, the expectation that *monetizing* self-expressive work is the
ultimate goal.

To earn a living solely through self-expressive/artistic means has
only ever been known to a certain few. The author is not claiming this is
an impossible task but that most people's understanding of their "perfect" lifestyle is incompatible with the realities of monetary expenses
and required working hours.[3] It is likely a symptom of social media
and the prominence of certain unique lifestyles on the many platforms
that appear to be sustained by writing and making videos around their
very living situation. (Consider "van life," a genre of YouTube videos
that idealize a combination of remote work and living out of a van, as
an example).

The viewer of such videos, especially an adolescent, is likely to
come to the conclusion that "following a passion leads to a fortune"
because all the popular content creators/influencers they watch seem
to be proof of it. In essence, they fall prey to survivorship bias—miss-
ing all the creators who tried but could not make a living from it.

So, unaware of this blindspot, the adolescent who watches a well-
known video creator playing video games all day may attempt to
mimic the path to financial independence of that person.

Even if the exact type of content is not mimicked, a pattern of
thought still arises that says, as a generalization, "If I do what I love
to do, and reveal the process in video form, then eventually I will
earn enough money to do what I love to do full-time." **Make content,
make money:** It seems to be the implicit motto of so many yet-to-be-
famous influencer personalities on the Internet.

This ideal, "To be creative for money's sake," which likely influences young adults and adolescents more than older adults, is treach-
erous to genuine self-expression and creates an endless wild goose
chase to find a socially acceptable "passion" that can be monetized as
quickly as possible.

For example, the author, though already doing what he considers
his "born-to-do" activities (e.g., writing and filmmaking), at one point
felt his self-expressive work ought to be designed in a way that earns

---

3   Let the reader note that this claim is open to debate. As one will see, the
point is not to quash dreams but to point out the most direct path to self-expression that exists. It is here now.

enough money to continue such activities. No such expectation exists any longer. As will be shown, the combination of earning money and making art (i.e., market fit vs. limitless expression) cannot be sought simultaneously. The very seeking of future wealth/popularity from an activity taking place in the present moment dilutes the power of that activity. It is possible that self-expression *can* lead to a sustainable income by means of the work, but this is a byproduct of present action.[4]

Although it may be obvious to the reader that focusing on earning money while making art will dilute the true expressive nature of the work, it is important to realize the more insidious ways that future-oriented thoughts *harm* the work taking place in the Now.

Money is not the only aim/fruit of action that one seeks when doing a self-expressive activity. Other fruits of action may include:

- To achieve a level of fame or influence
- To seek to out-do another artist
- To please a certain person or group of people

Seeking social inclusion is likely a stronger factor than seeking money as it relates to self-expressive work in the age of social media. ("Selling out" can mean selling out for likes and follows regardless of the prospect of dollars). **Even now, the slightest fear of how individuals will interpret this essay can completely disrupt what the author is attempting to say.**

The artist or writer who reads this now must consider, in their own life, times when they altered their work to appease a portion of the audience out of fear of rejection. Did it stifle the process?

---

4   To clarify, in the case of this book, the author does seek to sell copies for a profit. There are self-expressing activities that are more oriented to earn wealth than others. The likely goal of a business owner is not to break even in a year but to turn a profit. So how can this be rectified with the above point? Take this quote from the Bhagavad Gita: *"You have the right to work, but never to the fruits of work. You should never engage in action for the sake of reward, nor should you long for inaction,"* (p. 94).[4] Although the author seeks to earn a profit from the sale of this book, the primary goal is to write. There is no delusion that any future dollars earned are more real and precious than this moment now. In the case of the business owner, it is clear that not all businesses are forms of self-expression. Those companies seeking profit *above* serving the end consumer will not last indefinitely. In seeking the fruit of the labor over the labor itself, they will be easily surpassed by those who prioritize the work.

For online writers and video creators, of which the author has been both, whether a piece of work begins with the goal of "views" and "likes" or because there is a message that demands to be shared makes a monumental difference in the joy and ease in the process of creating.

If the reader realizes the truth that future expectations (i.e., seeking the fruits of action) dilute true self-expression, and now *desires* to do his or her self-expressive activity with a sense of ease, peace and joy, then how can such expectations be dropped? It is an important question to ask, but what answer could possibly suffice?

To *desire* to drop a future expectation still creates an expectation that to hold a future ideal is wrong or undesirable.

There is a paradox there, if it can be sniffed out. To seek to stop caring about future goals *creates* an opposing ideal. To say "I'm not seeking anything from this work. I don't care if I make money, I don't care if no one likes it, I don't care if people despise me for it," when there *was* a future expectation before, implies that the individual is holding all their greed and vanity at bay, stuffed below the surface, perhaps because they have a new ideal which states, "Not being greedy and vain is good for me and good for my artwork."

Ah, so the commonality, the inescapable truth that always follows the artist, writer or self-expressive doer is this: *I want to behave like "X" because I think it's good for me.* There is always the desire to avoid the bad and do the good, even if, at different stages in life, an individual could do the same thing convinced that it used to be good and now is bad, or vice versa.

If the above passage confuses the reader, that is okay. The author understands that it may be like running with your shoes tied together if this paradox has never been presented before. The gist is this:

1. Ideals, or future expectations, detract from self-expression and dilute the intrinsic joy of the creative process.

2. To attempt to drop an ideal, or future expectation, because of its spoiling of the present moment will only create a new ideal. That new ideal, though it rejects the old one, still carries the same deadening, diluting quality of the former.

3. All ideals, or expectations for the future, are based on the belief that "living in alignment with 'X' ideal is good for *me*." Seriously, test it with any held belief or habit. Nothing

is done *because* it is knowingly bad, in the subjective sense, for a person. Even physically destructive behaviors have an element of either repentance (i.e., justified suffering) or hedonistic pleasure.

4. Once it is fully understood that ideals cannot be escaped, avoided or suppressed with rationality, there comes a point of giving up the fight: Self-surrender. *That is the place of enlightened self-expression.*

The author, as it was stated in a previous footnote, would like to earn money from the sale of this book. The more dollars the merrier. Yet, the desire is secondary to the work being done now. It is given mental space. It exists, but the author does not claim the desire as his own. It is only there as a pattern of thought in the mind. There is no identification with it, nor a strong repulsion to identify with an opposite behavior. This is self-surrender.

The task, which is actually not a task at all (except when described in language), is to *surrender* and *give space to the desires that the mind has acquired from social influences.* Do nothing with them. Just see them as they are. Observe without comment.

☼☼☼

FINDING YOUR THING

Already the author has spoken to the budding or established artist or writer and sought to show how idealizing a future lifestyle dilutes the power of action done in the moment it's done. (It's distracted work, in its purest sense). The "dazed and confused" readers who hold this book, however, may be at a loss as to their very core drive.

It is important to note that every human being has this core way of living—that born-to-do thing—whether it's making art, films or music: writing, teaching, meditating at an ashram, feeding pigeons on a park bench, creating new businesses or some combination of many things. For a rule of thumb, the simple distinction between this activity and anything else is this:

If money were no object, if fame and influence were out of the question, would you still have the drive to do such activity?

As mentioned before, in the age of "content creators" making a living off "niching down" and posting content online, the people who desire to follow in the footsteps of such creators must separate pride and greed from intuitive drive. It has become common to consider "finding a passion" to be a necessary step *before* "taking action."[5] It is especially true for the adolescents who have grown up watching this type of content. Such people are in search of an activity that (A) they like, (B) is profitable and (C) they are talented at. These criteria are not wrong, but the individuals *in search of* their passion will always remain at an arm's length away from doing the self-expressive work.

At its core, no search is necessary. Only when faith in one's own intuitive actions is lost or stifled by authority figures does the need to search for "the right activity" arise. Only in comparing one's own means of self-expression to another does the illusion of the "right" and "wrong" way of doing arise.[6] The truth is that no reason is needed for the writer to write, or the painter to paint, or the entrepreneur to develop new businesses.

That is what has gotten lost in translation. Perhaps the many "thought leaders" retrofitting their pop-psych theories onto their stories of personal achievement creates the illusion that writing out one's *why* is the key to riches. It must be emphasized though that writing out a why is not wrong or incorrect. The author is only pointing out that writing a purpose-based "why" and not writing a purpose-based "why" are equal paths to being a unique, creative individual.

The author does find that attempting to articulate a life purpose—as self-help literature often encourages—can feel as if one is grasping at straws or pulling inspiration from the words of motivational speakers (and therefore such goals read with an inescapable phoniness). In that sense, goal setting is a double-edged sword: On one hand, it provides clarity and a rationale to one's daily habits and actions. On the other hand, it can bind someone to a future ideal based on some authority figure's ideas that does not align with their unique life situation.

---

5   The use of quotations is to highlight the phrases that have become hollow with overuse.

6   There is the idea of "right action" as part of the Buddhist eight-fold path. It's common sense what falls under the category of "wrong action" here: Killing, stealing, abusing drugs, abusing sex and lying. When I refer to the illusion of right and wrong action, I'm not refuting the Buddhist distinction. I'm speaking purely of externally approved actions and externally disapproved actions, not related to the law, as illusory. If parents think it's wrong for their child to go to art school over law school—that is an illusory "wrong."

"NOT" FINDING YOUR THING

The opposite way of realizing one's born-to-do activity (opposite of an external search for the "right" activity) summarizes to "anything *you* decide to do is the correct thing to be doing." For the author, he is writing because he decided to write. There is no use in saying that it's been his passion since childhood or because this or that author inspired him with this or that book. Even calling it a "decision" is a stretch—it's more accurate to say "I am writing because I am writing now," but it, of course, looks silly when the knowing-feeling is translated to language.

Although "no wrong answers" appears to be a reasonable compromise in a state of decision paralysis, in the modern world, there is, for many, an inherent distrust of one's own impulses. As much as one would like to go with the flow of things, the ego sprinkles seeds of doubt that "the flow of things" is not what's best for you.

Perhaps from a relative perspective this is true. If one is needlessly fired from a job, the pull of the thinking mind may have him planted in front of the boss's desk defending himself or begging for a second chance. It feels out of sorts to let external circumstances dictate one's life path. It feels as though one becomes stranded in the ocean without a sail or paddle to guide him; bound to the impulses of the waves—internal and external waves equally.

This appears to be the keystone piece of confusion—not the waves that push the personality/egoic self into different experiences, but one's inability to go with it. This resistance takes place at an internal level. It feels like a tightness in the chest and may be labeled as anxiety or anger. Now, there's little to be done, externally speaking—if one gets laid off from a job, if one's car is totaled, if a relationship breaks off—but internally one will either not go-with-the-flow or *choose* to flow with it. The choice only appears as a choice when one is *aware* there is a choice. Resistance implies no choice, or no awareness that a choice exists, because no sane person chooses to intentionally cause their own suffering (in the form of producing and sustaining negative emotional states).[7]

So although one may constantly *choose* to "resist" or "accept" what is, if there is no awareness of the two possibilities, then the nega-

---

7   There's a quote attributed to the Buddha that says: "Holding on to anger is like grasping a hot coal with the intent of throwing it at someone else; you are the one who gets burned."

tive occurrences in life will be resisted by default. This is to be unconscious in the spiritual sense.

If there is awareness, then the negative event will be accepted internally to the *extent* awareness is there. No one *chooses* to resist the present moment. If choice were always presented plainly, which implies two or more possibilities weighed against one another in clear terms (for example, [A] resist an unjust firing, feeling angry and embarrassed along the way, *or* [B] accept the outcome with the understanding that negative emotions will not change the outcome and move on), then acceptance would always be picked over resistance.

PREDETERMINISM AND FREE WILL

As far as predeterminism and free will are concerned, they are nothing more than mental concepts. At the most fundamental level, when one accepts the Now, those far-reaching, abstract philosophies dissolve away from the mind. As Ram Dass, the late spiritual teacher, would say:

"You have free will to the extent that you know who you are."

"Who you are" is the space in which *all that is occurring* exists. You are Awareness—observing all perceptions, thoughts and perhaps even Awareness itself. To say that one's life is predetermined points to the habits of behaviors and thought patterns that form as, or in tandem with, an egoic sense of self. It is the *ego* that lives like Bill Murray's character in Groundhog's Day, not You. To the extent You identify with the ego, your life situation might *appear* predetermined. The mind brushes over the past and future to generalize most days as the same as all the ones before and to follow.

Yet, upon coming into this moment now. Wherever you hold this book. This present moment is more unique than any memory that the mind could remember from the past or imagine about the future. *It is unique because it is all there is.* It has nothing to do with whether similar events have taken place before. (I'm sure the reader has read from the same place before, perhaps holding the same book). It has everything to do with ungraspability of the totality of one's perceptions of the external and internal world. By identifying a limited selection of memories as "unique moments," the actual uniqueness has been clipped at the wings and deadened by its association to a used-out word. Saying "unique" is not what constitutes uniqueness in actuality.

Labeling does not make it so.

The quote at the start of the essay points to this truth: The "eye" of the beholder is the eye of judgement and comparison, but the "heart" of the beholder does no such thing. There is beauty when there is beauty. There is uniqueness when there is uniqueness. That is all.

To claim to know, from memory, the *most* beautiful or unique thing, is a delusion of thought. To believe the verbalized thought placed on the memory *is* beauty or uniqueness is analogous to believing the tail wags the dog.

So it is here, wherever that is for the reader, in its absolute nowness, which *is* the space of free will. No, it is not how the term is commonly used, often with regard to big, life-altering dilemmas; to move away or to stay, to chug along in the mediocre job or to quit. Rather, this "space of free will" is the ineffable emptiness that underlies all "choice." In the case of the cliched dilemma, *should I stay or should I go*, the space of free will is the underlying stillness that observes the mental push and pull of thought-forms as they arise in the Now. This stillness (synonymous with Awareness or Unconditioned Consciousness) cannot take a side, and instead observes the totality of the dilemma.

It is the realization that You are Awareness: Aware of thought-forms as a stream of internal objects to behold.[8] Except, this "space of free will" doesn't appear to have the control that one commonly associates with free will. *I only observe what is occurring? And I do nothing about it?* The reader may think.

Upon first inspection, this realization that one is eternally in

---

8   As a way to realize this at an experiential level, stand in front of a mirror. Rather than looking at the body in center frame, become aware of the wholeness of your sight perception. Keep your eyes on the body though. It may be tough to *see* the body as one's own and to *be aware* of all to be seen; however, one can oscillate between the two. Wholeness and specificity; Wholeness and detail; Wholeness and ego. Realize now, as a visual metaphor, the body is one's stream of thought; all of sight perception is present moment awareness, which includes but is infinitely more encompassing than the contents of one's thoughts. Krishnamurti, and other spiritual teachers, describe this as the "vertical" dimension of consciousness, which occurs now and is transcendent of past identity and belief systems, as opposed to the "horizontal" dimension, which occurs now but is conditioned by past and future. It sounds esoteric, but it's intuitive when imagining an abstract timeline of history: "Horizontal" measures the span of time, "vertical" measures the spaciousness of everything occurring within the small sliver on the timeline called "now."

this so-called "space of free will" appears paralyzing, or at least like hyperbole: *It's not really all the time, is it?* Not only does the author's description appear passive and counter-intuitive to one's initial thoughts of "free will," but it also lacks logical certainty; the kind one feels when answering a question like "What's $2 + 2$?"

No rational argument could prove or disprove the truth of this "space of free will."

So why bring it up? Why point toward something that cannot be fully grasped by the rational mind? Because this is the space where all creative acts take place: Out of the empty mind.

This idea of "art arising out of emptiness" is important to remember while in the midst of *any* self-expressive act. **In knowing that intelligence can arise outside the boundaries of rational, causal arguments—outside the boundaries of linear thought—one is free to trust the process as it unfolds.** It is a black box system; it can be applied but not deconstructed. This is "faith" without the religious overtones. Faith that, as an example, as the author writes now, the lines that are written will read as coherent and evoke a certain set of insights within the reader.

That's not to say rules and constraints must be thrown to the wind. This is an essay and will transform into a fictional story on a whim. The rules and constraints (i.e., the structure) that relate to cohesion in a creative act/work are intuitive. It would be silly to scrutinize the confines of genre for no particular reason. The medium (e.g., a book in general or a nonfiction essay in particular) is only a vessel to carry a message to the reader's mind.[9]

---

9   The reader may have heard the phrase "The medium is the message," coined, and argued for, by Marshall McLuhan. It is true, the medium plays a role in *whom* an idea reaches: The number of potential book readers is smaller than the number of potential TV watchers or social media scrollers. It is also true that those book readers likely lead a different life than those who consume information only through television, which would influence *how* they interpret the content. Still, McLuhan's point has been taken to an extreme in modern times. Since McLuhan's declaration, the author believes too much scrutiny and college-level analysis is on the medium rather than the message. College students, according to the author's experience, are more adept at explaining the biases implicit in every medium than they are at explaining and scrutinizing the messages/theories that *shape their thinking* about those biases. In essence, higher education (in the humanities and social sciences) has created a culture of trainspotting rather than train conducting: *Too many reactive and reductive points about old ideas, and not enough new creative messages.*

The true impediment/constraint is *expectations* of what the creative work or activity should be or achieve (i.e., seeking the fruit of the action). That is ultimately what writer's block boils down to—a resistance to the current flow of creative ideas because it doesn't meet a certain standard in the individual's mind (again, this can apply just as easily to the golfer or gardener). That standard is guaranteed to be influenced by the society at large because, in a social vacuum, no ideas would appear as good or bad because they would exist without comparison.[10]

DESTINY

It appears as though the piece has derailed from the initial premise, *how does one find or discover or act upon their "born-to-do" activity (i.e., one's life purpose)?* The reader must intuitively know that the author is not able to write out a list of step-by-step instructions to apply to the general reader. It would require an understanding about each reader's unique life situation. Therefore, it is on you to introspectively know what is true.

All the author can do is strip the many social constraints that impede one's discovery. He will act like the archaeologist, brushing away the dust so that the buried bones of passion may reveal themselves in the reader's mind.

The allure of upward social mobility, near-infinite career choice, and the American credo of constant and never-ending improvement make this task of "finding one's passion" appear difficult. Even the word "finding" implies that one must discover their *thing* in the external world. What actually happens is that something in the external world awakens a latent passion in the person. "Awaken" is used to imply that it has been there all along. This is where destiny comes in. It is to connect the dots of the past in order to explain, in perfect

---

10   The author is not arguing that social comparison or quality standards on art or literature are *bad* or *counterproductive*. To the extent that present-day politics can be filtered out of these standards, they serve as useful benchmarks to improve one's artistic mastery. However, to the extent present-day politics, financial incentives and fear of social ostracization act like a mind-virus on the artist or writer—there will be a stifled, limiting quality to the work of that time. We are living through one of these mind-virus periods now. It will take individual courage to heal: Take a break from the contagious political collectives online. Come back to your senses.

retrospect, how one ended up where they are today. Faith in a personal destiny is merely to trust that the dots that connected in the past will also, somehow, connect in the future. Faith that one's life path, which is unknowable and cannot be veered from, is what is meant to happen. That is to be in the flow of what life offers.

HOW TO REALIZE YOUR "LIFE'S PURPOSE"

In concluding, it feels right to offer three heuristics to assist in uncovering one's born-to-do activity:

1. *"Your passion" does not need to be bound to one medium or one subject matter for an entire lifetime.*

It appears that the author is saying one is free to float from one thing to the next with no thought of coherence. That is true, though this points to the fact that any willful attempt to bottle in one's passion will constrain it. The author writes and will likely write another book in the future, but there is no pressure to be *only* a writer of the spiritual variety.

If one's life's work exists in one medium, focused on one theme, which is common, then it is a byproduct of uninhibited activity—who tells Stephen King to keep writing horror novels? One's personality will inevitably act like gravity in keeping one's projects within a certain sphere, but this happens without effort or willpower. It is the young reader who must be especially cautious about boxing in their natural curiosity before allowing it to explore freely. Social media, as a tool of social approval, is poison to this state of free exploration.

It is okay if the activity does not seem connected to any previous interests. There is no need to justify it.

2. *"Your passion" does not need to fill one with a manic joy for all of one's waking hours.*

Feelings, which rise and fall in the body with no clear distinction, are always bound to their opposite. The feeling of happiness or excitement will eventually bring the feelings of apathy or depression or calmness at a later time. High energy must flow into low energy, which must flow into high energy and so on. This idea that one must wake up with a manic eagerness to get back to their passion is only true in rhetoric.

Not every day can be fruitful and not every moment can be active. The rubber band of burnout comes for the exceptions.

To detest a moment of calm or rest goes against the flow of life. Not all seasons will feel like spring; not all days will be sunny. It is okay if the activity does not feel positive all the time.

3. *"Your passion" does not need to save the world, but it must change it.*

A great fallacy in realizing one's born-to-do activity is believing that it must alter the world in a monumental way. Not all people will be written about in the centralized history books or have work in the Western canon. This desire, or implicit assumption, that a life purpose must be *world-changing* is the ego seeking fame by virtuous means. That said, the activity or creations *may* end up in the history books (or the Western canon), but this is a byproduct of the work—not something to be sought from the get-go.

However, the work or activity must change something. It is not enough to talk about doing something. Action must be taken. The mirage of perfection must be confronted. It is the people full of ideas and opinions, but no outlet or discipline, who need to be high alert: Sitting on potential means nothing. Do not delude yourself with thoughts of "Someday I will …"

It is okay if the activity impacts only a few people or even just you. That is enough. No activity is too big or too small, so long as it changes something.

It is the author's deepest hope that the reader will feel an added level of reassurance in the art they produce and the activities they pursue. One's uniqueness is implied in their existence. The question of "What am I here for?" never requires a verbalized answer—it is always meant to be lived, acted out or held up to the world (in the form of a finished work) while you give your deepest bow.

Here is the gift. It is now sitting in your mind. It came from nothing, and it is dedicated to the existence of you.

CHAPTER 4

POLITICAL POLARIZATION: WHERE TO FIND WHOLENESS IN OUR SOCIETY OF DIVISION

Love and do what you will.

— *Saint Augustine*

It is almost satirical how divisive American politics have become. It has grown cliché. The author would not call it a skill any longer—if it ever was—for a writer or "tweeter" to use their words like a knife to cut bone-deep, leaving "us" on one side and "them" on the other. Rather, it is an impulse, and a childish one at that (no matter how big the vocabulary one uses to divide).

Not all individuals lust for a villain or scapegoat, however. There are attempts to reunite the "Divided States of America" made by politicians from time to time, but their speeches invariably carry the baggage of the speaker's party. The political bias is assumed of the speaker, whether the speech's content shows this or not. So, the citizens—the ones who root for the other team—will wait until their news channel or podcast of choice gives the recap of the event. Whichever news source is picked will have its own bias (that much is obvious), but, because it aligns with the viewer's sense of "who to trust," it appears negligible or non-existent: like finding a pair of glasses with one's exact prescription already fitted in.

Bias, specifically political bias, the buzz word which grows hollow with overuse, is important in the conversation of finding, or rather *realizing*, unity in a divisive society, but this will be touched on later.

There is—outside of the gradient of the overtly divisive op-ed journalist-activists (of any political affiliation) and the covertly biased politicians—a group who seeks to stand outside of bias: comedians. Not all, but some are wise enough to call a spade a spade, whether it's red or blue (for example, Bill Maher or George Carlin).

For the markedly biased comedian, they may always have an ignorant fan base who sees evil *only* in the opposition and cackles at their shortcomings. What is missed in this approach is that they not only cut ties with people aligned with the other political party, but such one-sidedness also erodes trust in the moderate and independent thinker (i.e., the silent majority).

THE NEW SILENT MAJORITY

It is this "silent majority," originally mentioned by Richard Nixon in a 1969 speech in reference to the conservative-leaning, non-revolting, modest citizen, whom the author seeks to speak to. Although, the group Nixon once referred to is no longer representative of *who* this quiet collective is. There is no war to protest, no Woodstock to attend and no Ram Dass events to see. On first glance, it may appear that a flip-flop has taken place. There is not a fight for free speech from the liberal voter but from the conservative one. (The author understands that this fight for free speech arises from a different place than the '60s Democrat). As a generalization, the liberal of the 1960s who embodied free speech, equal rights and peace has transformed to the liberal of the 2020s who embodies politically correct speech, group identity-based rights and safety.

This essay will not dwell on *why* such a stark shift has occurred. Rather, the shift in the outspoken liberal's values is pointed out because the author believes that the values held by the 1960s liberal represent that of the "silent majority" of today.

There is the possibility that the reader of this essay has self-identified with one political party as opposed to identifying as an "independent." Therefore, it may appear ignorant to refer to the silent majority as liberal (old-school liberal) leaning when the recent popular vote percentages do not reflect stark differences between the Democratic and Republican candidates (the largest popular vote gap since 2000 was 7.2% when Obama beat McCain in 2008).[1]

Merely referring to the modern-day silent majority as holding similar values as the old-school liberal, in social values specifically,

---

1   "United States Presidential Election Results." *Encyclopædia Britannica*, Encyclopædia Britannica, inc., 27 Aug. 2023, www.britannica.com/topic/United-States-Presidential-Election-Results-1788863.

does not mean they must identify or vote as a liberal today. Freedom of speech is possibly the primary example of an old-school liberal siding with a modern conservative over her own present-day counterpart.

THE PROBLEM WITH MORAL VALUES

The last sentence could unfold into a well-meaning, but ultimately divisive, essay railing on politically correct speech. Every reader would feel affirmed in their opinion on the topic, whether smug in agreement or enraged in disagreement. As was said at the top of the essay, such divisive writing is impulsive and, frankly, easy to do. It gives the ego an opinion to attach to (likely derived from an argument with no definitive answer to *ever* be claimed) and a group of moral adversaries to hate and fight against.

This is the kind of writing most often seen as it relates to politics. Make no mistake, *there is a place for it.* It demands critical thinking and prompts debate, which can be healthy. However, no debate at all is sickness and one which we are witnessing today. Everyone is sheltered in their own bubble of curated content. Most of that content, because of the nature of the attention-based, ad-based profit model, is made quickly, using clickbait titling, with extremist points of view and as a reaction to something else.

It's alluring and addictive. The consumer of information becomes like a digital rubbernecker who cannot help but hold their gaze on the enraging mess glowing from the smart phone in their hand.

Except, what makes one attracted to such content in the first place? **It is tension sparked by seeing one's personal beliefs attacked or further affirmed.** It may be argued that this content attracts attention because it sparks rage or fear in the viewer, but such a point ignores that every emotional reaction sparked by such content must be based in a personal belief/viewpoint (otherwise, the person would not care).

How the Conservatives Are Screwing over the Middle Class (Again).

How the Liberals Are Wasting Your Tax Dollars.

Two generalized political headlines. Given a bit more nuance, even the most sophisticated viewer would click.

It's important to note that such clickbait titling need not be bound to politics, but *any* opinion held close to one's self-identity. For exam-

ple: content about "how to become a millionaire," "how to study better," "how to manifest abundance," "how to be more anti-racist," or
"how to gain 10,000 new followers in 30 days," all have a similar
allure quality to a certain subset of people.

It's not the clickbait (i.e., the loaded promise of information)
which is alluring, but its relation to one's moral values. The author, for
example, would never be sucked into "study tips" as a genre of content
because it is irrelevant to his life. In using the word "moral," it likely
has a connotation of living rightly according to a religion or school
of philosophy. In the way the author is uses it here, the term encompasses something much larger. It can be revealed, for each individual,
in answering the questions:

"How do I live a good life? What is my purpose?"

There are as many answers as one can think of, and living according to
a religious creed may or may not be a piece of one's answer.

For the Christian of any sect, the answer to the previous question
may be "give charitably, serve humbly, and love thy neighbor with all
thy heart." The ego, which seeks nothing more than self-preservation,
feasts on such hollow, good-sounding words.[2] They are the ephemeral
standards by which the mind orients itself toward future action. These
morals serve as the carrot, which sits always one bite out of reach
of you: the ego, John or Jane Doe—the jackass. It is a carrot, which
you position out of reach for yourself; in hopes of "becoming a better person."

The carrot on the stick can also take on a more selfish or short-term
flavor: to attain the next high. To make the next million. To achieve
"celebrity-status" (which social media platforms have allowed us to
quantify via follower count). It is a goal/ideal/standard to be achieved
sometime in the future, no matter if it is considered morally good or
bad that creates and sustains *the trap* that keeps one dissatisfied with
the present moment. **The trap, in plain terms, is to be fully identified
with the ego.**

To reiterate, the term "ego," as used here, means all thoughts, all

---

2   The problem is not the call for charitable behavior, but the self-made pride
or guilt one feels based on whether they are in alignment with the doctrine or
not. The author believes these negative emotional states caused by self-judgement can dissolve while still orienting one's actions toward such altruistic
behavior.

aspects of one's socialized personality, and all references to "me." Every person, from the lofty saint to the lowly criminal, has an ego. Most human beings are trapped and isolated by it. It's heard in the phrases "I can't stand myself," or "I've got to get out of my head!"

At the core, ego is formed by the conceptual division between "I" and "other." This division affects everything from one's view of a politically opposed citizen to one's view of certain undesirable traits in one's personality (e.g., when a person "beats himself up" because he lost his temper).

However, for most people, this division is so fundamental to their worldview that an alternative has never been considered. Without introspection, the general assumption is that "I," as an individual, and the "others," as anything outside of one's self, is implied from birth. **The fallacy arises in being too close to the error.** The newborn baby has no mental division between "I" and "other," but you, in the moment you think of the belief, *project* that division onto everything you observe. That projection of division applies to the external world as well as any arising memories or hypothetical thoughts. It is the pair of glasses placed so close to the eyes that one forgets that it filters their current perception.

But can this dividing quality of mind be turned off or stopped? What would exist *outside* of this subject-object paradigm? What does it leave if one is no longer "totally identified" with his or her ego? *The Unspeakable beyond label.*

THE INDIVISIBLE WORLD

The reader is what is called the ego *as well as* the encompassing space that allows the ego to be. There is nothing larger, nothing smaller, nothing older and nothing younger than who one truly is. Both size and age depend on relative points. When nothing is measured (or when one realizes the unmeasurable, unlabeled, unspeakable world that is here now) the loftiest questions about God and Nirvana and "Wait, what came before the Big Bang?" are answered *in* silence.

However, such insight does not stop scientists from seeking to answer—though more often *explain*—the world human beings are swimming in. What invisible particles float in the air? What photons bounce around this room that illuminate the author's view? What wigging sound waves slither into his ears as he writes this now?

The impulse to know is beautiful, but only when a level of consciousness has been realized that allows for a sustained non-attachment to the egoic mind. Otherwise, scientific discovery follows the same pattern of religion's influence on the state: The scientists who "get it" take on a self-righteous attitude and, in time, hit a point of safeguarding the current consensus instead of seeking to falsify and improve it. Science then turns into scientism. This will be detailed in the following essay.

Although this seems far removed from healing an extreme political divide in a society, Self-knowledge, in the sense described above, is the first step to seeing past one's politics.

FACTS AND STATS

Facts don't care about one's feelings—or so the author has heard. Often from the most prideful tongue. That's common, is it not? To hear arguments of objective facts and infallible statistics (an oxymoron) from those who've staked their identity on such facts.

Well, facts and stats may not care about feelings, but they do spark them. Statistics have become weapons—fired off at the opposition in hopes of killing their argument. As has been said earlier in this book, when the mind is so attached to opinions and ideals (staking one's sense of self on these things), any attacks on those opinions will feel like someone is trying to annihilate *them*. This kind of verbal attack often makes the mind cling even tighter to its original beliefs and form a closer connection with the egos who affirm said beliefs.

It is no coincidence that social media (i.e., mass communication with little to no filter) has coincided with a culture of animosity and distrust of anyone with an opposing viewpoint. The reader is now able to exist entirely in whichever bubble of ideology they prefer. The algorithm is designed to give someone what they want to see (not consciously, but from the perspective of their ego-mind). Yes, it feeds us violence and negativity, but more critically, it has infused political polarization into *everything newsworthy*.

POSTMODERNISM AND OBJECTIVE TRUTH

Although the author pokes at the validity of supporting opinions with objective truth, this is not to be confused with the postmodernist argument, which says (as a generalization): Certain people, the oppressors, use language and narratives to shape other people's perception of the world (i.e., to do X behavior is good, to do Y behavior is evil) in order to gain power for themselves. This power is maintained through social institutions, which, as the postmodernist claims, must be dismantled if there is ever going to be equality (in however they define it). Also, social constructs, such as binary genders, which are [according to them] created by the patriarchy, are designed to maintain the roles of oppressor and oppressed (to maintain power for the oppressor).

The bleak irony is that, in the present-day postmodernist's retribution against "the oppressors," they become the very thing they sought to dismantle.[3] Language and narratives are now reversed to paint the oppressor (which is a collective identity and rarely directed to a single person) as the villain. Power floats to those who pointed to the powerful and called them evil. In essence, the ego identifies as the victim in order to provide itself with a purposeful fight for justice. (Another carrot dangled in front of the donkey).

In what the author is saying, all ideals and morals articulated as a dogmatic doctrine (whether secular or religious) are created by the ego to perpetuate its existence. This is not to say it is wrong to do, but it must be acknowledged. These ideals of "how to live a virtuous life" are subjective, open to debate and, ultimately, unfalsifiable. They can spark useful reflection for self-correction (e.g., how truthful have I been? Have I sinned? Where have I been too prideful?), but must be separated from scientific objective truth. They are not the same.

Yet, in the postmodernist argument, all objective truth is deemed the oppressor's language game designed to maintain power (thereby calling it subjective too). This is a corrosive belief that leads to the decay of social institutions.

If human beings give up the idea of objective truth, then the institution of science is castigated on the basis of ideology (e.g., Is this discovery politically correct? Were all identity groups consulted in the finding?). This disregards the fact that any scientific discovery can be verified by anyone with the education to understand it (making it objectively true, in common sense terms).

All debates once argued on the basis of reason, logic and evidence decay into moral arguments fought on the basis of emotion. Who feels the strongest about their point of view? In this change, the debate is no longer about *what* is factually correct and factually incorrect, but *who*

---

3   The postmodernist is more likely to be referred to as a "social justice activist" or "activist scholar." Such terms will be the focus of the next essay.

is morally virtuous and who is evil.

The societal response to the assertions of postmodernism has been to alter institutions to avoid or reduce feelings of discomfort for the self-identified victims (or victim-protectors, yet another ego identity). Protecting one from feeling certain emotions is a trap designed to keep the ego intact. Once it is realized that *You* are not the emotional sensations, but the observer of them, then all bodily sensations, which can be felt without thinking or complaining about them, are accepted the moment they occur. Therefore, no emotions are resisted.

As an analogy, the difference is whether one pulls out a thorn when it pokes them or if they keep it in the skin and guard it from further discomfort: The former is instinct, the latter is insanity.

THE COVID CLASH

Coming back to all things newsworthy, the author is reminded of the multifaceted COVID clash that took center stage in America from 2020 to 2022. There were political battles of lockdown vs. anti-lockdown, mask vs. anti-mask and, of course, the vaxxer vs. anti-vaxxer.

Yes, there was misinformation being spread by unqualified quacks. However, a vast amount of questioning and other possible solutions to a vaccine by qualified people were lumped in with those called quacks. Anti-vaxxers (of the mRNA vaccine specifically) were vilified, deemed to be of a lower IQ (to put it lightly), or looked upon with pity from self-righteous eyes. They were also lumped in with, and ridiculed because of, the more conspiratorial skeptics against vaccination.

There was hardly a breath after the initial confusion of the virus's rapid spread before two-sides formed—like repelling magnets—and began to rail on the opposition. In a way, misinformation became a catch-all term for "whatever *I deem* factually incorrect."[4] The people

---

4   The most blatant example of this was the ridicule of the drug Ivermectin in legacy media. A meta-analysis of the drug (which means multiple studies being reviewed to reduce the chance of bias) showed "moderate-certainty evidence finds that large reductions in COVID-19 deaths are possible using Ivermectin."[7] That analysis was published in June of 2021. In August of the same year, CNN published an article with the title "Right-wing media pushed a deworming drug to treat COVID-19 that the FDA says is unsafe for humans" in reference to the same drug.[12] The author will give the journalist the benefit of the doubt in saying that he wished to prevent citizens from buying bulk quantities of Ivermectin meant for horses (because it can be purchased easily

sought out those with expert status, trusting that their qualifications would act as their own citation for their opinions. There is nothing wrong with outsourcing intelligence in an area one has no experience—it's wise. The problem arose as the vilification of and inability to accept those who went against the grain of the mainstream consensus.

The author knows of at least one person who would, in jest, wish the disease on the unvaccinated just to convince them to get the shot. **In this unconscious pattern of political factioning, one loses all compassion for their fellow human beings even in the most universally trying times.**

The vaccine was not the keystone solution to ending the pandemic, but many treated it as such. Of course, the glaring analogy is that of the Christian missionaries, imposing their religion on the "savages" by any means necessary if it saves their souls from eternal damnation. And where did that road paved with good intentions lead?

There was no black and white solution to COVID-19. The people, the government and the media responded in the only way they could—unconsciously (that is not the same as saying "incorrectly"). The author does not wish to stir old resentments. It is only mentioned to point out that hypocrisy, a refusal to listen to new and/or opposing information with an open mind, and distrust and hatred for the "other" existed on both sides of the debate. To only see the flaws in the opposition's argument and not one's own is to deny a piece of one's self. This will be touched on in a moment.

It was not the virus or the vaccine that divided the people. The people were already divided, and COVID-19 was kindling for the flames of opposition. The collective response to the virus, and the opposing narratives which arose in America, will be a pattern that repeats with every large-scale event for the rest of history *until* the majority of people become conscious enough to see through the veil of good and evil:

---

online and is not meant for humans). However, he did not clarify that the drug also exists for humans, nor did he do any research into the potential validity of the drug. It took only one internet search of "Ivermectin for COVID studies" to find the meta-analysis in the National Library of Medicine. This glaring discrepancy took two minutes to discover. The author does not think many readers will actually look at the study linked, but it is there for those who demand evidence. Let this example of "misinformation" convey that there is a difference between a conspiracy theory about the media and pointing out a clear example of the media misconstruing and negating publicly available scientific research.

the illusion of "us" versus "them."[5]

BEYOND GOOD AND EVIL

To see beyond good and evil is quite a jump from the mind's incli-
nation to *be* good and its aversion to *become* evil. The response the
author has heard to such a claim—that good and evil are only labels
the egoic mind gives to things, and You are not the ego—is:

> *Won't everyone just indulge in all their vices and evil impulses if*
> *there is not an intention to be good?*

To answer that, it is important to bring in the ideas of Carl G. Jung,
the dream-interpreting psychologist—or so he is hazily known. In
his book, *The Undiscovered Self,* he explains that in one's refusal
to accept the capacity for evil within one's self, one will invariably
impose/project that shadow of evil upon one's enemy. The key word
is "capacity," not that one needs to act on the evil, but that one must
accept its existence within him or herself.[6]

**Only when one can *be aware* of the two sides at war within
one's own mind can there be a transcendence above good and evil,
or at least, a ceasing to project evil upon the enemy.** The two opposites are clarified to be like a house of cards: without one, the other
cannot stand.

It may enrage or confuse the reader to think that "evil" is necessary for "good" to exist within a single individual. *It is only necessary
to the extent that "being good" is necessary for you to exist.* One
cannot have a magnet with only one pole. It's the deal, Jack. Take it
or leave it. Opposites are inseparable, except in the mind that hides/
suppresses/resists/denies/projects one side of the whole.[7]

---

5   This does not imply that [spiritually] unconscious people are wrong or
inferior. Avoid the temptation to create a moral high ground to stand upon.
6   *But I could never do something evil,* the reader may think. The very fact
that the reader is a human being with biological instincts that often undermine
moral tendencies all but guarantee that the capacity is always there, even if it is
dormant now. The unconscious psyche can easily trick the person to engage in
evil and violence in the name of "peace," "justice" or even "scientific innovation." The creation of the atomic bomb is an example of the latter. Be on high
alert for the second-order evils that can arise from "good intentions."
7   This suppression is what creates the unconscious "shadow" in one's psyche.

In the same book, in an essay called "Self-Knowledge," Jung points to dictators of the State (in reference to the Soviet Union) intentionally isolating the individual person from their fellow neighbor in order to strengthen the authority and reliance on the dictatorship. The author is struck by how relevant his insights read today. In a point about self-criticism, he notes:

> "We can recognize our prejudices and illusions only when, from a broader psychological knowledge of ourselves and others, we are prepared to doubt the absolute rightness of our assumptions and compare them carefully and conscientiously with the objective facts."[8]

Right after, he points out that Marxist countries hold self-criticism in high regard, but only to the extent that the self is critical of its thoughts and behaviors in relation to the communist ideology (i.e., subjective/distorted truth).[9]

Again, this term "objective facts" comes up. Although, instead of in the weaponized sense of the word, as referenced before, the author believes that Jung's usage equates to a whole-picture view. Objectivity made objective by the nature of combining opposing, subjective views into a whole.[10]

---

8   Jung, C. G., *The Undiscovered Self*, p. 100.

9   The author wishes to make clear that, in critiquing a dictatorship versus a democratic country, there is clear distinction in the severity and intentionality of suffering caused under each government. Any critiques of American politics are attributed to the mass amount of unconscious people (i.e., people totally identified with the ego) involved rather than a handful of controlling overlords. Yes, there are corrupt people in the U.S. government, but the author is grateful for the bureaucratic slowness, which prevents swift ideological changes. It is worth thinking this out for yourself.

10   This "combination of subjective views" occurs in one's own psyche. In essence, Jung uses "self-criticism" to mean be humble even in instances where you feel absolutely certain about the rightness of your position in a debate. You need a counterweight to your pride! If you cannot find a flaw (or many flaws) in your position, then that is a sure sign that those flaws are being suppressed or ignored. Take capitalism vs. socialism, for example; proponents of each see the other perspective as not merely wrong, but evil and morally abhorrent. Self-criticism allows one to acknowledge the good and evil *within* their position, rather than using "socialism" or "capitalism" as a scapegoat for all the evils in a society. It is a matter of trade-offs and choosing the lesser of two evils—*not aiming for a utopian world.* The sooner one can acknowledge and

This may read like a paradox, or impractical common sense (like claiming "heads and tails make up a coin").

Though it is an individual's rejection of the "other" that keeps her from wholeness within herself. There is no point in aiming at political change when both sides are made up of rigid and dysfunctional egos oblivious to their own thought patterns (and ignorant of their instinctive capacity for violence). Denial of this, or more likely, to say "my side's not as dysfunctional as *their* side," misses the point entirely!

America may still be distanced from any overtly authoritarian government, but the road is being paved by our unconscious distancing and lack of compassion for those who think from a different perspective. The term "unconscious" is used—not to imply that people are blind to the moral splitting in the U.S. (it's all anyone ever talks about)—but that they are blind to how to rectify the split.

WHOLENESS

It begins and ends with the individual.

The reader, who may *get* and on some level *agree* with what is being said, may still find him or herself flaring with anger sometime in the next 24 hours because of the "stupidity" and "ignorance" of an outspoken person with an opposite viewpoint. Whether it's the truck or Prius's political bumper sticker, some piece of hate-bait on the internet or a conversation overheard at work.

As certain morals (which act as the foundation of an egoic sense of self) are manipulated online to gain viewers' attention, a person may become more aware of how they are being strung along because of their beliefs. **It is like the monkey whose hand fits inside a jar to grab a piece of fruit, but who cannot pull it out because their closed fist is too big to escape.** One's tightly held beliefs are *why* they are sucked into the polarized, fear/anger-provoking content so easily.

So, although divisive content creators may knowingly manipulate basic human impulses for money and attention, this is not a cry to condemn the people who profit off the moral splitting in America. There need not be a war waged against the extremists and their pundits (the urge to do so is an unconscious reaction from the egoic mind

---

accept the good and evil impulses within himself or herself, the quicker one can realize the ever-present peace within this moment now.

and not You).

If one is aware of the personal anguish and suffering caused by compulsive consumption of this divisive content; if one is aware that they are stuffing themselves with this content because they observe that their foundational beliefs, i.e., their self-identity, are being pricked like a Voodoo doll; if one is aware they are, in a word, trapped, then the important question to follow is, "What is one supposed to do about it?"

The answer, which is as difficult as it is simple, is awareness. Not *mindfulness*. Not *meditate*. Not *forgive*. Not *love thy enemy because it's "good for you."* Only awareness—awareness of what is happening in this moment now.

Awareness of *what is* brings a natural distancing of You from the ego as well as any collective groups it has attached to. With an understanding that You are not the ego, there is a natural reduction of hatred, fear and isolation. Even as those thoughts and sensations arise again (because a long-pedaled wheel will keep spinning for a time), it becomes obvious that total identification with one's own thought patterns only leads to suffering. Love arises when the tight clinging to beliefs and ideals are seen as perpetuating the reactive insanity in the opposition (as well as the suffering in one's own mind). The dis-identification from divisive beliefs happens without effort upon knowing thyself:

> *We are the same, You and I,*
> *Born and bound to simple frames.*

There is no ideal or moral code the author could write that would not inevitably become one side of a coin, which implies opposition or "other." Only by identifying with the underlying emptiness behind all thoughts can those reactive emotions, rooted in tightly-held beliefs, dissolve away.[11]

---

11   The author presumes that the reader will still have a variety of ideal and foundational beliefs in their mind that appear critical to maintain. The idea of no longer fiercely defending an ideal may equate to the pain of losing a critical [culture] war. This is a projection of fear from the ego afraid of its own dissolution. It is not You creating those projections of fear. As the Witness of the mind's arising counterpoints to the ideas in this essay, must you believe all that mental noise? What would happen if you choose to *observe* the thoughts without clinging to them as *your beliefs?* Simply, observe it as you would a stampede of animals whilst on a safari—let it pass; let the dust settle. Once the reactive, emotional energy has subsided, then clarify your beliefs

Awareness that you are not "your" opinions and beliefs. Awareness that, put in the same life situation as another, you would hold the same viewpoint as them.[12] Awareness that the capacity for evil exists in every person, and by denying this you only strengthen your fear and resistance against the so-called enemy (perpetuating the illusion of ego).

A fear of people deemed "other" (i.e., people of opposing belief systems) is a projection of the fear in your body and mind. This might take the form of vague thoughts of living in a dystopian future if the "other" were to win the [culture] war.[13]

The problem is not actually the end result, which you may imagine as an apocalyptic end of days, but your inability to be aware that such visions are merely thoughts arising self-so in your mind. It is created in this moment now. You are watching it. You are here, reading a book, breathing in and out. Notice that? Look around where you are at this moment. Notice that? That is more than the contents of the thinking mind.

THE WORST THAT COULD HAPPEN

If World War III were upon us now, where would your mind go? Still, the author presumes, it would project itself into the future. If you follow the fear-provoking thoughts all the way to the end, the core fear is *always* the obliteration of ego: Either actual death or death of the environment one has grown used to. Do not merely believe what is being said—think it out:

> Take a moment now to imagine and see the full picture of your worst fear, specifically, a fear that would affect society at large. What is the literal physical sensation that the mind labels as "fear"? What is the thing that you believe will alter your psyche beyond

---

and opinions.

12   Make no mistake, this does not condone or excuse violent behavior, nor does it prevent one from stopping or penalizing such behavior when it occurs.

13   How does the real and dysfunctional leadership in Russia and China factor into this? Any grievances Americans hold for them are likely reciprocated in their opposite toward us (even if only between governments). Also, the author does not have the power to stop any geopolitical conflict, only the power to open the reader's eyes to the duality within him or herself: Dysfunction is not conquered by gunning down the dysfunctional, it is superseded in Awareness. It is slow-dawning insight—not good-sounding but impractical advice.

recognition? If one is afraid of being a social outcast (which may be more common in this post-cancel culture era), what is the crux of the fear? What scares you the most about it? The author is not saying to imagine a grotesque gore-fest in your mind, but to keep asking, "Why do I fear this thing? Why do I fear that? And why do I fear that?" until it is boiled down to a physical sensation and/or a simplified fear such as:

- Fear of losing/not having love
- Fear of the unknown/death
- Fear of isolation
- Fear of losing freedom of choice
- Fear of intense pain
- Fear of chronic illness/trauma

That is one way to unmask the ego. In stripping away the theatrics of one's worst fear (often, the reader will not realize how foggy their worst fear is until one seeks to understand it), all that is left is a timid ego, which has been caught in the ruse.

Listen very closely to your mental monologue from this point on.

☼☼☼

Does the author seem to trivialize your fear? Does he just not get it? Does something feel wrong or incorrect about boiling a deep fear down to a handful of bulletpoints? What does that "wrong" feeling feel like in the body?

You need only feel the feelings until they pass. You can focus deeply on your body, not indulge in mental commentary, and realize every physical sensation, no matter how uncomfortable, *is all there is*. All you have to do is be here now and experience what is. Of course, there are techniques (breathing patterns, mantras, certain yoga positions, etc.) to stay present when the physical sensations are most intense, but that's not what this book is for. All you have to do is continuously fold every sensation and reactive thought into your non-judgemental awareness.

THE GAP BETWEEN THOUGHTS

Imagine, for a moment, that "who you are" is the silent space between thoughts rather than the contents of thought. If this were true, it would be simple and obvious to let go of moment-to-moment chatter in favor of silence when you realize you are caught up in a destructive, negative thought pattern (or even a "positive" manic thought pattern).

As an analogy, consider the "silent space" to be all the water in a river, whereas thoughts are the fish swimming within it. In such a place, let's say, you may decide to follow the path of a fish as it swims within you (i.e., a thought pattern). Over the span of the fish's journey, you may become so invested in its life that you *forget* you're the entire river. The moment you remember you are the water, not the individual fish, you now have a choice to stop looking at the fish: To let go. You do not need to *try* to stop looking. It is as natural as turning focused attention toward the *sensation* of being water rather than the *perception* of observing the fish.

You can, of course, continue to follow a fish, even as it swims into danger, while remaining conscious that you are the water. This is what occurred when imagining one's worst fear a moment ago. It's like watching a nature documentary. Right when the emotions are at a peak, when the fish is being chased by a predator, you can remind yourself (this is a sense reminder, not a verbalized thought) that you are only the water watching the whole thing transpire.

This analogy is not exclusive to thought-patterns (as fish) and You (as water). From the macrocosmic view, over the span of a lifetime, one's entire life—as a body and egoic personality—is akin to a single fish. You, in the absolute sense, always remain the water, which might be labeled Unconditioned Consciousness or Pure Awareness. It important for the reader to realize that understanding this *will not* change one's external fate or alter the fragility of the body.

Even in knowing that one *is* the water, not the fish, in the absolute sense, the thinking mind (i.e., the ego) cannot escape the fate of the fish. You will remain the fish, feel the fish's pain and fears fully, but will now have an inner-peace—an unexplainable assurance—that You are untouchable. That is, "to be in the world, but not of the world."

This might be merely a delusion, a shift in consciousness as a way out of the most intense pain, but how would you know until you have experienced the shift directly? To comment on it with abstract psychological theories on why "such and such an experience" occurs will always keep the reader from knowing what the author is pointing to.

Coming back to the worst fear imagination exercise, once you are able to sit and not be swept away in the imaginings of your worst fear, you have, in a psychological sense, walked across fire. That is not to say this will cause a permanent shift in consciousness. It is possible that a fear-inducing thought based on an illusory future will cause you to forget that you are only observing "the fish's journey." However, returning to identification with "the water" is the spiritual practice.

Be aware of everything you are perceiving now, and if a thought arises that "I don't want to be doing this. I don't want to turn this into a practice," fold that into your perception too. Not the contents of it, but the *is-ness* of it as a small, ephemeral thought-form in a big, expansive reality.

No other words can point to what it is.

✧✧✧

This disidentification from the thinking mind is *how* you can apply Jung's conception of self-criticism (i.e., humility with respect to one's own opinions) with ease. Only when one is not clinging to his or her ideological beliefs for a sense of self can there be an objective critique of those beliefs (acknowledging the good, the bad and the ugly). There is no longer an emotional barrier blocking this kind of self-reflection. Thus, one is free to acknowledge their good and evil capacities (both of which are part of human nature) without fear. You can remain watchful of your evil impulses—which arise, first, as ambiguous, arcane thoughts—without the guilt of having them and without the need to project them upon "the other."

You no longer perpetuate hate as a reaction to another person's hate directed your way, but instead, when the negative sensations rise up in the body and the mind starts to justify the discomfort (in the form of blame), you need only witness the theatrical, mental monologue of a scared little ego. *Feel the sensations in the body as they are and let it all exist.*

Every moment. Every perception. Even this one now. And this one too.

But what are we supposed to do about the evil which still exists in the world?

And that thought too.

Fold it all into your awareness of this moment. Only now can you act from a place of non-reaction. Only now is it clear that "shoulds," "ought tos," and "supposed tos" are empty chatter from a scared, shortsighted and selfish little ego. Only now is it clear what you are doing and how you will proceed: No trying, no aiming and no compulsion.

Now, whatever needs to be done gets done. There is no war waged for the sake of righteousness. However, for a more pressing issues like climate change, with apocalyptic stakes, there may be a compulsion to disregard the "deniers" and save the planet by any means necessary.

POLITICS AND CLIMATE CHANGE

If a reader feels compelled to "fight" climate change, then allow action to be taken without the baggage of vengeance, hatred or fear. The baggage of those emotional states are dropped when You realize, on an experiential level, that You are not the thoughts that arise in the mind self-so: You are the Witness Consciousness.

The thinking mind humbles itself upon the realization.

In that place of knowing, it becomes so clear to see that what can't be changed must be accepted and what *can* be changed must be acted upon in an unconditioned way: Not based in hate or fear, but what the present moment intuitively calls for.

Such action requires no justification. There is no "because" needed. There is no reason for it except that, as with writing this book, it is a joy in and of itself. The writing of this book is sometimes slow-moving. The author is not snapping his fingers to get this done in a day, but every moment spent working on it is trusted as what ought to be done.

But how can I do something without any purpose?

How can you breathe without a purpose? How can you think without a justification for why human beings think? How can you walk, eat, sleep or dream without a reason why?

The only difference in looking at "why" in terms of why we do our work is because there is an element of choice. But from the place of non-reaction (i.e., not caught up in ego), there is no choice to make. *Anything you do is the right thing to do.* Again, pain and the propagation of hate and suffering is minimized because there is no point in these things once you realize who you are; in the absolute sense. There is no hate within you that could be dished out.[14] There is no "other"

---

14   The bodily sensations of so-called hate may arise, but in knowing who you are, the sensations are felt in the body without the compulsion to blame the pain on others and justify the blame with thoughts.

to whom you could dish out the hate. Plus, the hate that is inevitably thrown your way is absorbed and accepted by you, therefore transmuted to love and compassion.

That last line may read as kitschy advice, except that it is not advice: It is what happens upon realizing what the words in this book are pointing to.

ACTIVISM

The simple point is this—no one will change *only* because you told them to. In an attempt to force a person into action, by commanding participation in initiatives to address climate change, you risk making him cling even tighter to his status quo (i.e., his existing beliefs, which are synonymous with his egoic identity). Specific measures to reduce carbon emissions *may* achieve their intended aim, but by declaring enemies and villains in the process, it only paves the way for future resentment and tribalistic division.

The solution, if it can even be called that, is to first know who you are, then do what you will. You are the Presence that is aware it is reading this book, aware of the thoughts passing through the mind and aware of the sensations of the body: The eternal subject to all passing objects.[15]

Feelings of hate toward politically opposed individuals will invariably arise, either as thought-forms, bodily sensations of anger or fear, or both. *The practice is to realize that you observe those feelings of resistance, but you do not willfully create them.* Therefore, you do not need to perpetuate them with emotion-justifying thoughts as soon as you are aware that the irritation is self-created and only worsened by the thinking mind.

☼☼☼

So be an activist, fight for policy change, stand against injustice—whatever action that takes for you—or do nothing at all. No matter the choice, there will be egos attacking you and egos praising you. *On both sides of every debate, there are human beings who really do*

---

15   This is not the full truth, but it will suffice for the target reader. For a deeper understanding, the author recommends the book *The Nature of Consciousness* by Rupert Spira.

not know their essential self that underlies the conditioned personality. That is why they fight so fiercely, for whatever they believe, with bared teeth and an existential fear stuffed deep below their outrage.

What else could be felt but compassion? They really do not know who they are. On the external level of life, you do not need to give the person once deemed a "moral enemy" a hug and give them everything they ask for—you would be pulled equally by two extremes anyway. However, you can feel a sense of awe for the wholeness of the debate in the midst of the firm stand you take. So, yes, you will still have opinions, but they will no longer based on short-sighted self-interest, but a true understanding of the nature of the problem.[16]

But this goes a step deeper than taking a firm stance on something while maintaining a respect for the morally opposed individual. Once you know who you really are, you don't need to *hold* a certain belief at all. There is no energy wasted on virtue signaling (i.e., expressing what you believe in social settings to establish that you are a good person) or attacking so-called ignorant people. The divisive political and morally based battles occurring on social media today are the smallest fraction of a shadow of reality. Only when one's eyes are so focused on the screen does it seem like defending and attacking beliefs is the whole, all-encompassing purpose of life.

But what about climate change? We must act now!

Yes, act now. Oh, you are reading this book now? Then you will have to accept that you are reading this book in the Now. When you are acting—creating some fundraiser or applying to some volunteer job, something specific—to reduce climate change, then you can act to reduce climate change.

Take action when the impulse arises, accept obstacles when they arise and take more action as creative insights arise in response to those obstacles. It happens with less forethought than one might think.

If, in the end, your actions help save humanity from extinction, that is good. If, in the end, your actions do not prevent humanity's extinction, that is okay too. You can seek one result over another and still accept all results when they occur in the moment they occur.

No blame to dish out; no hate or vengeance to spread. Know who

---

16   Even with this lack of selfish interest, there is always the chance of an opinion being misguided and wrong. Therefore, humility is essential no matter how altruistic you *think* you are.

you are, and act from that place of knowing. That is all.

CHAPTER 5

SOCIAL JUSTICE ACTIVISM: WHEN MORAL VIRTUE FUELS FEAR, HATE AND VENGEANCE

*I hate all politics. I don't like either political party. One should
not belong to them - one should be an individual, standing in
the middle. Anyone that belongs to a party stops thinking.*

— *Ray Bradbury*

I could finish *Off With His Head* without including an essay on the
topic of social justice. Perhaps the subject seems outside the scope
of this book. On the face of it, that is true. However, this book is about
exposing the ego, and, at this time in history, I see it hiding (or revel-
ing, rather) in the "social justice activist" identity embraced by many
of my peers today.

"I stand for the side of truth and justice," I hear, uttered with tone-
deaf arrogance, by the individuals impervious to critique and venom-
ous toward anyone with a dissenting opinion. It is difficult to con-
verse with these people in a productive manner. There is no room for
debate; nor even a willingness to agree to disagree. If anyone dares
to disagree with the activist, then they are deemed wrong, racist, big-
oted, homophobic, transphobic, xenophobic, misogynistic, and the
list trails on.

They fight for diversity, and yet they are homogeneous in their
thinking. They fight for equality, and yet they focus on group equity
over individual opportunity.[1] They fight for inclusivity, and yet they

---

1   When people focus on identity groups and how they compare statistically,
there is often a naive assumption that institutions should aim for total statistical equality and that this requires other people to step aside to "make room"
for the minorities. Certain groups demand or deserve "a bigger slice of the
pie," or so it is said. This pie analogy is used often in relation to wealth and

exclude and ostracize the so-called "ignorant." It is hypocritical to the nth degree, and yet many people see this "fight" as a noble pursuit.

Make no mistake, this essay is about the egoism implicit in the far-left political ideologies arising in the 2020s and the people identified with such viewpoints who walk with a morally righteous pep in their step (e.g., progressives, democratic socialists, social justice activists, etc.).[2]

Oh, the surety in their beliefs! How could anyone ever disagree! Let us turn to the activist scholars—who take it upon themselves to discover new injustices in society, so we may know how unfair life *really* is—to teach us how to atone for our sins! Haven't you heard, the good word: *The whole system is racist, and that's why these people do worse than those people!*

Great job, dick. Thanks for doing the hard work.

Of course, the true challenge lies in the real world application of abstract theories; in making actual changes and getting the whole population to go along for the ride. We forget, too often, that citizens are not chess pieces, and every social justice policy shift requires either imposing a burden or restriction on an individual's freedom *or* taking their money (in the form of taxes or forcing a land sale for government enterprise). People complain (or seek workarounds, as with tax sheltered investments). They take to social media. Mob mentalities form and the aggrieved gain leverage.

Let it be known that this digital tribalism is not exclusive to either

---

income distribution. It assumes the economy is a zero-sum game; to give a slice, a slice must be taken from someone else. Only in the case of government intervention is that true (this also includes any kind of government-sponsored grant funding or license distribution for businesses or nonprofits). Capitalist markets are based on a non-zero-sum game (or "win-win" scenarios). I give away my money because I believe I am gaining a good or service of greater value (otherwise I would not go out of my way to part with the cash). Monopolies are, of course, possible in free-market capitalism, but freedom of competition and freedom of choice (which governments must safeguard) are what prevent permanent monopolies.

2   I have intentionally omitted the word "liberal" despite its common sense usage because I am not critiquing liberals, in general, but rather a small subset of the group. Progressive or neo-progressive, as I am defining it, is equivalent to far-left. Classical liberal, centrist or moderate are all equivalent to the "old-school" liberal described in the previous essay. Understand that I am differentiating the groups ideologically even though they are both considered "Democrats."

political side (e.g., the conservative reaction to a simplified version of Critical Race Theory being taught to kids in elementary school or the liberal reaction to what was deemed the "Don't Say Gay" bill that related to Florida's K-12 education policies), but as stated before, the essay is focused on a critique of far-left ideologies.

So, to put it plainly, I believe much—but not all—of the activism embraced by my peer group today—those in their 20s and younger—is misguided, counterproductive to the economically disadvantaged (i.e., who they protest on behalf of), and has a quality akin to religious dogma (i.e., a set a principals to accept without question).

Does that mean conservatives have the right answer? Of course not! They are just as guilty of stifling free expression and rejecting people based on their own religious dogma (homosexuals, in particular) as the other political extreme.

> I focus on the far-left, whom I will call "progressives" or "neo-progressives" moving forward, because their views are currently mainstream in America today (the Overton window has shifted). Even the moderates who spot flaws in this group's thinking often concede that the neo-progressive is "good-hearted" and "selfless" in nature.

It's as if their mistakes and failed solutions (e.g., the backfire effect of rent-control laws and public housing projects, both of which disincentivized property upkeep, which degraded the environment of poor communities) were just some "oopsies!" created in the midst of fighting the good fight. Politicians are great at this public relations maneuvering—of severing the link between cause (previous public policy) and effect (specific economic inequalities), and proposing *more* public policy to "fix it." It's like selling band-aids with micro shards of glass in the cloth.

This tactical severance of government-influenced cause and effect is not exclusive to either political side: Franklin D. Roosevelt, amidst the Great Depression, created the origins of the welfare state (which admittedly has its pros and cons); Lyndon B. Johnson's administration declared the "war on poverty;" Richard Nixon's administration expanded Section 8 housing; and Ronald Regan's administration announced the "war on drugs."

If this essay were written 70 years ago, then I would write to the opposite side of the political spectrum (although my method of cri-

tique would be almost identical).[3] I am calling out *ideology* and showing, with evidence, how buying into this specific, modern ideology of
"social justice activism" is doing more harm than good.

This is a difficult topic to talk about with a level head. It is possible that anger, discomfort or something similar bubbles in your chest
upon reading this now. Stay with it. Feel it. Where is it located in the
body? Is it projected as hate (or something similar) toward the author?
Can you observe the stream of thought without interference?

☼☼☼

I ask the reader, no matter their political leanings, to read this essay all
the way through. I promise the rather provoking claims presented thus
far will be treated with nuance and sensitivity.

It is often presumed that any activist—even one whose contributions to "the cause" is exclusive to sharing social media posts—is
altruistic by nature of their "activist" label (this can also be swapped
with the terms "ally" or "advocate"). Activism equals self-sacrifice, or
so it is often conflated.

By the inverse token, it may be said that non-activists are *less*
self-sacrificing than activists. I don't think this is true, but I see this
as a common assumption in modern times. It is, of course, based in
historical truth—activists in every domain from racial equality to gay
rights in the 19th and 20th centuries did fight a dangerous, uphill battle (to put it lightly): These people *were* self-sacrificing because their
safety and reputations *were* put at risk.

Today, there is more reputation risk from silence or dissent against
activism, as a general topic of discussion, than the reverse. This is
not a hard and fast rule, and there are many exceptions (for example,
cannabis advocacy in America is still taboo in some circles), but I
refer specifically to any activist subgroups that might be lumped in
the diversity, equity and inclusion (DEI) box (e.g., activism related to
race, gender and sexuality).

---

3   *McCarthyism*—that time in American history in the 1950s when the government's fear of communism gave rise to congressional and FBI investiga-
tions of communist sympathizers (and those accused of espionage for the Soviet Union) for the sake of protecting American values—*is a prime example of
conservatives taking an ideology too far.* There was also a tie to Christianity
whereby the atheist values of communists marked them morally sinister.[2]

I am not saying these topics need to be advocated *against*, but I wish to point out that when dissenting opinions become taboo, then such activism becomes ideological. I will show why this is so destructive later on.

Coming back to self-sacrifice, the word is often held in contrast to self-interest: *Are you helping your community or helping yourself?*

It is commonly assumed that these two qualities are mutually exclusive, as if self-interest implies that the only way to help yourself is to cheat or harm others. This is the mistaken assumption that self-interest is equivalent to selfishness: *It is not.* Self-interest shifts the philosophical lens from seeking hedonistic, short-term pleasure to asking, "What behaviors are in my best interest?" To exercise, to eat healthy, to treat neighbors with respect and dignity, to read difficult books instead of watching mindless TV—all of these things *are in one's best interest*, but they are not pleasurable in the hedonistic sense, as eating a Krispy Kreme donut is.

The problem is that when people misinterpret the word, they assume that they must *try* to avoid becoming self-interested. They resort to secular ideals and philosophies (e.g., collectivism, socialism, secular humanism, etc.) to *convince* themselves to be self-sacrificing. These concept-heavy rationalizations "to be good" are akin to painting legs on a snake (i.e., to do more work than required).

> Genuine self-reflection allows one to see that sacrifice is in one's own best interest and *need not be justified with an ideology.*

In simple terms, when activism is equated with self-sacrifice, there arises a moral high ground for the activists to stand on that encourages division and polarization. The population becomes split between "good, morally superior people" and "bad, morally inferior people," but it's based on the superficial label, "activist," which grows hollow with overuse.

I will push back on the idea that [self-declared] activists are morally superior to non-activists with three basic points:

1. Social activists are self-interested too.

People who protest for, and are vocal allies of, the disenfranchised (i.e., an act of "self-sacrifice") do so, in part, out of self-interest. This is especially visible on digital spaces, like social media platforms, where there is zero cost for saying (or retweeting) the virtuous remark. It is an act of moral grandstanding and serves mostly to signal to the world which social tribe one identifies with.

I am not saying this is wrong, or that it needs to stop, but to point out that self-interest and self-sacrifice are inseparable in modern social justice activism. A good rule of thumb for whether an action is *actually* self-sacrificing (instead of a mask for self-interested virtue signaling) is to ask, "Is there a cost, or risk to my reputation, for speaking out or taking this action?"

2. **Self-interest *can* encourage self-sacrifice (so long as one has skin in the game).**

A focus on self-interest (i.e., individualism)—*when one is wise enough to play the long game*—actually encourages self-sacrifice.[4] This is true of social relationships in general, and business relationships, in particular (e.g., manipulating a customer for easy profit only assures a loss of future business). Self-interest, as I see it, is different from hedonism or short-sighted selfishness: A *self-interested* person has every incentive to treat the people around her well. "Reputation" or "moral character," one might say, is the glue that binds self-interest and self-sacrifice together.

The only time this isn't the case is if one pays no price for the consequences of their actions (i.e., no skin in the game). Politicians and public intellectuals often fall in this camp, whereby they can promote whichever public policies they want without taking responsibility for any adverse effects caused by those policies later on. Anonymous online trolls are another example of this.

3. **Moments of self-interest and self-sacrifice arise in every person, regardless of their philosophical views.**

Someone in favor of the *philosophy* of individualism (as opposed to collectivism) does not compel them to *always* be self-interested. If we distinguish the abstract philosophy from real world living, then it is obvious that one can be, say, a mother or father who sacrifices greatly for their children *and* a "rugged individualist" in

---

4   This is best expressed by the motivational speaker Jim Rohn, who said, "Whoever renders service to many puts himself in line for greatness - great wealth, great return, great satisfaction, great reputation, and great joy."

their other pursuits. In other words, self-interest can be prioritized in some areas of life and self-sacrifice can be prioritized (or done out of instinct) in others. It is more a gradient than a black-and-white division, and therefore there is no need to *force* oneself to be altruistic.

The important thing to note is that there is a difference between self-identification (i.e., words) and objective phenomena (i.e., behavior). As most people know, talk is cheap. Anyone can *say* they are "a do-gooder activist fighting for justice" and *behave like the most selfish person in the room.* On the opposite end, someone can claim to be an individualist and still take care of their dying mother, raise three kids, and donate a chunk of their income to a private charity every month. Self-identification, in this sense, is a slippery slope for verbal manipulation.

Words can mislead: Sometimes they understate, but more often they overstate virtuous behavior. This is true of words shared online or in person *as well as* the words arising in one's head as inner thoughts. To spot a false thought in one's mind is trickier to spot than a lie told by someone else; as the proverb goes:

> *Why do you see the speck that is in your brother's eye, but do not notice the log that is in your own eye?*[5]

In secular terms, the detective called "ego" can locate any crook, except when it is the *detective* who committed the crime!

Every person has a blind spot to the limits of their own foundational beliefs (moral, political and religious beliefs, specifically). The only way to acknowledge those limits is to observe those fundamental beliefs from an objective, non-judgemental point of view: To be the Witness of thought.

☼☼☼

My intention in this piece is not to insult, ridicule or vilify the people who have fallen into a state of unquestioning faith in the approaches of modern social justice activism, but to offer a new possibility—one that does not ignore the disenfranchised (as messages like these are

---

5   "Bible Gateway Passage: Matthew 7:3-5 - English Standard Version." *Bible Gateway*, biblegateway.com/passage/?search=Matthew+7%3A3-5&version=ESV. Accessed 12 Dec. 2023.

so often twisted to mean), but empowers them to go their own way. To steer their own ship and manifest their own destiny. That said, this piece is written more for the activists and allies of these social justice movements rather than whom they fight on behalf of.[6] My reason for doing so is two-fold:

1. The target reader likely is, or close to, someone self-identified as a social activist or ally (even if only in one niche like racial justice, climate change mitigation or LGBTQ rights).

2. The social activist or ally stands to benefit more from these words than someone in poverty. I am not offering practical economic advice, but a way to untangle one's mind from the guilt-tripping, problem-seeking entity called "ego." Without the awareness of the ego and its insidious nature, the activist becomes like a raging bull with eyes on red: *Their emotional passion has ensnared them to one moral-political direction without the ability to acknowledge its pitfalls and trade-offs.*

THE ELEPHANT IN THE ROOM ... OF ACTIVISTS

There is an even more important reason for this essay, one that is indirectly related to social justice activism. A reason that I believe is being *misdiagnosed* as a call for more mental health awareness (i.e., more activism) instead of a call for rediscovering our foundations of meaning (and, in doing so, developing a sense of emotional antifragility).[7]

---

6   I cannot emphasize this enough: The actual victims of discrimination, prejudice, or bullying deserve dignity and to be judged on their individual character and merits—not their identity group. I understand that racist acts still occur in modern times. The perpetrators of such overt discrimination— those who sow the seeds of their own destruction with their ignorance—they warrant their inevitable ostracism from mainstream society. I am critiquing the *methods* of social justice activism (namely, a fixation on destigmatizing "awareness" campaigns and protection against what are deemed harmful ideas), not their intentions. I, too, condemn close-minded prejudice where I see it.

7   The word "antifragility," popularized by philosopher Nassim Taleb, is one degree above resiliency whereby stressful events and emotionally provoking situations make the individual stronger than before. Things that gain from disorder are antifragile. Human beings have this ability, but an over-emphasis

Anxiety and depression are on the rise. I presume most readers know this intuitively, but there is strong evidence for it as well. A 10-year study conducted between 2008 and 2018 measured the rate of anxiety of those aged 18 to 50-plus as it changed in the population over time. In bracketing the ages, the most significant increase was in the 18-25 age group. The level of anxiety of that subset rose from 7.97% to 14.66%. For context, that's 4x the rate of increase compared to the total population.[8] This is staggering, and it occurred *before* the COVID-19 pandemic.

As for evidence of the increase in depression, a study measuring the rate of a past-year major depressive episodes (MDEs) between 2015 to 2020, in a population ranging from the age of 12 to 50-plus, found a similar upward trend in the younger age brackets. The 18-25 age group's rate increased from 10.3% in 2015 to 15.5% in 2019. For the 12-17 age group, their rate of depression increased from 12.7% to 15.8% in the same time. Again, for context, the groups' increases were around 4x and 2x greater than the total population, respectively.[9]

I focus on the rate of increase (ROI) instead of raw percentages of each age group because adolescents and young adults still figuring out who they are, how they fit in, and what they wish to do with their life (not to mention major hormonal changes) would naturally have a higher rate of anxiety and depression, on average, compared with older adults regardless of the decade. The ROI tell us that *something* (likely, many somethings) are changing in this specific culture to *cause* the meaningful increase.

Jonathan Haidt, author of *The Coddling of the American Mind*, has done substantial research on tracking the rise in adolescent mood disorders since 2010 while seeking to prove a casual link to social media use and its increasingly addictive iterations. It would take more than a few paragraphs to share his collection of evidence, so instead,

---

on social institutions adapting to the victimized individual (rather than the reverse) weakens the psychological muscle, so to speak.

8   Goodwin, Renee D., et al. "Trends in anxiety among adults in the United States, 2008–2018: Rapid increases among young adults." *Journal of Psychiatric Research*, vol. 130, 2020, pp. 441–446, https://doi.org/10.1016/j.jpsychires.2020.08.014.[18]

9   Goodwin, Renee D., Lisa C. Dierker, et al. "Trends in U.S. depression prevalence from 2015 to 2020: The widening treatment gap." *American Journal of Preventive Medicine*, vol. 63, no. 5, 2022, pp. 726–733, https://doi.org/10.1016/j.amepre.2022.05.014.[19]

his ongoing collaborative reviews will be cited for readers to view themselves.[10] Although even with the strong evidence, it is unlikely to change many people's media consumption habits significantly.

We, as a society, also run the risk of using "social media" as a catch-all scapegoat for America's woes: Blame Big Tech! Blame Mark Zuckerberg! Blame Elon Musk!

Hanging the CEO figureheads for the sins of their company may provide a moment of satisfaction to the aggrieved, but it does not fix the root mental health problem, nor will suppressing access to social media platforms. The cat is already out of the bag.

THE PENDULUM SWINGS: FROM STIGMATIZATION TO NORMALIZATION

To talk about depression and anxiety is touchy, no matter how well-worded. I must emphasize that my goal is not to *re*-stigmatize the people with such mental illnesses. If the reader identifies as having one (or both) of these, whether clinically or self-diagnosed, then there is no doubt that your mind will attempt to villainize the author as ill-intentioned or scientifically naive. Therapists will likely be on high alert for error too. Before going further, it feels right to quote the Nobel Prize-winning economist Dr. Milton Friedman, who was also in the business of writing against the grain of mainstream consensus:

> "When myths get established ... they tend to be so strongly held— they tend to become so much a part of you—that when anyone comes along and differs with them and contradicts him, he risks automatically being dismissed as a crackpot, but I shall nonetheless take the risk of being dismissed as a crackpot because it seems to me so urgent that we deflate these myths, recognize what the reality is, in order to be able to provide a basis for a change in our philosophy ... in my opinion if we do not do so, if we continue on the road we have been going ... if we begin to rely more on the government and less on the individual, we are condemned to a future of tyranny and misery ... let us see these myths for what

---

10   This first review focuses on trends in teenage mental health: www.tinyurl. com/TeenMentalHealthReview. The second review focuses on social media's tie to mental health: www.tinyurl.com/SocialMediaMentalHealthReview. For potential updates, refer to: www.thecoddling.com/better-mental-health and www.thecoddling.com/better-social-media.

they are and adjust our thinking to a correct perception of our present and our past."[11]

Although Dr. Friedman's quote prefaced his talk debunking the historical myths of the government's involvement in America's economy, the sentiment holds true for the contents of this essay. **We, as a society, need a change in our philosophy regarding social justice activism, in general, and mental illness, in particular.** The conundrum though, is that different people need different changes in philosophy.

If the reader imagines mental illness stigma as a pendulum, on one side sits the disbelievers and stigmatizers. Such types might write off depression as laziness—or anxiety as cowardice—and demand that people simply "pick themselves up by their own bootstraps." This mental illness denier is likely older, conservative-leaning, religious and/or comes from an ethnic background where such beliefs are common. Most importantly, they have likely experienced forms of external hardships (e.g., war, poverty, physical bullying, etc.), and therefore see the crisis of anxiety and depression as unfounded based on the luxuries of our modern, techno-centric culture (for example, cyber bullying would appear absurd to an older adult who considers bullying a physical act; *"Just turn off the phone, what's the real harm?"*). This is one end of the spectrum.

On the other end sits the activist/destigmatizer group who vehemently emphasizes safety, protection from discomfort (of "harmful" ideas, in particular), mood stabilizing medication, clear labeling (of one's diagnosed mental illness) and coping mechanisms. This is arguably the mainstream consensus in present times. Psychotherapy or prescription medication are often the first lines of defense when someone approaches their primary care provider with issues regarding their mental health.[12] These are effective tools, but, I would argue, too

---

11   Friedman, Milton. *Milton Friedman Speaks: Myths That Conceal Reality*, YouTube, Uploaded by Freedom to Choose Network, 31 July 2012, https://youtu.be/xNc-xhH8kkk?si=-ZjUILpAA72AFYQ_. Accessed 12 Dec. 2023.

12   To be clear, psychotherapy, like cognitive behavior therapy (CBT), and prescription medication, like SSRIs, both have their contrasting pros and cons (namely, high versus low cost, large versus small time commitment, and side effects/withdrawal effects or lack thereof), but I take issue with patients being prescribed specific brands of antidepressants upon request rather than based on a clinician's decision. In a study testing this kind of patient influence, it was found that, "antidepressants were prescribed far more often when SPs [standardized patients] requested them."[30]

narrowly focused. There are many other potential culprits for stressors that worsen one's mental health besides social stressors. This includes:

- One's diet[13]
- One's history of head injuries[14]
- One's average quality of sleep[15]
- One's exercise routine (or lack thereof)[16]
- Exposure to environmental stress (such as from mold)[17]
- Undiagnosed autoimmune diseases (e.g., gluten sensitive disorders/celiac disease[18] or hypothyroidism[19])

In ceding the physical for the psychological, one bypasses a series of interventions that could reduce mental illness with little to no side effects—or for little to no money. I am not saying the interventions are surefire, but why not experiment with cutting alcohol, sugar or gluten out of one's lifestyle for a month before starting a selective serotonin reuptake inhibitor (SSRI) with a host of known side effects?

The aforementioned list includes criteria often (but not always) disconnected from mental illness. I intentionally omitted mental illness roots like social isolation, childhood trauma and bullying because these are more obvious in connection to mental illness and align with the destigmatizer's philosophy of "when discomfort strikes—get help

13   Gibson-Smith, Deborah, et al. "Association of food groups with depression and anxiety disorders." European Journal of Nutrition, vol. 59, no. 2, 3 Apr. 2019, pp. 767–778, https://doi.org/10.1007/s00394-019-01943-4.

14   Howlett, Jonathon R., et al. "Mental health consequences of traumatic brain injury." Biological Psychiatry, vol. 91, no. 5, 1 Mar. 2022, pp. 413–420, https://doi.org/10.1016/j.biopsych.2021.09.024.

15   Ghrouz, Amer K., et al. "Physical activity and sleep quality in relation to mental health among college students." Sleep and Breathing, vol. 23, no. 2, 26 Jan. 2019, pp. 627–634, https://doi.org/10.1007/s11325-019-01780-z.

16   Ibid.

17   A rat study revealing the mechanisms behind mold exposure, which can be extrapolated to humans: Harding, Cheryl F., et al. "Mold inhalation causes innate immune activation, neural, cognitive and emotional dysfunction." Brain, Behavior, and Immunity, vol. 87, July 2020, pp. 218–228, https://doi.org/10.1016/j.bbi.2019.11.006.

18   Busby, Eleanor, et al. "Mood disorders and gluten: It's not all in your mind! A systematic review with meta-analysis." Nutrients, vol. 10, no. 11, 8 Nov. 2018, p. 1708, https://doi.org/10.3390/nu10111708.

19   Nuguru, Surya P, et al. "Hypothyroidism and depression: A narrative review." Cureus, 20 Aug. 2022, https://doi.org/10.7759/cureus.28201.

from others."

It is tricky to critique this kind of thinking because it is good advice *some of the time* for *some of the population*, but there are drawbacks—most notably, the potential for a self-fulfilling worsening of mental health problems.

THE PREVALENCE INFLATION HYPOTHESIS: TOO MUCH MENTAL HEALTH AWARENESS?

There is a question that cannot be ignored in the current approach to destigmatize mental illness: *"Is there such a thing as too much mental health awareness?"*

Lucy Foulkes (University of Oxford) and Jack L. Andrews (University of New South Wales) have taken on this question in the affirmative by offering up the prevalence inflation hypothesis. Their proposal is that "mental health problems and awareness efforts are affecting each other in a cyclical, intensifying manner."[20] The hypothesis arises out of two observable patterns from mental health awareness campaigns:

1. *Improved recognition:* This is the benefit and goal of these campaigns. Awareness of the symptoms of an anxiety disorder or major depression allows the symptomatic person to seek help. In the case of suicide prevention, it can arm teachers, parents and peers with signs to watch out for before a loved one makes an attempt to end their life.

2. *Overinterpretation:* This is the unforeseen drawback of these campaigns. Namely, that awareness and destigmatization efforts can potentially lead people to "unnecessarily consider milder or more transient psychological difficulties as mental health problems that require labeling, reporting and treating."[21] The problem is not merely too much labeling, but when self-diagnosis, as when using Google search to uncover

---

20   Foulkes, Lucy, and Jack L. Andrews. "Are mental health awareness efforts contributing to the rise in reported mental health problems? A call to test the prevalence inflation hypothesis." *New Ideas in Psychology*, vol. 69, Apr. 2023, https://doi.org/10.1016/j.newideapsych.2023.101010.
21   Ibid., p. 2.

for the root cause of a negative mood, leads to false positives (i.e., considering oneself to have an anxiety disorder without proper evidence) that *become* a self-fulfilling prophecy whereby one avoids fear-provoking events because of her proclaimed anxiety that then creates a *stronger* fear response to similar future events. The pattern establishes itself; the monster grows, so to speak.[22]

It must be noted that this is a hypothesis and has yet to be empirically tested—however, one can draw connections from other research as to its potential validity.[23]

To play devil's advocate, one could argue that the trade-off is worthwhile: If even one person is prevented from committing suicide (as a result of Suicide Awareness Month efforts), then it's worth 100 people becoming a bit more anxious and depressed. *Human life is at stake here! Have you no heart? No compassion?*

Such an argument is short-sighted. Why would the individuals originally in the "overinterpreting and self-diagnosing" category who fall into an anxiety or depression feedback loop be exempt from suicidal ideation in the future? This is a serious problem; a problem that requires empirical, scientific testing and not just anecdotal success stories.

It is not limited to school-based mental health awareness efforts, but the difficult-to-measure culture of mental illness normalization on social media. Yes, normalization is the byproduct of destigmatization. It is observable online from the popular social media accounts that focus on using humor to "cope," but more often glorify mental illness.[24]

---

22   This self-fulfilling process was discussed in more detail, based on the author's anecdotal experience, in the essay "Growing Pains: How to Loosen the Stranglehold of 'Personal Identity.'"

23   A study testing how misinformation might influence mental health symptom reporting, many people who reported their baseline symptom severity (reported on a 5-point scale) pertaining to anxious and depressed tendencies did not notice—and in fact, *justified*—researchers' manipulation of two responses by two full points when reviewing answers with participants in a post-survey interview. This included inflating symptom severity for questions the participant originally responded with 0, or "not at all." It was a small study, with only healthy undergrad students as participants, but it points to the possibility of overinterpretation of mental health symptoms when influenced by an external factor.[3]

24   Wong, Bonnie. "Social Media's Depression Jokes Severely Devalue and

Have these words begun to provoke the reader? Does it feel like an attack? On what? On whom? I will say it again that this is not an attack on individual's suffering from mental illness, but *a critique of the activist approach*; an approach often blind to potential drawbacks and iatrogenic harm (i.e., harm from medical intervention) caused by destigmatization efforts.

HOW IDEOLOGY EVOLVES

I am wary to step into any other domain promoted by social justice activists,[25] but I will offer a simple, seven-step model to show how, based on the critique above, "mental health awareness" could be swapped with any other topic that social activists campaign on behalf of and still reflect the core issue with their approach:

1. PROBLEM DISCOVERY:

An injustice must be identified for a collective to rally against. It may begin with anecdotal claims, political presumptions or an observance of statistical disparities (e.g., the gender pay gap or the suicide rate of transgender people compared to the general population).

2. THEORY IDENTIFICATION:

When someone debates a neo-progressive, the critique is rarely on the data itself (for example, from a 30,000-foot-view, without the gender pay gap is indeed notable), but rather the *conclusions drawn from the data.* This is where a scholar must offer an existing theory or invent a new one to *justify* the statistical disparity (e.g., differences in median black and white family income differ *because of* systemic racism).

Theory is important in science because, without a potential reason as to *why* a social disparity (or any observable phenomena for that matter) exists, the data is impractical. A theory proposes the "root cause," which ideally serves as a focal point to create non-profits, businesses,

---

Normalize Mental Illness." *Study Breaks*, Study Breaks Magazine, 17 Feb. 2018, studybreaks.com/thoughts/depression-jokes/.

25   The book *Cynical Theories* by Helen Pluckrose and James Lindsay covers the many specific domains in depth.

or, in rare circumstances, government intervention to remedy.

The problem with the activist approach begins here. **Theory, while important, ought to be the aspect of research *consistently* open to testing and falsification.** The purpose of theory, in plain terms, is to offer an idea as to why a disparity exists *in order to test* if that is causally the reason. By that, I mean designing an experiment (or reviewing historical data) to check, did A and B arise simultaneously? Did one occur before the other? Can we remove A and still observe B rising? For example, 3+ hours a day of social media use is correlated, in adolescents, with mental health problems based on a cohort study of more than 6,500 participants.[26] However, before jumping to the *theory* that social media use *causes* such problems, we must first consider reverse causality: Could mental health problems *cause* someone to spend more time on social media?[27]

3. Improved Recognition:

Once theories are established and justified with data, the evidence of injustice can be spread to the public via journalists, intellectuals and influencer laypeople. The problem becomes a "crisis," and citizens, far and wide, are made aware of it.

For example, after the death of George Floyd, there was a collective repentance in America for its racist history (a racial reckoning, if you will). Once journalists and laypeople found the pattern—that calling out racist behavior (even from one's own past), no matter how out of context, unintentional or trivial, is praiseworthy—many hopped upon the virtue signaling bandwagon.

I truly believe there were many justified cases of calling out #whiteprivilege and #systemicracism, but over time, it became less about calling out overt prejudice and more about signaling group

---

26   Riehm, Kira E., et al. "Associations between time spent using social media and internalizing and externalizing problems among US youth." *JAMA Psychiatry*, vol. 76, no. 12, 1 Dec. 2019, pp. 1266–1273, https://doi.org/10.1001/jamapsychiatry.2019.2325.

27   Although this question is not worth dismal, a small study has shown Facebook's causal link to a reduction in well-being by testing changes in well-being of a group abstaining from Facebook for a week (tested against a control group).[40] It is an imperfect study for a handful of reasons, but it gets us closer to causal proof of social media platforms' harmful effects on mental health.

affiliation (because, in this new ideology, all white people are racist by default, and only anti-racist behavior, like posting a black square on #blackouttuesday, can bring atonement).

4. Build Consensus:

To stay on the Black Lives Matter (BLM) movement—and the racial reckoning in general—after George Floyd's death, consensus built fast:

- Protesters good, cops bad.
- White guilt good, colorblindness bad.[28]
- Being quiet is racist (and evil), being upset and brazen is anti-racist (and virtuous).

By "build consensus," all I mean is that anyone not living under a rock could point out the two sides of a current hot-topic issue *and point out the side of "the good guys."* Once this impression of morality comes in (i.e., one side of a debate appears morally superior to the other), which arises out of a media firestorm of opinion, anyone who cares about their social standing will choose the virtuous side of the argument: regardless of their actual nuanced opinion.

Social media plays a big role in this groupthink behavior because #cancelculture was nothing new by the 2020s; most people knew the consequences of speaking an unpopular opinion—no matter how carefully worded.

5. Enemy Extermination:

When I say "enemy," I am not talking about the obvious: the reactive conservatives. Such people have reacted to the major anti-racist upheavals in social institutions with the same knee-jerk attitudes as their (mainstream) opposition. They speak with no nuance, and parrot the BLM movement with gleeful irony: #whitelivesmatter.

Again, I am not referring to that group.

---

28   Coleman Hughes makes a case for colorblindness in a TED Talk from 2023.[26] The point, he says, is not to ignore skin color or disregard the history of injustice perpetrated on black people (he is a black man himself), but to limit race-based public policy as much as possible.

The "enemies" I refer to here are the centrist, and even left of center, citizens who saw signs of overzealous morality at work. The people seeking liberalism, in its original meaning. What happened to the jokes? To poking fun at people? Moreover, what is the effectiveness of this censorship of ideas? Of anti-racist workshops? Of punishing microaggressions (no matter how unintentional)? Can we look back at the science? Can we re-validate or invalidate these original theories with new, data-driven research?

The original theories were based on statistics showing disparities based on identity groups (i.e., identity politics, in a nutshell). However, by this point, the consensus that *America is systemically racist and the only way to change that is a total overhaul of institutions* was sticky and politicized.[29] The mainstream view had solidified and turned science into scientism.

To remind the reader of the distinction: *Science* is open to, and encourages, falsifying a dominant theory to explain the data if a more accurate one is proven, but *scientism* freezes the current scientific theory from being falsified because its defenders' identity—which have become linked to certain viewpoints—is at stake. Individuals now have personal incentives to uphold the dominant social theories (e.g., DEI employees and consultants, popular activist authors and influencers, and social science academics doing research and teaching activist-influenced courses). In a sense, it is no longer science, but an ideology (or political philosophy) with *unquestionable* statistical evidence as its base.

But questions will be asked once the ideological status quo (i.e., identity politics) becomes the monster it once sought to destroy (namely, the reaction to real, overt marginalization and discrimination throughout the 20th century has been *populist-driven* marginalization). The strategy to deal with such question-askers—who've become the enemy by means of their skepticism—is to resort to defamatory character arguments: *Racist! Bigot! Transphobe! White supremacist! Incel! Fascist! Misogynist!*[30]

---

29   I ask the reader to not get hung up on the term "systemic racism." It is only one ideological viewpoint out of a basketful. Here are two others, from their respective political sides: A. The best way to prevent war is through military disarmament and promoting pacifism (progressive) or B. Christian morals and values ought to be instilled in every American institution (conservative).

30   "Fraud! Hypocrite! Snowflake! Socialist! Radical!" So cries the other side. Ask yourself, which labels carry the harsher sting in the 21st century?

No matter how unfounded, irrelevant or provably wrong the claims are—because the downside (of being sued for defamation) is rare and the upside (of conflating critiques of the far-left ideology with being an evil person)—they are spoken as casually as one speaks common sense facts. What are the repercussions? How many people have been #canceled for baseless slander aimed at someone's reputation? I imagine the list is short because blame is so easily diffused: *I heard it from so and so, who heard it from so and so, who can't be called for comment.*

6. OVERINTERPRETATION:

As "enemies"—in particular, the centrists who refuse group affiliation (with either political extreme)—are defamed to oblivion or pushed out of the public spotlight, neo-progressive ideologies can flourish among like-minded peers. I can personally attest to this groupthink behavior among my friends in college, all of whom I like and respect on a personal level. These people are good-hearted and good-intentioned. (I speak of my community, in particular). They have an impulse to live morally. They want to do good. They want to change the world; to rid the place of evil. They have found truth, meaning and purpose in activism. That is no small feat. I say all this to emphasize that social justice provides a cookie-cutter answer to "What is my purpose in life?" It is not merely a political philosophy but a moral crusade.

In that respect, social justice activism is nothing unique. Crusades have existed before: National Socialism in Germany; Fascism in Italy; Imperialism in Japan; Communism in Russia, China, Cuba, Cambodia, North Korea, etc. Even in America, there is a history of Christian dogma being imposed on others regardless of their religious affiliation in secular spaces like public education.[31]

But what have been the consequences of unchecked crusades? History is full of examples: genocide, mass starvation, rampant poverty, corruption, suppression of speech, and totalitarian governments, to name a few. As for this particular social justice crusade—which, to be clear, is nowhere near the extreme cases mentioned above—the consequences are still evolving: Every week another phrase must be

---

31   A clear example is the history of state laws banning Darwin's theory of evolution in schools. In 1925, John T. Scopes, a Tennessee high school teacher, was convicted and fined for teaching the subject.[36]

scrubbed out of mind because of its uncovered #racist or #homopho-bic origins. The list of blacklisted speech grows. The cognitive disso-nance, between political correctness and common sense, widens. The threshold for "offensive" behavior sinks to trivial levels (though the reputational fallout is just as crippling).

The ironic turn of events is that once overt "enemies" of an ideol-ogy are rooted out, the group begins to turn on each other. They police their peers and censor themselves as if it were an act of service. The most offended (or the most offended *on behalf of* a minority group) now control the flow of conversation. A power dynamic develops whereby the most victimized (more accurately, the "thinnest-skinned") sit on top: *In the name of historical retribution, of course.*

Friends begin to call out other friends for microaggressions. Fear of saying the wrong thing sets in. Political correctness is no longer a polite gesture, but a protective measure to avoid social ostraciza-tion. Common sense is no longer reliable to determine racism from non-racism (or homophobia from non-homophobia). Call in the experts! Departments must be established. Consultants must be hired. Training seminars must be attended.

This self-evident truth is a tough pill to swallow,[32] especially if one's personal identity and social group is tied up in social justice activ-ism today. I will repeat it again, I am critiquing only the *ideological movement*; not individuals who are, say, volunteering their time at a women's shelter or Big Brothers Big Sisters of America. I ask that the reader avoids jumping to conclusions that activism is *always* good or

---

32   The self-evident truth is this: Intersectionality (i.e., dividing the popu-lation into subsets of race, gender and sexuality, or some combination of all three), when applied to public policy, creates a social hierarchy with the most historically victimized intersectional groups on top and the most historically oppressive groups on bottom. It ignores individual differences (namely, eco-nomic differences), so that, with a straight face, one can say a homeless white male has more privilege than a wealthy black transgender celebrity. Intersec-tionality is an important consideration for expanding compassion for others—yes, a black woman has uniquely difficult experiences dissimilar from being *just* a woman or *just* a black person—however, it's an awful way to design public policy because intersectionality, by definition, fragments the categories of identity, which makes it difficult, and inherently unfair, to create economic policies that help, say, *only* black women or *only* Asian trans people. That said, it's a complicated topic and one worthy of more nuance than can be given in this essay.

always bad. Such impatience and lust for moral certainty is how ideologies develop in the first place.

7. Rinse & Repeat:

The current stage of the modern social justice movement has not reached the "rinse & repeat" phase, but I will give a clear example of a past ideology that mirrors the present-day social justice ideology to illustrate how such movements transform once public opinion wanes.

Some readers may be familiar with the bogus, racist pseudo-science called "eugenics," an ideology that sought to prevent the survival of "genetically inferior" races. What is likely unknown, even if the term is familiar, is how popular it was among the Left in general, and intellectual progressives in particular, in the Progressive era of American history (1890s to 1920s).

In 1916, Madison Grant, a Progressive-era conservationist, released *The Passing of the Great Race,* in which he details a theory of Nordic superiority and claims that Nordics are the most superior race. It was a book Hitler called "his Bible." Grant was an activist regarding things one would associate with the left today; namely, the preservation of endangered species and the creation of national parks and wildlife reserves. In founding the American Bison Society, he is credited with "saving the American bison from extinction."[33] He was invited into a social club established by Theodore Roosevelt and exchanged letters with Franklin D. Roosevelt in the 20s.[34] This man was by no means fringe or an enemy of the left.

That book—and the eugenics movement, more generally—is a clear example of racism, white supremacy and an abuse of statistical data to support the "in vogue" social theory of the time. To pretend Grant and others in that movement were conservative rednecks is willful blindness. They were suave intellectuals with strong connections to left-wing leaders.[35]

---

33   Wheeler, Jim. "Madison Grant and the dark side of the conservation movement." *The Public Historian*, vol. 45, no. 3, 2023, pp. 75–82, https://doi.org/10.1525/tph.2023.45.3.75.

34   Sowell, Thomas, *Social Justice Fallacies*, p. 37.

35   Of course, the conservative party of that time had many racist party members, too. Of course, the "Southern rednecks" were racist too. The point is that it wasn't a redneck who wrote a best-selling book that used cherry-picked statistics to make racism appear "scientific."

It may appear as if I am cherry-picking or attempting to associate the modern progressives of today with that of the past: Far from it. I believe the social activists and far-left politicians of today are as anti-racist as it gets. The fact that the word "progressive" can be applied to both groups is not to call them equal in ideology. **However, the *pattern* of ideological development is the same.** To quote Dr. Thomas Sowell, who documented the history of eugenics' popularity in America in the early 20th century in his book *Social Justice Fallacies*:

> "While these different generations of Progressives reached opposite conclusions on the reasons for racial difference in economic and social outcomes, they shared very similar views on the role of government in general ... They also had similar practices in dealing with empirical evidence [by using only data that confirmed their theory]. Both remained largely impervious to evidence or conclusions contrary to their own beliefs."[36]

Dr. Sowell also notes:

> "There were hundreds of courses on eugenics in colleges and universities across the United States, just as there are similarly ideological courses in college and university campuses across the country today, promoting very different ideologies as regards race, but with a very similar sense of mission, and a very similar intolerance toward those who do not share their ideology or their mission."[37]

I'm willing to bet that *every single reader* would denounce eugenics as the racist, bogus ideology that it is, but is there enough awareness and humility to see the dangerous overlap with the social justice movement of today? At what point would it become clear, if not already apparent?

"Rinse & repeat" occurs when an ideology's negative consequences can no longer be swept under the rug: For example, communism is perfect in theory, but in practice, its flaws and horrendous consequences cannot be ignored (to the point that propaganda can no longer hide the truth). Once an ideology has been so thoroughly proven destructive, the once bullish intellectuals (e.g., professors,

---

36   Sowell, Thomas, *Social Justice Fallacies*, p. 38.
37   Ibid., p. 35.

activist-journalists, sociologists, economists, etc.) jump ship, dust off, and go back to the drawing board.

An academic can support every "in vogue" social theory without ever taking responsibility for the fallout and real-world consequences of the previous one. They may acknowledge how misguided/racist/cold-blooded their predecessors were, but they never seem to understand that it is unchecked *ideology*, regardless of how well-intentioned, that causes catastrophic problems in the long term.

To state it clearly, I define an ideology as a system of beliefs based on a foundation of unquestionable premises. The key word is "unquestionable" because science (as opposed to scient*ism*) is based on a collection of premises, but has foundational underpinnings that are *always open to critique and falsification*. It's always looking for a better alternative. **With science, the proof is in the pudding; with ideology, the proof is in the recipe—no matter how awful it looks and tastes by the end.**

As the saying goes, "The road to hell is paved with good intentions," the current social justice ideologies are no exception. How long until the intellectuals and activists of our time wake up and note the road signs—which, historically, have been passed before—that point to our final, hellish destination?

LET US DEBATE: THE LONG AND WINDING ROAD OF LIBERAL PROGRESS

Thus far, I have done my best to write from a place of centeredness. Not centered from the view of the Overton window of 21st century American politics (I'm sure I've been marked as "far-right" already), but centered in light of a much wider time horizon.

As stated before, the social justice ideology is considered by many as mainstream today (specifically, the focus on politically correct speech regardless of context/intention; the expanding definition of words like racist, homophobe, transphobe, etc.; and the blackballing of critics of these ideological shifts). By comparison, this essay may appear to support "right-wing" viewpoints. It would do the reader no good to categorize the work as such.

Anyone who grows disillusioned with the identity politics of the far-left runs the risk of running "out of the frying pan into the fire" of the far-right. *Do not mindlessly run into the arms of another ideological movement.* Arguably the straight, white male is on the short end of the identity politics stick in America today; however, it would be a stupid mistake to think the solution requires a reassertion of "white maleness" or, more generally, "Christian dogma." **Tribalism got us into this mess, and it will *not* get us out of it.**

But what will? What ideology will unify the culture—or at least allow a tolerance of opposing ideas? As far as I know, there is only one: **liberalism**. Yes, liberalism! It is the *only* ideology that opens itself up to critique. It is the *only* ideology that allows for a unified nation full of different opinions and beliefs. It is the *only* ideology where intellectuals can offer up revolutionary ideas and novel political systems (such as communism) without persecution.

The last line is worthy of further inquiry. A liberal nation is the *only* place where Karl Marx could write *The Communist Manifesto, a* book that would inspire totalitarian regimes *where that kind of freedom of expression could not exist.*

So we must blacklist people who further new ideologies? So we must suppress anti-liberal writing? No and no! We must allow for information to flow freely—for debate and ideological critique to happen openly—in trust that genuine knowledge is self-evident and can withstand any amount of scrutiny (or adapt based on new information).

Liberalism, at its core, is freedom of expression, freedom of debate, free-market economics (i.e., freedom of competition), belief in the worth and dignity of the individual, protection of individual rights and private property by the government, and limited government intervention in private affairs. It could be summarized in a single word if need be: "Freedom." It is an ideology arising out of the Enlightenment period in the 17th and 18th centuries in Western Europe, and it acts more like the "rules of play" in the game of knowledge production and politics rather than a singular, dogmatic worldview.

The disheartening rebuttal to classical liberalism (and the Enlightenment values, in general) is that it is systemically racist and/ or Eurocentric because it was developed by straight, white men in Europe (as Jamelle Bouie summarized in a Slate article).[38] It is a fair critique to say the Enlightenment values *have* been misused to justify Western Europeans treating other populations as inferior because such people lacked their abstract reasoning abilities, but can that truly be

---

38   Bouie, Jamelle. "How the Enlightenment Created Modern Race Thinking and Why We Should Confront It." *Slate*, Slate Magazine, 5 June 2018, slate.com/ news-and-politics/2018/06/taking-the-enlightenment-seriously-requires-talking-about-race.html.

a reason to oppose those core values? We do not blame the sword, but the swinger of the sword for wrong deeds committed: *Liberalism is that sword, neither good nor bad, but a tool to be used by good or bad actors.*

If liberalism can truly be blamed for sparking racist beliefs, which have existed all throughout history across all cultures, then it ought to be blamed for all the horrors of communism and fascism because the intellectuals who developed those ideologies did so in liberal nations.[39]

Can the reader see the absurdity in this claim?

Liberalism can be blamed for the good *and* bad qualities of any liberal nation because the ideology makes no centralized attempt to suppress the bad opinions in favor of the good opinions. (Who would get to decide anyway?). The same is true of its economic cousin, "free-market capitalism:" For every finger pointed at the millions who rose out of poverty because of it, a cynical finger will point at the handful of "robber barons" who turned lemons into monopoly-ade.

To paraphrase the late writer David Foster Wallace:

A wise old fish passes two young fish and says, "Morning, boys. How's the water?" The two young fish nod and continue on a while longer, then one turns to the other and asks, "What the hell is water?"[40]

In this case, water is liberalism—the ideology that contains within it all the more forceful, dogmatic belief systems that activists, advocates and

---

39   In Bouie's defense, he doesn't call for a dismantling of Enlightenment values; in fact, he advocates that they be taken seriously. His analysis, however, focuses on the hypocrisy of the philosophers of the Enlightenment Era, like John Locke and Immanuel Kant, (which he makes a strong case for); and yet, it seems to conflate their ideas regarding classical liberalism with racist ideology. I see his point that these thinkers invented bogus "scientific" racial hierarchies—based on philosophical reasoning—to justify the subjugation of black slaves, but I struggle to make the connection between those philosophical reasoning tools (removed from the original philosopher) and racism. I see "scientific" racism as a misuse of the tools, but those very same tools can and have been used to *rectify* the original racist ideologies that arose out of that period. Therefore, I don't think the two things—namely, the Enlightenment values and racism—should be treated as interwoven. Racism arose out of Enlightenment values, true, but so has all the evidence and reasoning *combating* racism.

40   Paraphrased from Wallace's commencement address at Kenyon College in 2005.[43]

ideologues assert as "the Truth." Critiquing liberalism and free-market capitalism by pointing out inequalities is *absolutely valid*, but calling for a different ideology, like socialism, to underpin American institutions (e.g., government agencies, public education, media organizations, private enterprises, etc.) is naive and short-sighted. This is a self-evident truth, and I welcome all debate against it.

DEALING WITH DISPARITIES

As mentioned before, activists often focus on very real statistical disparities between different identity groups. I believe it is with a good (and self-righteous) heart that these people shed light on those disparities and offer some postmodern and postcolonial theory to explain their root cause. However, once these disparities are brought to light, there is a naive assumption that it is *possible* to create equality among demographic groups in proportion to the population (for example, if around 14% of the US population is African-American, then that group should make up around 14% of the academic professors, CEOs, scientists, engineers, etc.).

Where does this presumption come from? What nation in history has ever achieved demographic equality of outcome? Search as long as you would like, but you will not find one example of this type of equality in any country at any point in history.

But we must do better than the past! It is a worthy ideal to aim for!

Is it? According to whom?

Only someone too smart for common sense could believe this is a worthy ideal (e.g., progressive scholars, public intellectuals, activist-journalists and the like). If we were dealing with abstract people in an abstract world, then yes, aim for this kind of equality. When one's eyes are glued to statistical metrics, then the ideal is merely a handful of percentage points away.[41] However, it becomes easy to lose sight

---

41   An important distinction must be made between *voluntary disparities* (e.g., differences between men and women in the STEM field) and *involuntary disparities* (e.g., sentencing length differences between white and black criminals for the same crime).[36] The former does not warrant social policy changes, but the latter does. This is in line with the tenets of liberalism because *involuntary disparities* imply that the individual is being discriminated against because of their group identity (instead of by their individual character), but

of the fact that each "data point" is a flesh-and-blood person with personal motivations living in a unique environment. The choices these individuals make are their own, not the result of some sinister "invisible hand," except where that "victim of circumstance" story is *directly taught to them* (via schools, social media or entertainment media) as justifiable, morally good and even praiseworthy.

When has a message of victim versus oppressor based on racial affiliation ever been culturally uniting?

Two decades into the 21st century, every newsworthy event involving a white person and a black person is being "racialized," and the cultural reaction is not to try to see past skin color (because most interactions in life have nothing to do with the race of the people involved), but to focus on how the incident is either racist or anti-racist. Why is being anti-racist more important than focusing on improving your individual character as a good person, regardless of whom you interact with? Why over-correct? Because, says the all-knowing, white author Robin DiAngelo,

"To not act against racism is to support racism."[42]

But the world doesn't revolve around her … nor I, nor you, nor any other person. You may choose to believe her and hold her thoughts in high regard, but that does not make her opinion "the Truth." It is open to debate and to be tested against other solutions, *if it can actually be called a solution*, to reduce the disparity gap.

Liberalism supports freedom of speech and freedom of belief, but it *rejects* freedom of knowledge. In other words, core to this ideology is that there *is* an objective/empirical reality, which cannot be dismissed for moral-based, emotion-based, or even linguistic-based, reasons. For example, to say the Earth is not round based on the relativity of the term "round"—with its multiple meanings— *does not* disprove the empirical observation that the Earth is a spherical shape.

Although one may hear that we live in a postmodern, post-truth

---

voluntary disparities imply that the individuals within a certain group—all of whom had the freedom to choose any career path—disproportionality choose against a certain career field (in this case, the STEM field).

42   Diangelo, Robin. "Basic Tenets of Anti-Racist Education." *Robin DiAngelo, PhD*, Robin DiAngelo LLC, 2016, www.robindiangelo.com/wp-content/uploads/2016/06/Anti-racism-handout-1-page-2016.pdf.

era—that there is no such thing as objective truth, only social constructs and lived experience—high-minded rhetoric such as that is just that: rhetoric. (If the name Jacques Derrida means nothing to you, then this small section about language can be skipped.):

> Derrida's idea of deconstructionism—the theoretical framework used to *deconstruct* the structuralist view that in binary oppositions of words (e.g., order/disorder, speech/writing, or reason/passion) one word of the pair is assumed to be "privileged" over the other—makes sense, barely, as an abstract critique of language. He, in essence, pointed out the silent space that underlies language from which to view binary oppositions in a detached way (allowing one to wrestle with any binary of terms from many perspectives). It is complex, and therefore, bound to be misinterpreted. It is from this framework that we get the *deconstruction* of the objective/subjective binary so that "objectivity" is no longer "privileged" over subjectivity (despite this being a fundamental precept of the scientific method, and, by extension, our understanding of the physical world).

> This language game creates the illusion that objective/empirical truth is equal to, or even lesser than, subjective truth (i.e., "lived experience") in our culture. By language game, I mean the context in which Derrida's ideas are taught—namely, in the humanities department of university campuses—provide a safe environment to explore the deconstruction method in the abstract. **A method so far removed from reality, from *objective truth*, that there is no danger of someone getting hurt, *objectively hurt*, from his ideas.**[43] Just imagine some deconstructionist structural engineer who designs a bridge whose calculus privileges "incorrectness" in the correct/incorrect binary. I'm joking of course, but this absurd scenario points to how the humanities department in schools supplies a safe space to explore ideas that have zero bearing in reality. No one is applying postmodern or deconstructionist ideas to

---

[43]   I would argue that these postmodern ideas do more harm, from an existential perspective, than any other philosophy. It is as if the postmodern French philosophers like Jacques Derrida, Michel Foucault or Jean-François Lyotard, diagnosed all of Western culture with an incurable case of nihilism. I reject it and see no benefit in accepting their cynical conclusions except, perhaps, intellectual gratification.

applied physics, engineering or medicine because people would literally be killed. Therefore, I take issue with the postmodern claim that there is no objective truth because, in practical terms, it does exist and flesh-and-blood people must adhere to it.

I understand that the words we use to describe objective reality have certain connotations—some positive, some negative—but that in no way invalidates that, say, gravity exists (even if we invent a new word like *beltra* to represent it). I don't think Derrida would deny the existence of gravity or other objective phenomena, like weather, but his work has been misappropriated to *deconstruct* certain aspects of science like biological sex (the fact is that the duality exists, even if we invent new words like *smerg* and *fremma* to represent the two sexes).
The deconstructionist philosophy may allow for some intellectual gratification if the concepts are grasped (which, paradoxically, misses the point of deconstructionism), but as it is combined with other postmodern ideas and travels downstream to the general public, or even undergrad students, it translates to: **All language is inherently meaningless, *therefore*, the meaning and connotation of words are invented and maintained in order for identity groups to assert power over other groups** (i.e., the victim/oppressor binary)**, *therefore* language and its manifestations** (e.g., the Western literary canon, works of Western history, scientific literature, classic Western philosophy, etc.) **must be adapted to redress the power imbalance, *regardless* of whether the alterations adhere to objective/empirical truth.**

In short, the conclusion that language is merely a struggle for power and control reflects a narrow and cynical worldview. It creates needless existential confusion to what would otherwise be a common sense statement: Language is used to communicate. (Of course, one doesn't get to be a professor in philosophy with mere common sense).

Implied in the phrase "objective truth" is that it can be *falsified*. For example, two people in a debate about an objective phenomenon (e.g., is the Earth round or flat?) must have enough humility to concede when the empirical evidence is against their viewpoint. Anything else is pseudo-religious and ought not be portrayed as "scientific."
The consequence of the modern, *egoic* delusion that truth/knowl-

edge (of the scientific variety, in particular) is subjective is that "people lose the ability to speak ... on shared terms and have no objective means ... to settle differences of opinion."[44]

I cannot emphasize enough that objective truth does not require that people suppress non-truth: The better method is to teach reasoning skills (i.e., the Enlightenment values of rationalism, skepticism and empiricism in addition to literacy and basic statistics) so that *anyone can verify the truth for themselves.*

> It is the knowledge version of "teaching a man to fish vs. feeding him for a day." Public education ought to teach students universal "fishing methods," and not serve up ready-made fish and chips with tartar sauce on the side.

I began the essay talking about ego hidden within social justice activism because the ideology implies that society must bend to the will of the most aggrieved or victimized (or, as with DiAngelo, aggrieved *on behalf of another racial group*).[45] Only the ego could imagine such a "utopia" arising out of centralized, censorious control. The truth is that "society" is not a malleable ball of clay that a few hands can mold into any shape they like.

As Dr. Thomas Sowell has been quoted, "A fool can put on his coat better than a wise man can put it on for him."[46] Moreover, the fool *prefers* to put on his own coat (as would any self-sufficient person).

Yet why is the goal of research outlining group disparities to inspire some grand and sweeping, top-down public policy change? Why not inspire individuals to *voluntarily* make their own choices by presenting the information plainly and letting them decide what is objectively true based on evidence and reasoning?

Might it be a lack of trust in others? Might it be a craving for control? Might it be an arrogant belief that intellectual prowess and academic achievement give one the right to socially engineer a better world?

---

44   Pluckrose and Lindsay, *Cynical Theories*, p. 250.
45   Even though I am not writing about the flip side, religious conservatives are just as liable to cherry-pick evidence or anecdotal news stories to support claims that homosexuality is evil or immoral. Such rejection of certain people and ideas is an egoic impulse too.
46   Sowell, Thomas, *Intellectuals and Society*, p. 229.

EGO AND SOCIAL JUSTICE: A RECIPE FOR DISASTER

Ego lacks trust in others. Ego demands control. Ego makes enemies. Ego seeks conflict. Ego focuses on future perfection (at the expense of the present moment). Ego decides who is morally superior or inferior. **Awareness observes all that is.**

I know this essay has not been so "spiritual," in contrast to the rest of the book, but it is written for the express purpose of dissolving the political tribalism that has led to the socially dividing, irrefutable ideologies at the expense of scientifically derived, *falsifiable* knowledge (*this can and does occur on both ends of the political spectrum*). Any moments of upset, anger or physical discomfort felt upon reading this piece *reveal the ego hiding behind the social justice activist mask.*

No doubt that certain things are disagreeable in this essay, but any emotional response (and corresponding thoughts of "This is blasphemous and false!") is evidence of mistaking one's thoughts for one's true identity (i.e., confusing "mind" with "Awareness"). This is not calling it right or wrong, but the reader must become aware of what ideas spark emotional outrage, and—rather than demand their suppression—observe the arising emotion as *not "I."*

✧✧✧

I want to return to an earlier point regarding the rising rates of anxiety and depression in the young population. We can point to a number of potential causes unique to the 21st century (social media being a prime example), but this knowledge helps only to a small extent. Yes, we can craft policies to regulate social media in this or that way to protect against adolescent overuse, but what about the individuals overusing the addictive technology presently? What if the reader is one such person?

Put another way, does hearing that Gen Z is more depressed or anxious because of this or that reason empower the person afflicted with a mental illness at this moment? Does it inspire *any* form of personal responsibility to change one's lifestyle habits (such as social media overuse)? **Or does it instead justify that state of suffering as inevitable** (*Well, I'm anxious and lonely, but at least I'm not the only one*)? I don't know the answer, but it is a question worthy of personal inquiry.

The evidence is strong that personal technology (smartphones, in general, and social media, in particular), while providing much good and prosperity, can intensify mental health problems, notably when face-to-face interactions are reduced:[47]

> *Okay*, thinks the mental health activist, *so let's design engaging media campaigns that explain the evidence about rising rates of anxiety and depression. We'll invite the youth to use cool hashtags in order to #StopTheStigma!*

> *It's working! Look how many likes these posts are getting!*

Yes, and next we'll show how fast food leads to obesity and stamp the statistical evidence on Big Mac boxes: Right next to that mouth-watering burger. *It's working! Look how many people are buying the Big Mac and commenting on the new box design!* Gee, how clever ...

The activist approach is fallible, plain and simple. It is naive to pretend no harm can come from it.

I believe most (but not all) people who identify as activists, advocates or allies *are* good-hearted people, but that does not mean they understand the second-order consequences that their proposed solutions may create. If history reveals anything, it is that **every generation has examples of intelligent individuals convinced that a utopian Earth has not yet been created because *they* were not around to design it**. How else could history's countless examples of ideologically driven violence and group subjugation be evaded except through the arrogant rationale "*I* will do things differently."

It is for this reason that common sense can so easily evade the smartest people: *Intellectual prowess often goes hand in hand with a big ego, that is, a massive sense of self-importance.*

OPTIONALITY: A LIBERAL APPROACH TO MENTAL HEALTH

I have done enough critiquing and would now like to present an alternative to the current "raise awareness & destigmatize" approach so commonly presented as a solution to the problems identified by social justice scholars. The new approach is simple:

---

47   Abi-Jaoude, Elia, et al. "Smartphones, Social Media Use and Youth Mental Health." *Canadian Medical Association Journal*, vol. 192, no. 6, 10 Feb. 2020, https://doi.org/10.1503/cmaj.190434.

Teach resourcefulness and personal responsibility, not ready-made resource guides and social reform "solutions."

The reason for this shift of focus, from external to internal transformation, is somewhat counter-intuitive. Most social justice campaigns—mental health-related movements, in particular—prioritize *external* change for the sake of the victimized group (e.g., increasing access to medication, therapy, destigmatizing information, and increasing excusability for mental health issues impacting work or school)[48] but negate the importance of upholding *courage* and *personal responsibility* as virtues needed to live and thrive in a challenging, chaotic world. The internal values are more important than external, institutional changes because the internal begets the external:

> Someone with the *internal values* of courage and personal responsibility not only has the fortitude to take personal problems into their own hands, but such a person is *uniquely primed* to build systems (i.e., external changes) that help others with a similar strain of problem. I am speaking of the **entrepreneur**: the individual who creates private businesses and non-profits instead of campaigning for political change. In this way, the citizens have the *freedom to choose* to engage with the enterprise or not. Profitability becomes a proxy measure to affirm whether people want the offer or not. In this "voluntary participation" approach, a political solution need not be taxed upon everyone's way of life.[49]

Coming back to the mental health activism, both external and internal strategies can be emphasized in, say, a public school environment: they are not mutually exclusive. However, I think developing the *internal skills* and *values* of students is a better use of teachers' effort in contrast to sharing pre-packaged solutions to mental health problems (all of which can be accessed with personal technology anyway).[50]

---

48   I am not saying these are wrong, but I *am* saying that such "social prescriptions" are not correct by default merely because they are *attempting* to help. Good intentions are no guarantee of good results. Test and reassess.

49   There are plenty of exceptions that I don't have time to list, but a good rule of thumb as to whether a political solution is required or not is to ask, "Is something in the private industry harming others or limiting their freedom of choice?" If yes, then the government may need to step in. The Civil Rights Act of 1964 is one example of this.

50   But how does one *teach* internal values? One method would be to create

Resourcefulness (i.e., the teachable skill of garnering resources to solve difficult or unexpected problems), **optionality** (i.e., a state of having many choices) and **personal responsibility** (i.e., taking ownership of one's actions, emotions and their consequences) all go hand-in-hand. I see the three as interconnected tenets that must be understood and upheld for an individual to thrive in this life. And when one is removed, the other two are rendered ineffective. For example:

- Someone may be **resourceful** and have **many choices**, but without personal responsibility the negative consequences of those choices will be blamed on someone or something else (and likely, feel a corresponding sense of "justified" anger or upset). Therefore, *without personal responsibility an individual loses their emotional autonomy and sense of free will.*

- Someone may be **resourceful** and have **a sense of personal responsibility**, but without optionality one's skills and virtues cannot be maximized. This combination may occur in a prison, a totalitarian state or, at a lesser extreme, a public school where a student is forced to learn via an incompatible teaching method. Therefore, *without optionality an individual loses their freedom of choice and must resort to radical acceptance of the present moment (which is easier said than done).*

- Someone may have **many choices** and **a sense of personal responsibility**, but without resourcefulness it's like being in a cave with no way to mine to the gems below the surface layer of rock. To have many choices (or *access* to many resources) is *useless* if there is no ability to "mine" for information and make it practical to one's specific problem. Therefore, *without the skill of resourcefulness, an individual loses their problem-solving autonomy and must resort to others for "solutions" to their personal problems (which also leads to a loss*

---

more opportunities for open-ended projects. Develop constraints and targets in a dialogue between teacher and student, which challenge the person. From there, have the teacher act both as a coach and referee (to prevent cheating) as the project evolves. Ideally, establish some kind of event to present the projects in order to create additional stakes and a formal deadline. Although this method is only indirectly tied to mental health, I see it as a potential antidote to the evident boredom students feel about their schooling, as shown in a nationalwide survey.[32]

of critical-thinking skills).

It is obvious by now, I'm sure, that I am not naming specific solutions to specific (or abstract) social justice-related problems. I firmly admit that I have no perfect solution to "fix" the rising rates of anxiety and depression in the younger population or, for that matter, the very real disparities among identity groups. *However, I must underscore that this is deliberate.* All attempts to propose grand and sweeping solutions are ideological because, by their nature, they refuse to acknowledge the multifaceted, unique circumstances of every individual. **Put short, "one size fits all" fits almost no one at all.**

So what do we do? Wallow in the cynicism of statistical disparities? Accept them as predetermined? Give up all hope for positive change? Turn a blind eye to the impoverished in American society? I ask all this in jest. Ideologues are prone to treat the conversation of progress, in general, and social justice, in particular, as all or nothing. *If you're not with us, you're against us.* But if I am not with them, nor against them, then where do I stand?

It is the ego that cannot understand such a paradox.

The truth is, once a person takes their attention away from the macro—i.e., focusing on nationwide statistical disparities as well as anecdotal news stories across the country—then all those good intentions begin to manifest on the micro level, in local communities and in one's personal life, where change is human-to-human or self-improving, where results are seen with one's own eyes. However, to the chagrin of scholars and intellectuals seeking a place in the sun, change that affects only a handful of flesh-and-blood people—though tangible and meaningful—is unlikely to pave the way for a spot in the annals of history.

While most laypeople pursuing a good life for themselves and their families will eat the metaphorical elephant (i.e., life's challenges) in small bites over a long period of time, public intellectuals attempt to eat the elephant in one big bite (i.e., solve complex social problems with a one big, abstract solution). It is rooted in the egoic impulse to stand out as superior to others—that, and carve out an advantageous career "selling" ideas instead of value-based products or services. I see that it is public intellectuals, like Robin DiAngelo and Ibram X. Kendi, as well as the journalists and influencers who parrot their viewpoints, who sow the seeds of polarization in the modern culture.[51] This

---

51   On the other side of the political spectrum, there are people like Tucker

is not unique to this era though. Flashback a hundred years, and it was *intellectuals*, such as Madison Grant and predecessors of a similar bent, who propagated racist ideologies that encouraged disunity among individuals in that time.

The rise of social media has allowed people to short-circuit what it means to be "a good person," because sharing popular social justice opinions is so easy, but it is a shrewd from of morality. Let us stop kidding ourselves. It takes almost no effort or risk and ought not be conflated with true courage.

Of course, there are times to have black-and-white opinions. Of course, there are times to virtue signal online. Of course, there are times to "raise awareness and destigmatize" certain topics. I'm not saying to stop sharing one's opinions with others. The point is that activism can quickly turn from *an altruistic and courageous pursuit* to *a destructive ideology in which all dissenting opinions are treated as evil and all debate is "off limits."*

You must be able to make the distinction! It is not easy, but the question, "Am I taking a reputational risk in speaking out about this thing?" is a good way to distinguish between true, selfless activism and ideological, self-serving activism.

Importantly, you must be willing to question your own preconceptions and belief systems. **Humility, as a cultivated virtue, is a critical piece of the equation: To be okay with being wrong or lacking all the answers.** To seek what it is true despite the consequences. But is it that simple? Well, yes and no. F. A. Hayek, author of *The Road to Serfdom*, expressed the central hold-up well:

> "It seems almost as if we did not want to understand the development which has produced totalitarianism because such an understanding might destroy some of the dearest illusions to which we are determined to cling."[52]

So long as one's "dearest illusions" are part of their sense of self (e.g., "I am a social justice activist!" "I am a mental health advocate!" etc.), any critiques of the underlying ideology will feel like an attack on one's self. In simple terms, if I feel like the world will go to hell if I

Carlson and Sean Hannity. I wish to make clear that the divisiveness occurs on both political sides.

52   Hayek, Friedrich A., *The Road to Serfdom*, p. 60.

"give up my cause," then I will fight until the bitter end to defend it. The illusion of ego is behind it all.

CRITICAL THINKING AND AWARENESS

These words are not meant to ignite some new social revolution; nor are they a call to villainize the ideologues of our time. I don't care if you utter a word to anyone about this essay. These words are written solely for You: the Awareness behind the thinking mind.

Can you hear me over there, from the other side of the page? Past all the noisy, swirling judgmental thoughts arising in the mind? Behind all the filters of political bias (yours and mine both)? Beyond the fictitious, egoic self who guards your foundational beliefs with a pointed spear, always on high alert for an attack?

Or have I, the limited personality, "Sean Patrick Greene," already been marked a malicious bigot and disregarded accordingly? Can you, as yet, sense that which makes us the same behind our unique form identities?

To close, I will state the purpose of this essay one final time, in clear terms, so there is no confusion as to why it has been included in the book:

1. Good intentions (a mask often worn by the egoic self) can have horrendous consequences when left unchecked and unquestioned. The only way to prevent those consequences is to allow free-flowing debate, to protect freedom of speech (even if some of it is unsavory) and to accept dissent of main-stream views (even if a small percentage are bogus and con-spiratorial).

2. Trust that the truth that remains open to critique and falsifi-cation is *always more accurate* than "the truth" that demands the suppression of non-truth. If there is a fear of misinforma-tion, then teach people proper reasoning skills so they may discover what is true voluntarily.

3. Point out statistical disparities if and when they are observed, but do not lose sight of the fact that the goal of a liberal nation is to establish equality of opportunity (as well as protect competition systems to prevent monopolies) and to protect

individuals' liberty—it is not improvement for some identity groups at the expense or disregard of others. *Tribalism got us into this mess, and it will not get us out of it.*

4. Have humility: I don't know everything, nor do you. The production of knowledge will never be finalized, and the direction of discovery is not linear, so stay open and skeptical ("strong opinions, loosely held" is a good motto).

5. Self-knowledge (i.e., knowing who you are beyond name and form) is an antidote to remove yourself from one dubious ideology *without* falling into another reactionary ideology. For as much as was critiqued about far-left politics, I see far-right politics as just as ideological (and with more potential for physical violence).

I don't think this social justice crusade is over, nor will it be the last of its kind, but that is okay. Domineering ideologies come and go like cold winters. The question is not, "How can they be stopped for good?"—which would only lead to *another* ideological reaction—but rather, "How can I cultivate enough awareness and humility to avoid being drawn into one myself?"

Come back to your sense: Here and now.

The ego is only an illusion,
but a very influential one.

— *Wayne Dyer*

CHAPTER 7

Q&A: ON THE INSIDIOUSNESS
OF THE EGO

*To realize that you are not your thoughts is
when you begin to awaken spiritually.*

— Eckhart Tolle

The second to last essay will take on a Q&A style. My intention is to pose questions and remarks that have arisen as I have discussed the contents of this book with people close to me. There are also questions that arose in my mind that I presume will apply to most readers in spite of them never being asked or answered aloud. *If certain ideas in this book have confused you so far, this essay seeks to clarify.*

I must remind the reader as they go through this piece that the focus is on the direct experience of Self-knowledge—not the author and his words. Any usage of the pronoun "I," in reference to the writer, is designed to bring the seemingly abstract concepts to the level of personal, day-to-day living. I hope this will allow the reader to dissolve any prejudices they may have regarding *who* is deemed spiritual and *how* such a person must behave. I imagine the biggest hurdle to integrate the book's message into one's own life is the thought: *Well, this is great stuff, but I'm not that type of [spiritual] person. I've got bills to pay, mouths to feed and people to see.*

I do too—perhaps to a lesser extent, but I have by no means "dropped out" of society, nor do I feel compelled to. Self-knowledge can be realized and integrated into *any* lifestyle.[1] Only upon true reali-

---

1 What about the person who steals cars and robs houses? What about the lawyer who defends white-collar criminals? What about the CEO who lays off half her workforce just to make the company's stock rise a few percentage points? Self-knowledge can be realized in any life situation: One's prior

zation is that clear. See, it is one thing to grasp abstract concepts from a book like this (and parrot those words to other people), but something entirely different to *experience* the realization that the words point to.

This reference of words that point—which Eckhart Tolle calls "signposts" in *The Power of Now*—is critical to understand before diving into questions. All of this talk of Self-knowledge and spiritual awakening are *words*; not the actual thing. So, although someone still caught in the grip of ego can conceptually understand the metaphors littered throughout the book, that is not true understanding. In fact, the lust to conceptually understand the Self (or the pride felt upon this form of understanding) is a great hindrance to realizing It.

Conceptual understanding is like trying to observe the reflection of the sun on a small pond, but instead of allowing the water come to stillness, the person splashes the water in the naive hope of grasping the sun in his hands.

The thinking mind is itself the water in the pond; one's stream of thought ("I want to know ...") is the splashing hand; and the sun is God (or the Self, Presence, Love, Consciousness, Bliss, etc.).[2] In a state of ignorance, the individual is compelled to find everlasting bliss (i.e., the up with no down; the love with no opposite) in an existence that *is* up-and-down. It's a fool's errand. It's like scouring the Earth in search of one's own eyes.

In the modern world, where God is a four-letter word, most people have nothing *except* existence: namely, the mundane experience of their daily life; the bleak outlook of humanity in the media; and the scientifically verified nature of reality. This keeps the secular individuals stuck between a rock and a hard place: Seek pleasure—or

---

behaviors have no relation to realizing one's true Self (as Unconditioned Consciousness) in this moment now. This doesn't imply that guilty criminals who awaken ought to get a pass in the eyes of the legal system. Self-knowledge is entirely different from the cause-and-effect relationship of action. (Action is also synonymous with karma). As a metaphor, good karma (i.e., being selfless and charitable) and bad karma (i.e., being selfish and greedy) are like good and bad weather to a plant: Good weather can be helpful to growth, but it is external to the process of a seed blossoming into a flower (i.e., spiritual awakening).

2   Ultimately, the word used to symbolize the Consciousness that illuminates everything in the material word is irrelevant. These words are signposts, and I use many terms in hopes that one will be free of preconception from the reader. Also, the instances where a word is capitalized (like "You" or "Awareness")—this too is used as a signpost for Consciousness and to differentiate the term from its common usage.

meaning—through substances, people and status (all of which contain peaks and troughs)[3] or fall into a state of cynical despair.

The good news is that this bleak-sounding dilemma is illusory! It is literally invented and perpetuated by the mind in the form of thought. Therefore, to get to the root of the problem—the true hindrance to spiritual awakening and the true cause of mental suffering—one must be aware of the nature of thought; specifically, egoic thought (e.g., "I am this. I want that.").

What is the nature of thought?

In a state of ignorance, one believes they are the thoughts that arise in their inner space. If the thought says, in reaction to an event, "That guy just cut me off in traffic. What a jerk!" Then the person now *believes* the other driver is a jerk. She might go out of her way to cut *him* off or drive beside him to curse him out. Only after doing the immature action does a feeling of relief wash over her. If, through sheer willpower, that driver did *not* lash out with reactionary behavior, despite those thoughts arising, then a lingering set of thoughts will likely arise throughout the day (e.g., *"I can't believe that driver. People on the roads drive like idiots these days. I'm the only cautious driver left. God, he could've killed me. My car would've been totaled. I bet he would've sped off, too. He doesn't even care. He's going to get someone killed. I hope he rots in jail for killing someone."*).

At some point, in a place far removed from the initial event, the person will realize, *"Wait, this is crazy. Why am I still thinking about that moment? That happened five hours ago. I can't do anything about it. I need to just let it go."* Although the person may attribute this second-order thought pattern to self-reflection, it is, in fact, Awareness that observes the insanity and futility of the original stream of thought. Said another way, she doesn't need to "think" about how crazy the thoughts are, but just become aware that she had not been in control

---

3   I don't wish to make this sound as if all atheists and agnostics are caught between a drug high and a deep depression. There are countless people whose community of friends and family is strong enough to weather the storm of life's darkest moments. (I would imagine such people have *some* spiritual tendencies—even if they use scientific language to describe them). The important point is that secularism can build strong, well-functioning societies, but it cannot comfort the existentially afflicted in absolute terms.

of the mental monologue prior to that point of coming back to Pure Awareness. From there, the thought pattern can dissolve *because* she is now aware those thoughts are not who she is.

From this anecdote, one can observe that **thoughts arise in reaction to a phenomenon** (like being cut off in traffic) **and perpetuate themselves from that point.** By perpetuate, I mean one thought flows into the next in a semi-coherent way. To pull from the early example, to go from "I can't believe that driver" to "I hope he rots in jail for killing someone" is a huge logical jump, but, by reading all the thoughts in sequence, it makes sense.

Now, most people think *all* the time, but it's often mundane and runs like background static. It's usually only seen as a hindrance when a strong (negative) emotion is sparked in the body and the corollary thought patterns take on an intrusive quality. That is what occurred with the hypothetical driver from before. A bodily fear response arose instinctively in response to being cut off (and possibly harmed), a stream of thoughts then *justified* the uncomfortable sensation, and those thoughts projected the discomfort onto the other driver (in the form of blame and anger).

But what are you supposed to do when those intrusive thoughts take over?

The way to dissolve such thought patterns, which is difficult in the moment when the physical sensation is strongest, is to become aware of them as *not "I."* Identify as the Silent Awareness that underlies the thoughts. You can observe your thought pattern in an objective way—like jumping off a bike and watching it roll a bit further—and realize, *without verbalizing it as another thought,* that you no longer want to identify with those thoughts any longer. This becomes easier the further distanced in time one is from the mental-emotional trigger event. However, if, in the moment bodily sensations are still strongly felt, you are able to disidentify from the thoughts spinning in the mind, then, from there, *feel* the bodily sensations (e.g., the breath, the heart beat or any tingling sensations in the hands or feet) without *labeling* them with more thoughts.

It sounds wordy on paper, but the process is intuitive and often occurs without a person knowing how they do it.

There is such a thing, though, as suppressing a thought pattern or emotion instead of dissolving it. This occurs when someone realizes, *"Okay, I don't want to think about this anymore,"* but, instead of observing the thoughts in a detached way and feeling the bodily sensations, he uses *different* thought patterns to distract from/ignore/ cope with the initial thoughts. As a metaphor, this is like putting out a small fire by throwing heavy timber on top. It may appear to have worked—the flame is out of sight, but at some point later on that fire will come back with a vengeance.

I thought coping was a good thing. How does a thought grow in strength when we ignore/cope with it?

I use ignore and cope interchangeably because coping often, though not always, implies resistance to the situation, thought or feeling. It treats the thought as inevitable. It treats the emotional response as inevitable. It validates the fear as an implied aspect of your existence.[4] It implies you must identify and label the sensations that arise in the body as good or bad. We learn coping mechanisms when anxiety strikes, when panic attacks, when anger boils the blood, or when grief heavies the heart.

Why must one cope with these emotions? Because they are painful? Yes, panic can create the sensation that one is short of breath, and anger can create the sensation of physical irritation. But is that what pain is? I find that the "pain" that arises from energetic emotions (anxiety and anger, in particular) is not the same type of pain as stubbing one's toe or burning one's hand on a hot plate. Often, this emotional pain arises from resistance *to* the physical sensations arising in the body. This is what one might called "suffering." Suffering is the egoic

---

4   I don't wish to speak arrogantly about the most severe mental illnesses: PTSD, bipolar disorder, schizophrenia, borderline personality disorder, etc. Although I believe diet and nutritional imbalances (and epigenetics as a whole) play an understated role in these illnesses, the fact remains that I have not experienced the most severe of these afflictions, and I have no medical acronyms behind my name. I urge the reader to look at the book *Nutrient Power* by William J. Walsh, Ph.D., for a better understanding of chemical imbalances as they relate to severe mental illness. This essay is written for everyone, though it may be most impactful to someone with general and, I shudder to say, normal neuroses and anxieties. This message can be understood by someone with a more severe illness, but it may not become practical until the biochemical/ physical aspect of the illness is understood and stabilized with help from a trained professional.

mind creating irritation by suppressing one's mental-emotional reaction to a certain event. Suffering strengthens a negative thought pattern because every time it is successfully suppressed or "coped with," the belief that *I do not want to feel that again*—that, in fact, *I am afraid to feel that again*—grows more solid. Therefore, it's not merely that the physical sensation grows more intense when it is triggered by a situation in the future, but that one's thoughts (which, for most readers, are ego-centric) resist the sensation even more intensely than before.

As an analogy, it's like standing next to a trash can and noticing an unpleasant smell. The natural response is to distance oneself from it—nothing special or significant to the movement. Though, later on in a new environment, the smell returns; the same smell, but now with the attachment to "this is a bad smell and I want to distance myself from it [because I have done so in the past]." It's not that one literally thinks, "I'm going to do something *because* I have repeatedly done it in the past." It is implied. It is the point that is missed by the unexamined mind. **More likely, a person projects their reason for repeating a behavior onto the conventions of good and bad; pain and pleasure.** It is ego that desires to repeat the behaviors and thoughts of the past because those patterns validate and animate it.[5]

To finish the analogy, let's say the smell arises one more time, in yet another location, except now there are no trash cans in sight. There's nothing around to point to which might "cause" the smell. (Stop me when you know the punch line). With no options left, the person pulls a tuft of his shirt up to his nose and takes a big breath in.

It was him all along.

It's not that the smell of the trash can was bad (relative to the flowers, perhaps, but not in actuality—not in being without comparison), but that the mind created a story for *why* the person moved away. From that point on, the story plays on repeat when the smell returns. The story is something you attach to. The individual *identifies* with the story. If, at a later time, the person would choose to remain next to such a smell, the mind would start to chatter (e.g., "Why aren't you

---

5   This is a bit tricky to understand because you are most likely reading from the point of view of John or Jane Doe. I am talking above the ego, and yet the ego thinks it is the personality reading this. Ego arises out of repetition. The only reason I am called "Sean Patrick Greene" is because a decision was made, the pattern was repeated many times and conventions of speech took front and center stage against the soon-forgotten backdrop of Awareness.

moving? You really want to smell gross? Everyone's going to think you smell like trash. Why won't you move?"). That chatter is automatic! It's not You! That is the ego attempting to preserve its existence by keeping one's actions in line with the previously invented stories/justifications for past behavior. As one begins to awaken to the illusion of ego, these moments of mental chatter reveal how feeble the ego truly is: It is a small dog with a loud bark.

The key, though, is not to fight fire with fire. To begin thinking "I'm *choosing* to stay here because I've built up the discomfort of standing near this bad smell for too long," will only invite a counterpoint "Well, it does smell bad, doesn't it?" And You have already sunk back into the ego-mind. Ego conversing with itself. You, the Awareness behind the thoughts—the collection of which creates the ego— remain the ever-present observer.

Say nothing.

Say nothing more.

The mind will talk regardless ("Oh, this is Awareness. Wow, is this enlightenment? Am I enlightened now? This is what the Buddha felt, isn't it? I'm like the Buddha—that's crazy."), but as that insane monologue plays on without interference, You watch. You watch until the thoughts subside. You watch until Awareness is so focused on Itself that no thought can pull the attention away. You become like a river bed: observing every fish and pulse of water move while You remain still. As the mental stories lose their power (because You no longer resist the sensations that the mind labels as uncomfortable/painful, like anxiety or anger), bodily sensations are felt and accepted the moment they arise. Thoughts like, "When will this go away? This still feels uncomfortable. This is hell. This is agony," may still play like sounded alarms, but from the perspective of the Watcher (the seat of Witness Consciousness, Presence, Awareness, Being, etc.), the thoughts are unmasked as the ego afraid of its own death. That death is nothing more than the ego (i.e., collection of stories that include "I, [the body], ...") dissolving into no-thought.

So, the ego has to die? I don't understand that term: ego death. If I become the Watcher or Awareness, does all my personality vanish? Do I become like a monk who has to meditate in a cave for the rest of his life? That sounds like a boring existence to me.

This fear of lifelong boredom is a reasonable one. Reasoned by the mind as a sort of warning sign to "not look behind the curtain." I use curtain as a metaphor, but in actuality, all I am speaking about is the gap *between* two thoughts and the gap *between* a set of physical sensations and the mental labeling of said sensations in the mind (as a good or bad emotional state). *The silence and stillness.* It is not so ephemeral that the mind cannot figure out what I am pointing to: It is just that the ego creates fantastical (and often fear-provoking) ideas of what lies within the silence and stillness.

Hell. Eternal damnation. Everlasting boredom.

Of course, nothing is there. It's Awareness only; formless and senseless. This is something that cannot be understood by the mind. It is a feeling, yet it is not sensory in the way of pressing two fingers together and noticing that. It is noticing the noticing. Being aware of being aware.

Yet, those last two sentences may read as so pointless that the mind labels such a statement as "meaningless" or "boring." That's because the egoic mind cannot *feel* what it means to be aware of being aware. The ego is this black text; You are the paper. It may look trivial in written language, but as an actual state of mind it is incredibly rich in feeling.[6]

But if "everlasting boredom" is the ego's rebuttal against its own dissolution, isn't it important to understand the fear?

What is boredom?

Being unsatisfied with the Now and wanting to be somewhere or some-time else. It's a state created by desiring something that is not here (e.g., entertainment, sensory pleasures, drugs, alcohol, etc.). It may be a low-intensity suffering, but it is a form of suffering.

By accepting every aspect of this moment (including thoughts, and associated feelings, of "This sucks. This is boring. Nothing is happening. This is so lame."), it is possible to see past the mental labeling that makes life seem so bland.

This is especially apparent in young people, including myself in

---

6   Yes, it is a state of mind to understand that You are not the mind. It is a paradigm shift to say, **I am not the mind, but the mind is a small piece of "I."** Once this is realized, *the mind*, the ego, John Doe, can live with the understanding. The thinking mind understands that it cannot go beyond itself. It settles into its role without overreaching (i.e., without the unquenchable desire for infinite pleasure, wealth and everlasting life). The ego knows it is an illusion, constructed by thought patterns, and so it no longer fears its own dissolution. *This won't make any sense if you identify solely with your thoughts and conditioned personality.*

my adolescence, when it comes to being around nature. To think, even unwittingly, "I've been in the forest before. I've seen that tree before. I've heard the birds chirp before," negates and ignores the uniqueness and wonder in every moment.

Again, this *cannot* be known as a concept.

In the process of spiritual awakening, the thinking mind is like a backseat driver while You drive cross-country. If You listen to and believe the incessant background chatter of "Are we there yet?" then the ride becomes hellishly long.[7] If, even for only a handful of intervals, You can accept the background chatter (accepting it as you would accept—but not act on or ignore—the driving instructions from a well-meaning 7-year-old) and *realize* there is nothing to be done about it, then You are free to focus on the road. **The drive becomes a rich journey when there is no *believed* thought that "I should be over there when I am here." The thought will arise, but there is nothing that says You have to *believe* it.**

Boredom is nothing more than mental chatter that You have identified with.

With regard to personality changes in the process of ego-dissolution, the idea that the personality will dissolve and one will become like a pious catatonic monk (i.e., motionless and mentally stupefied) is yet another fear conceived by the ego to preserve its existence. Any reader of the book who knows the author personally will not see dramatic changes in his outward appearance or personal hobbies. Yet, his fingers type out this book regardless. A book whose message is self-evident.

By seeing the ego for the hollow bundle of thoughts that it is, one's personality—in the conventional sense—is able to shine to its maximum potential. When there is no mental concept of "this is who I ought to be if I am ever to be happy/wealthy/healthy," then one can trust with certainty that who they are, in terms of their life situation—hobbies, career, relationships, etc., is *exactly* who they ought to be at this moment.

---

7   Often, in modern, pseudo-psychological terms, "ego" is considered only the negative, self-sabotaging aspects of the personality. The author is speaking of ego, of the thinking mind, as *all* thoughts and conceptions of egoic identity (even positive self-talk). Even the self-aware thought that says, "Shut up, ego! I know you're a destructive force in my life, and I won't listen to you," is the pot calling the kettle black. Only You, the Silent Awareness, can observe all aspects of the ego, no matter how it reveals itself.

But what about the people stuck in dead-end jobs? What about all the people who don't know their purpose in life?

The total acceptance of "not knowing your purpose" is required before any progress can be made on this front. So often people do not examine the exact, present situation they are in. Every moment is spent in projected future or past moments. **By *seeking* your purpose in life, you will never find it.** Why? Because the idea—the thought you identify with—that you are "someone seeking something" is what keeps you bound as a perpetual seeker. *Think on These Things* by Krishnamurti is an excellent read to go deeper on this topic.

If you are able to stand outside of the question—to be in "no-thought" or Pure Awareness for a single moment—it becomes clear that there is no need to articulate a life purpose for the sake of the egoic mind. It can never be satisfied anyway. What good would the answer do? How would you ever be certain there is not a better, more impactful life purpose waiting just around the bend?

That is deeper (or "higher") consciousness; not thinking about thinking, but *identifying as the Silent Awareness* while all thoughts run their natural course. This is not some esoteric thing except where draped in symbolism—as with organized religion.

Hell, it's only total acceptance of the Now.

I say "only" as if it's easy. It is, but it's made difficult to the extent that you *believe* in shoulds and should nots.

What about violence and injustice? Should I just accept it? Wouldn't that make me an accomplice of evil?

Ego must be dropped, or at least distanced from, before a proper analysis of any situation can be made. With regard to witnessing violence (most likely to be violent language because physical escalations are short-lived), intervention may be necessary, *if* one can see through the thought patterns that say, "I am an intervener," or "I am a bystander." What the situation calls for in the moment cannot be premeditated. (Obviously, this is not referring to people who make a career of protecting or saving others).

When it comes to violence—in the abstract—the ego crafts hazy, unexamined "evils" as distant contrast points to give one's self a moral high ground to stand upon. Violence—in the specific—does exist and, when it arises, ought to be diffused as soon as possible. I merely am pointing out that proclaiming something like, "I stand against injustice!" is a pseudo form of virtue.

In simple terms, talk is cheap.

But what about racial injustice? That is the issue of our time!

Obviously, as Sean Patrick Greene, a white male who grew up middle class in the Midwest, I do not have a direct understanding of racial injustice. Call it white privilege or not—whatever allows the reader to reach the end of the essay.

In looking at this topic, it is important to separate empathy and compassion. Empathy implies I have similar memories of pain on which I can draw from to feel what I "think" the other person is feeling. "I know how that feels, I'm sorry. I can relate,"—it doesn't apply here. There can only be compassion: *Compassion is like empathy but without bringing in a sense of self.*

I can know pain exists—without experiencing it myself—and still wish to relieve someone's pain. I may see someone's face strained in pain, and if I too strain my face, and draw on painful memories of my own, then that is empathy. **If, though, I do not strain my face— beyond what is instinctual—then I can cultivate *compassion* by being present with the other person and doing what the situation calls for.** It may be shedding tears. It may be a warm hug. Or, being there with a quiet, non-judgemental presence may be enough.

As for racial injustice specifically, I must remain aware and distanced from my stream of thought because every "answer" that springs from the conditioned patterns of my mind are bound to lead to polarizing interpretations. Although is that what the reader wants? Is that what the ego seeks—to know whether the writer of this book is woke or racist? Compassion, kindness and acceptance arise in moments they are called for and are only hindered by premeditated ideologies.

Are some cops unconscious—seeking status and power by choosing to play that role? Yes. Are all cops? No. Can something be done? Yes, but vilifying collective identities is far from the answer.

Legislation may allow for a more fair starting line to account for generational divides in collective groups, but that is not the true problem. The problem exists in every individual; both the perpetrator and victim of *specific* unconscious behaviors. I emphasize "specific" because too often the activists, intellectuals and politicians seeking retribution for historical injustices craft notions of "absolute right" and "absolute wrong" in ways that make enemies out of collective groups, regardless of the *specific* behaviors of the individuals within.

For example, the Republican Party (or any conservative) is often implicitly or explicitly considered racist by the opposition. Black Republicans are seen as an enigma and, sometimes, traitorous. This generalization is imposed by a collection of egos who see themselves as anti-racist (a label which gives the ego a justification to attack "racism"—going so far as to search for racism in the recesses of people's unconscious in order to expunge it from society). Who is the perpetrator and who is the victim of such a situation? When victims attack the perpetrators, it becomes easy to see that the ego is using whichever mask seems most effective to maintain its sense of self. Victimhood is in vogue in the 2020s.[8]

The irony of such attacks is that self-identified racists (you know, the neo-Nazi types) would not take offense by being called racist. Often, it's self-identified liberals or moderates who are most in fear and susceptible to shame if labeled by others as "racist." *Precisely because that isn't how they identify themselves!*

This distancing of the ego from the abstract notion of "evil" was mentioned in the essay about politics, but to be specific, when one denies one's own capacity for evil, one projects that evil upon the decided enemy (e.g., a liberal or conservative) and perceives their behaviors as malicious or ill-intended; regardless of how they act. *This mental filter distorts one's view of the world in a way that promotes division and fear.*

Anyone, regardless of skin color, is *capable* of doing a racist thing or thinking a racist thought. Anyone. To realize this does not mean you condone or engage in violence or racism in any form, but that you can feel compassion for even the most evil, spiritually-unconscious human beings. There is oneness behind the duality of good and evil. This unity cannot be rationalized with words, but only felt as the spacious emptiness from which words and thoughts arise.

Does your mind refuse such a thought at this moment? Does my

---

8   Often, an ideological thinker will side in favor of such a statement and cry out, "Liberals are wimps! Snowflakes!" This is yet another mask of ego trying to maintain itself. I am not pointing out that victimhood is a more common identity in modern times in order to insult anyone; only to express how insidious and deceiving the ego can be.

privilege, which I speak of without spite, create resistance to the message presented? Do your conditioned thoughts wish to lump the author into the category of a right-sided ideological thinker?

Just notice the mind's inner-monologue for a moment before you read any further.

☼☼☼

That is not You. **You do not think the thought; You merely observe it.** In a state of ignorance, most people identify with the thoughts in their mind as "who I am and what I believe." That is how an egoic sense of self is created. Its origins begin in our upbringing as implicit or explicit lessons taught to us by role models to (A) maintain a consistent identity (something that one must "try" to do) and (B) resist and avoid pain at all costs.

There is value in these lessons, just as there is value in developing an ego in adolescence. Without ego, there can be no spiritual awakening. It is much like the transitional, cocoon stage of a caterpillar before transforming into a butterfly. However, too many people in modern society remain in this cocoon their entire life.

The media, political media in particular, is a major hindrance to people going beyond this transitional stage. When the egoic mind seeks to know where another person sides with regard to a hot-button issue (e.g., abortion, trans rights, gun control, climate change policy, etc.), it is only seeking to strengthen its position, and therefore strengthen itself.

The real You does not vilify the unconscious person (in this example, someone who is racist). It has no need to. It needs no opposition because it has no identity to uphold. If, the moment a racist act is occurring with the intention to harm another, then action will be called for. (How that action is taken cannot be premeditated). Until then, all that is asked of you is to *be aware* of what you seek to strengthen or validate when you vilify or praise someone else's opinions/behaviors.

What about planning for the future? I understand that we must be present, "be in the now," but won't that allow evil people to grow in strength while the spiritually conscious people do nothing?

This is a two-pronged question about the ego's craving for the future. The first prong is about planning versus being present. The second prong is the ego's "save the world" mask asking about stopping bad actors from acting bad.

In looking at the first question, how can one rectify the paradox of "living in the Now" and "planning for the future"? It requires you to be present *while* planning for the future. As a visual metaphor, it is like looking into a crystal ball while scenes of potential future scenarios play out, but *being aware* that you are only watching a crystal ball that still exists in the Now. The breath still rises and falls; the AC still hums somewhere in the background; the weight of the body can still be felt—all of this is occurring now.

One can still plan meetings on their Google Calendar, set alarms and use clock time *without being used by those things*. By "used by it," I mean becoming swept up in the drama of future imaginings, which often create physical sensations of resistance in the body in the Now (e.g., heart palpitations; shallow, upper-chest breathing; bodily agitation around the arms and chest; etc.). That is what people call "stress," although almost *no one* looks past the catch-all word in order to inspect what is physically occurring. When one remains present, even as the sensations that the egoic mind labels as stress are noticed, those sensations can occur and be processed on a moment-to-moment basis. The "future" in the conceptual sense can still be planned for, but You are no longer caught in the drama of it. *The Power of Now* by Eckhart Tolle is an excellent read to explore further the distinction between "clock time" vs. "psychological time": The former is necessary, the latter is poisonous to the psyche.

What about the second question? How can we save the world from bad people if (and this is implied in asking) all spiritually conscious people are absolute pacifists?

As one becomes more conscious, internal resistance toward emotions lessens and therefore those "uncomfortable" sensations are not projected onto the external world. I no longer scream out in anger when I am aware of the sensations as it is felt in my chest before thoughts label and intensify what is there to become so-called anger. To put it more simply, once You realize that thoughts arise self-so, then You no longer choose to intensify the ones that poison the body and strengthen the illusion of ego.

The sensation still exists though. The ego may try to delude itself with a "mind over matter" philosophy that thinks, *I don't need to feel this. I'm not actually angry. I can overcome this.* This is not what I am saying. I am saying that You, the Awareness that is and underlies thought, must inspect the sensations and thoughts by experiencing them as they are. *Why is this mental chatter so focused on avoiding these physical feelings?* Do not wait for a thoughtful justification. Go straight into the bodily sensations. Sit with them. *Is this what the mind keeps running from?* Only as the Silent Awareness is it crystal clear that there is no purpose in projecting the uncomfortable sensations outward because it only prolongs and intensifies them (and often sparks pain in other people).

But how do we know these negative sensations will go away?

You don't. The very thought of "when will this feeling go away" while the sensations are felt *is* resistance. When there is full acceptance of the sensations and thoughts (which means detached observance of them)[9]—when it all becomes one process, one unlabeled *is*—something arises. It cannot be known by reading these words, but I will attempt to explain it anyway:

> When there is full acceptance of this moment as it is, the Watcher of all thoughts and sensations is aware of Itself. There arises a natural distancing from the thoughts and sensations without needing to push them down and away. It is not distance in the physical sense, but in the psychological sense of *this is not the entirety of who I am.*

A fair rebuttal to this description is to ask, "Isn't that a form of depersonalization? Isn't that a dissociative condition caused by trauma? Isn't that a bad thing?" In this line of critique, the mind has already begun to resist what is.

In what I am saying, I am not telling the egoic mind to step outside of its emotions. I am talking to You. **Depersonalization still involves a sense of self, of ego, which perpetuates thought patterns by constantly interfering with them.** It is the ultimate form of ego convinced it is beyond itself—convinced it has gone behind the veil of so-called reality and has become depressed or anxious because there is seemingly nothing there. It is like trying to see microbes and galaxies—the smallest and the largest—with a meager pair of binoculars.

---

9   It is the same as watching the breath without *trying* to change the rhythm from what it was prior to focusing your awareness on it.

To further distinguish depersonalization from "being aware of being aware," here is an analogy:

Imagine you, the ego, [insert your first name and last name here], as a tightly clenched fist. You, believing you are nothing more than the fist, have developed the belief that you must hold yourself, the fist, as tight as possible to hold your identity together. Every achievement, every personality trait, every new like and dislike, tightens the grip. As all this accumulates, as your knuckles grow white, there develops a terrible fear that if you ever do relax, if you ever release the grip, then all of those things that you have accumulated will vanish. You believe you will become a speck of dust forgotten in the ether. This fear may grow so strong that the fist grows numb to sensation; as when cold weather turns one's fingers stiff and blue.[10] The fist suddenly *feels* detached from itself—in spite of it gripping tighter than ever.

But lo! Every fist belongs to a body. This body cannot be understood as a mental concept to the fist because it firmly believes it is in control of itself. *The fist can only sense it is connected to the body.* By feeling the sensation of fear, which keeps the fist tight-gripped, the fear is unmasked (namely, as a thought/emotion that exists only in the limited scope of the mind/body) and rendered powerless. This non-resistance—free of concepts, rationalizations and justifications—*is* the truth. This non-resistance sparks spontaneous change. The blood re-circulates, so to speak.

The blood re-circulates? Does that mean going into our heart instead of our mind? I think I've heard that's what spiritual people do.

I too have heard that the heart has an intuitive, "spiritual" knowledge to it. Our emotional states (which measurably alter our heart rate and heart rate variability) cannot be stopped by the rational mind. Suppressed for a short while, but not stopped entirely. When something as trivial as finding dirty dishes left in the sink occurs, the hot, tight sensations of anger may arise in my chest. I don't *rationally* want

---

10   "Cold weather" represents an acute traumatic experience.

to feel that, but I have been conditioned to. This is not a diss on my upbringing. There are too many factors at play to place the blame on a single person, and such blame would only negate my ability to process the emotion in myself the moment it arises.

I am using the phrase "process the emotion," which is part of the modern psychology lingo, but I wish to make clear that all that means is *feel the sensations as they are in the body*. It requires no "technique." Of course, certain coping tools can help at the start, but they must eventually be dropped for direct, unlabeled experience.

As a short aside, one hidden form of clinging I have been letting go of is the associations I have to the term "love." Love in the spiritual "that which has no opposite" sense. Though I'm not sure where the expectation grew from (perhaps from a vague understanding of Eastern symbolism like the big-bellied Buddha formed in childhood), my mind once equated a certain feeling-sensation that it believed to be spiritual love. That means other sensations are *not* spiritual love. That means my conception of spiritual love is false because spiritual love can have no opposite. Following so far?

I, therefore, became closed off to [spiritually] loving pain and suffering within myself.

This is an important and paradoxical point. To love pain and suffering? It sounds masochistic. Though, in that masochistic sense, "love of pain" refers to [sexual] pleasure. That is not spiritual love, in the all-encompassing sense, but rather a limited form of love that implies an opposite.

Understanding spiritual love is difficult in the West because, in the written word, love is always directed toward something else: the object of love (i.e., the beloved) and the subject of love (i.e., the lover). Even this idea of self-love, of "I love myself," turns the individual into a dual thing—the "I" who loves and "myself" who is loved. The English grammar structure makes it difficult to see past duality: The basis of an active sentence requires "a *subject* verb-ing an *object*." However, this structure does not obstruct our awareness to the point that we are incapable of seeing past it. It only makes it difficult to realize *until* someone else points it out.

This is where the sentence "I [spiritually] love the pain within myself," gets sticky. Love, in that sense, is synonymous with *total acceptance*. Though, as I type this out, the grammar structure still imposes that I include "I" as the subject and "pain within myself" as the object, so as not to sound incoherent to the reader. A more accurate, though grammatically incorrect, way of writing the aforementioned statement would be:

"Paining."

Silly as it sounds, total acceptance/spiritual love is the dissolution of subject and object. The thinker and the thought is only *"thinking."* The pain and the "I" in pain is only *"paining."* There is no distance (between subject and object), and there *is* no distance (as in it does not exist except as a mental concept). If this makes the reader dizzy, then it is worth intuitively feeling what is being said instead of trying to grasp it as a mental concept.

As you read this book (and may explain to another, *"I*, [the subject], am reading *this book*, [the object]."), what is actually happening? "Reading," yes. Although if you defocus your eyes and become aware of the breath, what then? "Breathing," yes, but does that encompass all of what you are aware of? What about the visual blur? What about the sounds in the room? What about the subtle sensations in the body? What about the thoughts that arise in the mind?

Set down the book and become aware of *everything* within your sphere of awareness for a moment. Become still.

☼☼☼

As one keeps opening and expanding, it is obvious that no verb, sentence or even an entire book could express what *is,* right now, in all its entirety. Any spoken word about reality is an inherent compromise of the whole thing. This book is a clear example. I *cannot* express everything that "I am aware of" even if I had all the pages in the world because *words are not the same as direct experience.*

In spite of the communication compromise, the reader can be aware of everything they are capable of being aware of right now. *I can point, and you can be aware of what I am pointing to in an instant.*

It seems trivial, especially if the reader ignores the author's request to do the practice, but this is total Self-knowledge! Awareness is *who you are* behind the mask of ego!

Distinction (of subject and object) dissolves when the thinking mind is left stupefied by its own incapability to *think* what is happening. If one is especially watchful of one's own stream of thought right now, then it becomes quite interesting how thoughts stop on their own:

But I'm still thinking abo...

Oh, this is what is meant by obser...

Okay, I get that I'm not the thought that I'm thinking right n...

When the flashlight of Awareness is held to a mirror of introspective thought, one can see that there never was a hand pointing to the light. There is Awareness only!

But, I don't get how I can be aware about not actually being the thinker wh...

No answer. No need for it. No need to resist or suppress the thoughts either because they dissolve, without effort, when the light of Awareness is not pointed away, but turned on upon Itself.

☼☼☼

Is this love? Is this the love with no opposite? I would never be able to say or think about the answer. Do you understand why now? Does such a simple absurdity make you grin? Or does it confuse and scare the hell out of you?

For the latter reader, I imagine your perception of the unspeakable world is thickly filtered by concepts, theories, and perhaps religious precepts. Such "seeing beyond the filters" requires You to observe that thinking is not an act of will that *you do* but an organically growing phenomenon.

A stream of thought is akin to a tree's expanding roots, just moving on a faster timescale. As long as this truth is avoided, the reader will live in an isolated, fearful state of mind, which can never feel love or joy and always carries the underlying fear of death.

This is where the intuitive heart-feeling comes into the picture. All intuitive tightness in the heart (which may be called, from a scientific lens, heart palpitations or acute anxiety) represents a resistance to the present moment. It is obviously not a black-and-white feeling (is my heart racing or is it not?), but a scale that signifies one's degree of fear. This fearful resistance can take on countless forms and rationalizations. No one would say anger *is* fear, but it *is* a way of suppressing/ignoring fear. Depression, as well as apathy, is not seen as fear, but it is a way of resisting fear by means of distancing/numbing out from fear.

But is it an over-simplification to say all negative emotions and mental suffering boils down to fear? And fear of what? Similar to how I distinguished spiritual love (which has no opposite) from sexual love (which is a pleasurable state that has an opposite), there is existential fear (which a wide-range of layered emotions) and there is acute fear (known by the fast-beating heart, tightening body, tunnel vision, shallow breaths, etc.).

Existential fear is the fear of death. Ego death, that is. To *be* without identity.

What about day-to-day living? If our thoughts are always "ego" thoughts and we're trying to get rid of the ego, then how can anything be done? Can I even think a thought without doubting myself?

The idea of "trying to get rid of the ego" is a common paradox that arises in the attempt to *know thyself.* "Okay," the reader may think, "I get that I'm not the ego. I know I'm something in the silence or the watcher or whatever, but how do I get to that place?" This is the point in a spiritual journey when there is conceptual knowledge, but no experiential understanding. This is the asymptote point (i.e., when the curve on a graph gets infinitely close to a specific line, but can never cross it)—the point where no more conceptual progress can be made without repeating old ideas over and over again.

Nothing can be done about it. There is not another quote or phrase that one needs to hear before *click*! the combination lock opens the "portal" or whatever metaphor one's mind pictures in this moment of satori (i.e., sudden awakening).

The only thing you *can* do is live and let be. That said, meditation, or whichever vehicle you choose to discipline the mind, can assist in developing a sense of awareness that does not interfere with anything:

It is to notice one's breath as it is *without* willfully changing the pace or intensity. It takes practice and patience. In doing it now, at my desk, the first exhale seems almost too long like I'm holding my breath and I don't know when to breathe in.

Take a moment to do this practice now. Start with one breath. Become aware of it without consciously altering it.

☼☼☼

The goal is not to direct the breath toward a certain rhythm, but to remain watchful as a rhythm arises on its own (most likely, but not always, deeper than when you were not focused on the breath). To master that—to breathe, while being fully aware of it but *without* consciously interfering—represents what must be done in all areas of life. Thoughts, sensations, urges, actions, spoken words, the breath—all of these can go on without conscious interference. The practice is to treat everything you experience with the same focused, non-interference that you just gave to the breath.

At some moment, it may dawn on the reader that even in times when the egoic self interferes with a behavior (e.g., creating a dilemma between the fear of embarrassment and taking courageous action), even *that* will go on without conscious interference. Every moment, no matter how metacognitive, will go on without conscious interference. In fact, that is how it has always been. *Did You forget?*

As that stillness becomes more developed and pronounced, as all thoughts—the good, the bad and the ugly—are no longer held in relation to each other, but in relation to no-thought (i.e., mental stillness), wisdom arises. As everything in existence is always held in relation to non-existence (i.e., emptiness), there is an openness to beauty and an intuition to honor what is. As You witness the unfolding of the Now without falling into the illusion of ego (which *thinks* it controls the movement of the body and mind), there is a deep sense of joy and play.

You can rest in the stillness (or rather, realize that the Stillness is who you are, in your essence!), and yet, everything on the level of material form will keep pace. Linguistic conventions still exist; you may still say, "This book was good," or "This book was awful," but there is a lightness to it all. This is the game. When did it all become so serious?

Compassion arises without effort because you know, with certainty beyond thought, that every person is caught in the spins of the egoic mind just like you. Acts of evil are unmasked as the naive attempt of a fearful (or deluded) ego trying to preserve itself.[11] Good is unmasked as a relative concept (which implies its opposite, evil, in order to exist). This world, Now, the literal space you are in as this book is being read, is rich in depth to the extent that no mental comparisons are imposed on it. If you cannot help but compare this moment to a "better" one from the past or one that may happen in the

---

11   Again, "to have compassion" for evil people does not prevent you from condemning and holding them responsible for their actions.

future, then accept it. Wherever you are—not in the external world, but in the spins of the egoic mind—accept it.

There is nothing to do except what you are doing now. Become aware of it: It requires no thought, only still, alert presence.

CHAPTER 6

THE INFINITE NARRATIVE:
FROM UNWITTING ACTOR
TO CONSCIOUS PARTICIPANT

You can be still and still moving.
Content even in your discontent.

— *Ram Dass*

The American frontier once stood as the land of discovery, of risk with potential reward—symbolic of exploration in the truest sense. Alhough by 1912, the lower 48 states had found place in their proper borderlines and the hopeful vision of a frontier on the West had all but dissolved. Nearly 50 years later, John F. Kennedy reanimated the ideal with his reference to the "New Frontier" in his 1960 acceptance speech at the Democratic National Convention. Among many ideals, he pointed to outer space, and more generally, scientific discovery as a place that could spark the sense of awe and exploration once embodied by the Wild West.

To this day, it is not as if the moon landings have been fruitless to scientific insight, but because of the costs and complexity of the science involved, there are no space cowboys looking to settle on the big gray rock as there were people venturing west of the Mississippi River following the Homestead Act of 1862. Space has not been a satisfactory alternative to the ideal of the Western frontier of the 19th century.

Though, even the Western frontier was far from a universal ideal in that time. Native Americans and African Americans would have no such fondness for this exploration. That is not to say exploration, as an action, is prejudiced, but the zero-sum nature of land exploration and ownership meant that toes would inevitably be stepped on (which is the biggest understatement in the whole book).

So the Western frontier once served as a purposeful ideal in America, even with the contemporary understanding that it could not be a universal vision for all groups of people. The ideal of "exploring the unknown" provided the sense of meaning; land just happened to be the physical symbol of it during that time in American history.

Today, the author would argue, the exploration ideal is tied to scientific discovery and technological innovation. There are practical benefits to this, but because most individuals do not have the time, resources or intelligence to explore the many subsets of science to the same extent as a trained researcher, this is not a universal ideal either. It is now the layperson, regardless of their age, gender or race, who gets the benefit of science and technology *without* the sense of possibility and wonder that the ideal of discovery is meant to evoke. Such a person may enjoy the fruits of discovery (i.e., inventions with practical, commercial applications), but it seems, from the author's point of view, that the cost of such discovery has been a growing numbness toward what is new.

The rate of technological innovation has hit such a pace that "newness" is the status quo. In this, there develops in the mind, an apathy (or worse, a cynicism) toward the future. No matter what comes down the pipeline, save for the discovery of sentient AI, there is nothing that can induce a sense of shock and awe in the modern individual anymore.

People are listless. There is no longer a sense in the culture that some technology will save humanity from its misery. Moreover, the question increasingly asked, even if only covertly, is, "What is all of this technology for?" Why create another iteration of an iPhone with a nicer camera and longer battery? Where is it leading us?

This is to say nothing of the billboard apps (i.e., social media platforms), which most people now understand to be a product for advertisers—not the end user.

So, if not in technological innovation, where is one to put one's hope? Which frontier still inspires wonder?

It appears, from a cynical eye, that there is nothing left unconquered, nothing new to discover, no niche untouched and no truth untold. **The culture is collapsing into nihilism, despite technology all but removing the inconveniences of daily life.**

Although, it may be because of that very thing.

It may sound radical to say the cost of all the useful things provided by science and technology is a sense of nihilistic despair for the layperson, but it's not a matter of one causing the other. Rather, because scientific discovery has dethroned religion from its pinnacle point of cultural respect, it has essentially refuted the ideal of faith [in the unknown].

In 2023, in the time this essay is being written, science is at its apex of societal dominance. All the biblical theology of the origins of humanity and the universe have been debunked by a number of scientists with the tools of mathematics and the scientific method. Such discoveries include, but are not limited to:

COPERNICUS' HELIOCENTRIC MODEL OF THE UNIVERSE (NICOLAUS COPERNICUS, 1473-1543):

This model defied the mainstream, geocentric view of the time that the moon, the sun and the other planets all orbited around a motionless Earth. Attempts were made by the Roman Catholic Church to frame the work as hypothetical and inconclusive. This included an unsigned "letter to the reader" in the book *De Revolutionibus Orbium Coelestium* added by the theologian and political figure Andreas Osiander (who was entrusted to publish the manuscript) to invalidate Copernicus' findings.[1]

GALILEO'S OBSERVATIONS AND SUPPORT FOR HELIOCENTRISM (GALILEO GALILEI, 1564-1642):

In addition to supporting Copernicus' model (in the face of severe persecution by the Roman Catholic Church), he greatly improved the power of telescopes for astronomical purposes. With this tool, he furthered the scientific method by emphasizing direct observation, controlled experiments, evidence-based reasoning over tradition or authority, and a commitment to publish his findings with the scientific community.[2]

---

1   Westman, Robert S. "Nicolaus Copernicus." *Encyclopædia Britannica*, Encyclopædia Britannica, inc., 11 Nov. 2023, www.britannica.com/biography/Nicolaus-Copernicus.
2   Helden, Albert Van. "Galileo." *Encyclopædia Britannica*, Encyclopædia Britannica, inc., 25 Nov. 2023, www.britannica.com/biography/Galileo-Galilei.

NEWTON'S LAWS OF MOTION AND UNIVERSAL GRAVITATION (ISAAC NEWTON, 1642-1727):

Although best known for the three laws of motion, he was also the original developer of calculus even though his contemporary Gottfried Wilhelm Leibniz published first on the topic in 1684. He also made strides in our understanding of the spectrum of light by reflecting white sunlight against a glass prism. This translated to him developing the first reflecting telescope, which used mirrors instead of glass lenses for magnification. This invention improved image quality by reducing chromatic aberrations caused by the curved glass in the older, refracting telescopes.[3]

DARWIN'S THEORY OF EVOLUTION BY NATURAL SELECTION (CHARLES DARWIN, 1809-1882):

Darwin's theory has arguably been the most controversial of the discoveries listed because it relates to the human species directly as opposed to the distant, insentient stars and planets dotted in the sky. In spite of its accusations of blasphemy because it contradicts the divine creation myth, *On the Origin of Species* became a best-seller after its publication in 1859. Darwin's work has, at times, been grossly misappropriated to justify racism and eugenics (i.e., "Social Darwinism"), but this by no means invalidates his core claim that plant and animal species evolve based on which have the traits best suited to survive and reproduce in a specific environment. After Darwin's death, studies of DNA would uncover the mutation process by which trait differences emerge among same-species animals.[4]

HUBBLE'S DISCOVERIES IN COSMOLOGY (EDWIN HUBBLE, 1889-1953):

The Hubble telescope may be more familiar to the reader than the actual discoveries of the man it was named after. Not only

---

3   "Isaac Newton's Achievements." *Encyclopædia Britannica*, Encyclopædia Britannica, inc., 23 Sept. 2020, www.britannica.com/summary/Isaac-Newtons-Achievements.
4   "Charles Darwin Biography." *The Biography.com Website*, A&E; Television Networks, 29 Mar. 2021, www.biography.com/scientists/charles-darwin.

did Hubble prove that other galaxies exist beyond the Milky Way, he, alongside Milton Humason, published a paper that theorized a linear relationship between the size of a galaxy's redshift and the distance from the observer. In simple terms, this paper provided the fundamental equation to support the idea that the universe is expanding and validated the Big Bang theory as the origin of the cosmos.[5] It also led to the estimation that the universe is around 13.8 billion years old.[6]

The list above hardly scratches the iceberg of scientific knowledge, but having already refuted the naïveté of the Bible's relation to the physical universe, all additional discoveries do not serve the purpose of this essay.

These discoveries are incredible and have put humanity's role in the universe into perspective many times over, but because they are known and proven through theory and mathematics—not direct experience—the average person may feel as though the patterns of the universe are known (which admittedly some of them are) with little to no understanding of how the scientific method led to such conclusions. It is that experiential knowledge, that sense of exploring the frontier of an unknown piece of life, that the author believes satisfies the quest for meaning. **It is not conceptual facts that give purpose to life, but *experience*, in general, and *discovery*, in particular.**

To some readers, this framework for a meaningful life, which the author will soon layout, may read as if he's putting legs on a snake (i.e., trying to overexplain something that doesn't require explanation).

Aren't there already libraries full of man's supposed "search for meaning"? Do we really need another book about it?

In what the author is saying, he is claiming that since the "death of God," and in less poetic terms, the rise of secular atheism,[7] some-

---

5   "Edwin Hubble Biography." *The Biography.com Website, A&E;,* A&E; Television Networks, 20 May 2021, www.biography.com/scientists/edwin-hubble.
6   "Expanding Universe." *Encyclopædia Britannica*, Encyclopædia Britannica, inc., 2 Nov. 2023, www.britannica.com/science/expanding-universe.
7   As mentioned in a previous essay, those who identify as Christian have fallen from 78% to 63% over a dozen or so year. To put it in context, Christians outnumbered non-religious people around 5 to 1 in 2007. It was down to 2 to 1 in 2021.[38]

thing must replace the pieces of religion that science does not and cannot supplant (namely, an implicit sense of life purpose, faith in the unknown and an experiential connection to nature—human nature included). To emphasize, it is not the scientist who is likely to suffer the crisis of meaning from imagining and testing scientific theories, but the layperson, whose understanding is weak, muddled and/ or grossly generalized. It is this kind of person who is likely to turn science into a ideology; what might be called "scientism."

SCIENCE VERSUS *SCIENTISM*

Science is verifiable, falsifiable, ever-changing and impartial toward moral issues. Scientism (which is an ideology held, often unknowingly, by intellectuals and laypeople) turns past scientific discoveries into infallible, unquestionable truths. In scientism, there is an impulse for the layperson or intellectual to default to scientific experts when pressed on why they believe a given claim and a knee-jerk reaction to vilify anyone who speaks against the current consensus of a given theory. Although science itself is not designed to convince people of its discoveries, it is those with an ideology based in scientism who go out of their way to convince people of certain scientific truths.[8] Often, these truths are framed in support of a specific moral claim, which gives the illusion of scientific correctness of said claim.

Anyone, scientist or non-scientist, can be drawn to this ideology, but the author focuses on the non-scientist because they make up the larger group of the two.

This ideology is incredibly dangerous when it is allowed to run unchecked. Similar to line of critique in the last essay, it is not science and the scientific method that are being called out, but the conclusions (many of which are capable of being disproved)[9] being used

---

8   The key phrase is "go out of their way." Has the rational, scientific argument been presented to the ignorant person? Are they unwavering in their belief? Is their ignorance harming others? If yes, then make the lawful case needed to mitigate the danger they are causing. If no, then accept that some people think the Earth is flat and move on with your life.

9   Black Swan Events, a term coined by Nassim Taleb, explain why many established conclusions based solely on historical evidence are capable of being disproved. The analogy goes like this: Someone may claim "all swans are white," having never seen a different colored swan; but all it takes is a single black swan to falsify the rule. In instances where science is based on histor-

as declaratory truths that have an unfalsifiable quality akin to the 10 Commandments. It is these "infallible" conclusions (which are often based on statistical analysis—which *is* fallible—as it relates to science being used to defend public policy or moral claims) that allow an intellectual or layperson to justify their disregard and belittlement of the so-called ignorant population (this group, referred to later as "the skeptics," will be detailed later).

It might seem as if the goal ought to be to bring everyone to the level of understanding of actual scientists, so everyone can exist on the same playing field of knowledge, but that ignores the mundane reality that not everyone is willing or able to study science at an advanced level. There's just not enough incentive for those without an innate curiosity. That's not to say that the push in K-12 education for STEM programs and more digital literacy is pointless—it is purposeful, to the extent that it applies to everyday living. It is analogous to "personal finance" versus "finance" classes; the former is universally applicable, but the latter is relevant only to the individuals aiming for a career in the financial sector.

That is all to say that scientific progress is not a frontier that everyone can garner meaning from. There must be an alternative path of exploration (or many paths), which allows an individual to stand on the razor's edge of discovery without the technical skill that science demands—and without negating or denying scientific insights as they apply to the general public (for example, the medical breakthrough of vaccinations).

Let us explore what this may look like.

SCIENCE: THE BEST EXPLAINER OF REALITY

The author would argue that science exists on the same plane of explanation as religion because they both seek (or have previously sought) to explain the origins of humanity and the universe; as well as the phenomena occurring in the natural world.

Science is more valid as an explanatory framework for making

---

ic data or anecdotes (quite apparent in the social sciences), it takes only one "black swan" to disprove a given theory/claim. With this understanding, it is possible to make *via negativa* claims with certainty: "All swans are *not* white" can be said with certainty upon seeing a black swan. This "semi-skepticism" or asymmetrical certainty is a powerful tool when examining expert claims presented in the media (p. 56).[41]

sense of Nature[10] than religion, but that does not change the fact that, from a 30,000 foot view, they exist for the same purpose: *Explanatory language is used to provide an individual with a sense of what is true.*

The shift from religion to science is akin to the shift from polytheistic cultures (i.e., belief in many Gods) to a monotheistic ones (i.e., belief in one God) over the past 2,000 years.

Monotheism, in general, and Christianity, in particular, are far from extinct frameworks, but the author is making the claim that science (and its pseudo-religious descendant "scientism") is to monotheistic religion (e.g., Christianity, Judaism and Islam) what Christianity was to the Roman Empire in the first few centuries of the Common Era.

Science, over the past century, has replaced the previously dominant framework—organized religion—for how we rationalize our beliefs and determine what is true.

The author is not attempting to reinstate a certain religion as the dominant force that influences American culture and politics. His own beliefs are unbound by any religious dogma. **In dovetailing science and religion in terms of their usefulness to the individual, the author seeks to offer the possibility of a framework that is completely different in purpose from science *or* religion.** If science and religion are plotted on the X-axis of a graph (as a visual), then what is being proposed is a framework that may be plotted on the Y-axis.

If the reader accepts the proposition that science and religion are connected in purpose in that they both use explanatory language (including numeral systems) to help a person make sense of Nature, then what would a framework *devoid* of language look like?

Perhaps "framework" is a misnomer because, without using language, the very idea of a "framework" could not exist. This is where language becomes a hindrance rather than a tool. For now, this framework will be referred to as the "Infinite Narrative," and the reader must maintain the understanding that it is pointing to a space of unspeakability.

NATURE IS UNSPEAKABLE?

This is not as esoteric as it presents. The "space of unspeakability" is

---

10   Nature is capitalized to represent everything that has spawned from planet Earth (including human-developed inventions and social institutions). That means, in the context of this essay, government organizations and iPhones are just as much a piece of "Nature" as the Amazon rainforest.

as mundane as the life of a pollinating bee, or a lion in the savanna or even the movement of clouds. These things grow, change and transform whether or not explanatory language (i.e., human thought) is imposed on their movements.

It is not so much of a jump to realize that human beings—in their prehistoric, pre-thinking stage of evolution—also acted without the need (or even possibility) of imposing explanatory language on their behaviors or any other natural phenomenon. All of the life that existed *before* the rise of language existed as the Infinite Narrative, though there was no capacity for self-awareness of this. There was no subject-object division. It was all self-fulfilling.

As language arose, so did religion in its disparate, animistic form (i.e., a belief which assumes all objects in nature have a spirit essence). From there, the polytheistic religions arose (e.g., Greek and Roman gods) and from there the monotheistic ones.[11]

Fast-forward many thousands of years and the pattern-finding ability, coupled with written language and the scientific method, appear to invalidate animism because science has allowed for human beings to *predict* natural phenomena. In the book *Finite and Infinite Games* by James P. Carse, he notes an irony in this shift:

> "By depriving the gods of their own voices, the gods have taken ours. It is we who speak as supernatural intelligences and powers, masters of the forces of nature."[12]

It is now the scientist, not the booming voice in the clouds, who warns of apocalyptic events; the phenomenon remains the same. Therefore, the evolving search for absolute/objective truth—and a riddance of heresy/unscientific truth—exists in the confines of language. The heated debate between two scientists, or a scientist and a Christian,

---

11   The author does not find it necessary to cite sources for this evolution. Evidence of such kinds of religion is abundant in mythology. It is not that all of humanity has had a clean-cut evolution from animism to polytheism to monotheism to science: It is merely that most contemporary, western civilizations have evolved to this point. A good heuristic to measure where a certain nation is at is to ask, "What justification does a government rely on to make its decisions?" The U.S. government is not swayed by some messiah claiming that God demands X policy change, but it can, and continues to be, swayed by some scientist claiming that the data demands X policy change. This is not good or bad, it is just what is.

12   Carse, James P., *Finite and Infinite Games*, p. 101.

is a battle of crashing waves on the surface of the ocean, while the Infinite Narrative rests below, akin to the entirety of the ocean.

THE INFINITE NARRATIVE: WHAT IS IT?

This phrase has been mentioned multiple times already, but the author has yet to offer any practical words about what it means for the present-day reader. The Infinite Narrative, though already clarified to mean the unspeakability of Nature (or that which language *does not alter*), is the space in which *any* and *all* explanatory frameworks for Nature arise. This includes myths, religion, philosophy, science and literature. **The very development of language** (and by extension, thought) **arose within this unspeakable domain.**

To realize this is to realize that absolute knowledge can never be arrived at—at least, in a way that could be known or explained in words. This refutes the teleological explanatory framework of Nature, which says, as a generalization, all action is in service of a future end goal.[13]

The silence of Nature is that which gives rise to all these theories, doctrines, philosophies, ethics, virtues, vices and proposals to live a meaningful life. Here is the critical part to understand: *By maintaining the understanding that no framework—neither religious, scientific, nor philosophical—will provide absolute certainty for one's existence, the unfolding of the Infinite Narrative can occur with a sense of play*

---

13   This occurs often in explaining Darwinian evolution: *The wolf evolved to have sharp teeth* for the purpose of *hunting*. Although this simple statement represents the layperson's assumption and not necessarily the nuanced view of the evolutionary biologist, it negates the reality that animals are constantly mutating and the lineage that survives *happens to have* these certain traits (like sharp teeth). Therefore, explaining any past natural phenomenon as occurring *for the purpose of* some present-day (or future) environment is fraught with intellectual hubris. It is nothing more than a story. The danger occurs when a story such as this, using scientific language, is written for the future (i.e., scientific predictions) and treated as prophetic. Those stories are no guarantee of the actual events in the future but they are treated as such because of scientists' ability to connect the dots between the past and now. This can be referred to as the "narrative fallacy." In simple terms, *the past does not equal the future* with regard to the evolution of plant and animal species (humans included); predictions can provide guidance for future action but they are not prophecies.

and joy. One can explore all the explanatory frameworks of Nature, but find solace standing on the foundation of Nature's absolute silence, which is another way of saying "the foundation of not [conceptually] knowing."

For one reason or another, there arises in the author's mind a negative association with "not knowing." It feels as if accepting defeat. But in fact, it is its opposite—of feeling absolutely certain about everything—which is the true poisoning of the psyche!

Nihilism, as was mentioned near the start, is the sense that life is inherently meaningless, that all existence is chaotic and random, and that consciousness is some fluke arising from inherent matter. The author and someone with a nihilistic-leaning worldview are in fact making the same observation but with near-opposite interpretations.

THE INFINITE NARRATIVE: AN ANTIDOTE TO NIHILISM

Both the author and the nihilist realize that no explanatory framework can wholly encompass all natural phenomena. However, in this realization, the nihilist regards their limited existence as detached, random and devoid of meaning. The author regards his own limited existence as a self-aware form of play with infinite possibilities (by means of exploring all the explanatory frameworks for the silence of Nature).[14]

The difference stems from the nihilist's ignorance of the fact that all individuals—the author and the nihilist included—exist in, and as part of, the silence of Nature. If, for example, the author began to develop cynical thought patterns based on how meaningless and pointless life is, then he *realizes* that he is not bound to those thoughts. The author is aware that he could view the silence of Nature through the framework of a nihilist, an existentialist, a Christian, a Muslim, a Jew, a secular humanist, a stoic, a hedonist, a pragmatist, etc.[15] The list is infinitely long because when all the frameworks have been exhausted, new frameworks will arise self-so. **To clarify, "framework" or "explanatory framework" means using language,**

---

14   This is not merely "play" in the childish sense of playing hide-and-seek, but more encompassing to mean playing with different ideas. It is akin to exploring all of one's curiosities.

15   The process to "internalize" a certain framework—presumably swapping a cynical POV with a more optimistic one—is as simple as consuming vast amounts of media that explain, rationalize and validate said philosophy/religion/framework.

whether empirical or symbolic, to explain *why* Nature (which includes one's thoughts and emotions) is the way it is.

☼☼☼

It is difficult to imagine what emotions arise as the reader moves through this essay. Assuming at least a small portion of readers feel an unwanted sense of fear or despair at the thought of humanity never reaching a state of absolute conceptual knowledge of the universe (or complete denial of that fact), the author would like to clarify that such feelings cannot be willed away even if the desire to do so is strong.

Without Self-knowledge, one is bound to which ever explainatory framework social influences have imposed upon them. *Therefore, the emotional reaction one has to this essay is the only emotional reaction one can have at this moment.* The desire for a different emotional state is what makes the current state *feel* negative by relation. **Only by surrending to this moment Now**—which means placing focus on one's bodily sensations, like the breath or the external senses, to draw awareness away from the mind, where all explainatory frameworks arise—**is it possible to "step into the silence" of the Infinite Narrative and allow something new to arise in the mind.** It is from this spacious emptiness that discovery, creativity and growth arises.

Growth, or "outgrowing" something, must happen on its own. To *will* growth—as in brute, forehead-straining willpower—is a waste of energy. Gardening is a good analogy here because a wise gardener develops an environment for growth but would never be so naive as to claim that their effort is what *made* the plant grow. To will oneself to change is like trying to crack open a seed in order to pull out the flower.

The reader may sense a paradox.

The author regards his existence as "a form of play with infinite possibilities" but also notes that "growth must happen on its own." Who, then, is causing the growth? How can there be a sense of play if there is no willful choice in which possibility arises at any given time—i.e., how can there be a sense of play when negative things arise?

Ah, and it is these two rebuttals that have made religion and science such exceptional, culture-influencing explanatory frameworks for Nature. The author will touch on each rebuttal separately.

1. Who is causing the growth?

The craving to attribute effect to a cause is what leads to attributing natural phenomenon to any number of deities or a single Almighty God. When scientific discoveries refuted the Bible's depiction of the natural world, the question shifted to "*What* is causing the growth?" In that question, it still implies a cause-and-effect relationship with natural phenomena.

Is it too difficult to imagine that things grow self-so? It is not difficult, but it is inherently unsatisfactory, because it doesn't seem to provide a concrete, universal answer that could be written in English. It offers no secondary proof or rationale. It feels incomplete. Yet, it is inherently complete because only with language does the *idea* of incompleteness exist.

2. How can there be a "sense of play" within the infinite possibilities if there is no willful choice in which possibility presents itself at any given time?

This boils down to a craving for certainty on demand. All the innovations in machine learning, computer graphics, virtual reality and software development are, in essence, attempting to provide the average layperson with such control. The problem is that software is bound to a digital screen and, therefore, will always have an inescapble artificial quality.

So the fruits of science and technological innovation are made commercially viable by their ability to provide a product with willful, on-demand choice to the end user.[16] The end goal of technological innovation could be said to be for every human being to have perfect control over their environment for their ultimate satisfaction (like having a perfectly matched personal AI assistant). It is unlikely that the reader will see this realized in their lifetime, but regardless, this essay seeks to show the futility and meaninglessness that arises as a result of the total certainty implied in this techno-centric utopian vision:

As a brief thought experiment to cement this idea, imagine a world in which every night you fall asleep you are able to dream about

---

16   There are plenty of exceptions, but even those people who desire uncertainty (as when one sees a new film) are still choosing that option. They are spending money with the *certainty* that they will get something unexpected.

anything—from any perspective, for a lifetime's length every time. It's likely that you would dream many lifetimes of hedonistic pleasure and ultimate success to start, but eventually become bored by the certainty of it. You, as the dreamer, may then desire to dream with an element of randomness, but maintain the knowledge that you are the dreamer. From there, you may desire more elements of danger and fear in the dreams, while still maintaining the lucid quality of your perspective. After enough nights, you may decide to dream from a random perspective and without the knowledge that you are the dreamer of the dream. It would only be upon waking that the element of safety, that it was all "just a dream," would strike you. After countless nights of this kind of dream there may be a particular dream in which you are reading a book called Off With His Head *in the exact place you are right now.*[17]

The author is not claiming that you, or he, are in a dream right now (an unfalsifiable proposition anyway), but the thought experiment above is meant to illustrate that total certainty would not be desired for eternity and that total *uncertainty* has many joyful elements within it. So the "sense of play" felt by the author is not dependent on any specific possibility, but the joy of discovering an infinite amount of new possibilities.[18] **This points to the idea that experiential knowing, mentioned earlier in the essay, offers more meaning than a life known only by concepts (i.e., factual knowing).**

THE INFINITE NARRATIVE AND PHILOSOPHY

Even if one grants relevancy to the Infinite Narrative—i.e., allowing natural phenomena to unfold without seeking a definite framework to explain *why*—there appears to be a passivity implied. *So what if it's there or not?* The reader, who will eventually set this book down and go about their daily life, may feel a vague sense of inspired freedom

---

17   This thought experiment was paraphrased from an Alan Watts lecture.[45]
18   Yes, painful situations may still arise, but they will not last forever. The price for seeking pleasure is moments of unavoidable pain because what goes up must come down. Although most people are trained to reject any pain, it is wise to understand that this pain and discomfort allows for growth and transformation—the natural kind, not dependent on willpower. Without intermittent gusts of wind, the stem of the growing flower would atrophy, or at least be snapped amidst the first big storm of the season.

but with no understanding on how to act to "make the feeling last."

For many readers, some kind of philosophy may be needed to grasp the *importance* and *relevance* of expierencing the Infinite Narrative in daily life (again, this is not the same as "factual knowledge"). It is similar to how having certain constraints in art—such as limiting the amount of available colors—can inspire more possibilities for creation versus no constraints at all. As this philosophy is laid out, please keep in mind that:

(A) The Infinite Narrative is beyond language, and therefore, beyond what can be explained in a book.

(B) This philosophy is a jumping off point and not a definitive answer to life's great mysteries.

As mentioned above, natural phenomena occur whether the voice of God or the voice of Science explains their occurrence. What can be said in either case is that challenges arise that affect an individual from his or her subjective viewpoint. When these challenges are resisted, they are labeled as "problems" and so a tension develops in the person—a tension between the present moment and when that problem occurs, whether already past or in the future. This tension takes the form of thoughts based around the problem. Let's call this suffering, although "stress" may be the contemporary equivalent; suffering is not in reference to the physical pain caused by a certain problem, but *the mind's aversion to said pain.* This is suffering created in the mind *by the mind* of the individual, though this fact is likely not realized by the sufferer.

Again, external pain inflicted by someone else is not falling under *this* definition of suffering. **There is pain, and there is a mental aversion to the pain—the latter is "suffering."** The distinction is important because, while pain is unavoidable because of the body's fragility, suffering can be transcended with Self-knowledge (i.e., the experiential knowledge of who you are beyond name and form).

So what can be said in the definite is that natural phenomena challenge us—from a subjective point of view. These challenges are not marked only by nature (e.g., a house-destroying tornado or a flash-flooding storm), but also by other people or society at large (e.g., an unexpected breakup or a major financial crash). Remember, "Nature" encompasses all phenomena we can observe because human beings are just as much a part of the silence of Nature as the birds and the trees.

There are two filters through which to interpret these challenges (with an obvious gradient between the two extremes):

1. One can assume these challenges are both, caused by random chance and cosmically insignificant, and therefore, all the more infuriating to deal with (the objective stance).

2. One can assume these challenges are intentional, purposeful and are integral to one's personal growth and humanity's evolution as a whole (the subjective stance).

The scientific community, at this point in the early 21st century, takes the former view by presuming every phenomena can be explained casually and objectively (i.e., without little to no relationship to the observer).[19] Any claim of a meaningful coincidence is written off as superstition or sheer chance (just as a monkey with a typewriter can punch out *Macbeth* given an infinite amount of time). This discounting of the subjective in favor of the objective in science is a double-edged sword. On one side, it allows for as unbiased an explanation of natural phenomena as humans can collectively assert, but on the other, it denies, contorts or simply ignores everything that cannot be held close to the light of the scientific method.

To give an broad example, experiments that measure flashes of brain activity on an fMRI have been used to "demystify" subjective perception by contorting it to the limited confines of scientific observation, but does that truly explain *why* subjective perception is the way it is?[20]

---

19   Many readers may have some vague understanding of how this breaks down at the quantum level (i.e., phenomena smaller than an atom). The observer has been proven to affect the result of experiments. The point is that on the whole, as a generalization, causality is the default assumption of all phenomena: If a ball rolls down a hill, then it is *because* something or someone pushed it.

20   See the endnotes for an example of a study of this kind.[24] What that study and others like it implicitly propose is that intelligence exists only at one focal point (i.e., the human being). Zoom in on one section of the brain and it becomes electric, mushy matter. Hence, "consciousness" is often referred to as an "emergent behavior" because the intelligence in all other phenomena (including the pulses of electricity in one's own brain) are dissimilar from the language-based, concept-based intelligence of human beings. It is no wonder

Although unscientific (because of its unfalsifiability), if you, the reader, can temporarily accept the premise that the phenomena of life are designed to challenge you—the self-aware observer of events—then the question to follow would be "Why is this so?"

THE PURPOSE OF CHALLENGE

What is the point of facing challenges? To grow. Forever? No. Then for how long? The growth being discussed is dissimilar from the linear growth of a tree trunk. It is rather a growth similar to measuring one's maturity "level" based on habits and attitudes. Remember, though, "maturity" is only a metaphor.

This growth—which subjective challenges in this world catalyze—is designed to awaken Consciousness to the illusion of the limited, egoic self. It's the evolution of human consciousness. The freedom of Unconditioned Consciousness is being realized. Humanity goes from (1) a pre-thought, animalistic stage, to (2) a thought-based, rationalistic stage, to (3) an unconditioned stage of inner peace balanced with intrinsic doing.[21]

This third stage of the process may sound as if the author is describing a utopia. Of course it does from a rational point of view. And, from a rational point of view, the most rational thought is believed to be a piece of one's identity. There is no choice involved. The person is enslaved to conceptual pursuits of truth and a prisoner to self-serving, guilt-tripping, isolating thought-forms. Such unconscious identification with rationalism and secularism is having disastrous consequences (albeit *less so* than unconscious identification with religious dogma).[22] That is different from saying those things serve no function; they do, so long as they are not misused for ideological purposes.

What the author seeks to show is that spirituality (in essence, accepting life without labeling it) does not require the dogma of a certain

---

humans are the most intelligent life form … it is *we* who defined the word by *our* standards using *our* language.

21   In this third stage, one can still use thought—and science and reason, more specifically—as a tool for creation, but one is not trapped or tricked by certain thought patterns.

22   This refers to when science—the social sciences, in particular—morphs into scientism to be used to justify moral crusades and violent political revolutions.

religion, nor does it require that one denies the importance and validity of science and technology.

Yet, too often, an atheist is quick to dismiss talk such as this as
new-age, metaphysical bullshit. (Although the author has made cau-
tiously few metaphysical claims). **It is this denial of the spiritual
aspect of life—or, more commonly, choking up spirituality to mere
brain activity—that is poisonous to the denier.** Spirituality is nothing more than experiencing the silence of Nature without imposing a
conceptual, explanatory framework upon it. It requires surrender and
a humble acknowledgment of the limits of rationalism (or any "-ism"
for that matter).

> To surrender to this experience, without labeling it, is to feel
> the inner peace that individuals naively seek through external
> experience.

The bliss of Being is what is sought in the constant seeking of positive sensations in the material world of "doing." Realize the futility of
seeking what cannot be found externally and, in the moment you are
reading this now, You—the Consciousness aware that it is reading this
now—can return to your unconditioned state of Being. In that space,
there is an indefatigable freedom that cannot be shaken by anything
in this world.

THE INFINITE NARRATIVE: THE CHALLENGING PART

In spite of the realization above, challenges will arise. If they are not
sought voluntarily, then challenges will find you. In accepting the
earlier premise that life's challenges exist in order to "awaken you"
to your true self (which is Unconditioned Consciousness or Pure
Awareness), it becomes much easier to weather the difficult winters
of life. It may even inspire the pursuit of *voluntary challenges*: To do
something difficult on purpose as opposed to choosing comfort and
safety at all costs. These voluntary challenges (e.g., writing a novel,
producing a film, starting a business or non-profit, etc.) often have
the added benefit of inspiring other people to pursue their own difficult endeavors.

Once ego is out of the way, then Unconditioned Consciousness
can use the mind for creation. It sounds scary, like some kind of dystopian hive-mind, but that fear implies identification with the limited
egoic self. The author cannot convince the reader of anything that they

do not intuitively know. If a reader happens to be convinced that the author is sowing seeds of doubt in the institutions of science and religion for his own malicious intentions, then it would be best for such a person to cling as tightly to his own beliefs as possible. Therein, one will see the futility of one's mental clinging by self-generated means, as opposed to blind acceptance of the author's words. Perhaps this essay will be read again after such an experience and make sense in a way it had previously not.

BECOME THE CONSCIOUS PARTICIPANT: AN OVERVIEW

This whole essay could boil down to a single sentence: *Human beings exist to be challenged.* It can be verified empirically, but, because it is based on subjective experience, it stands outside the culture validator of our time called the "scientific method." This method, though purposeful in a multitude of ways, is not designed to comfort the existentially afflicted (despite eroding the credibility and sacredness of religious beliefs and institutions, which have historically provided that existential security).

In observing where science diminishes the human experience, as it relates to turning subjective, individual meaning into objective, meaningless explanation, **there must be something that supersedes science *without* invaliding its discoveries and utility in society.**

When comparing science with religion, it's clear that both have served the purpose of explaining the phenomena of Nature, but, as science and the scientific method have done the most exceptional job as an explanatory framework for Nature, it is clear that something well outside the scope of "conceptual explanation" is required to supersede science. The author proposes that this new "framework" is beyond language and merely observes natural phenomena without the unconscious impulse to explain it with mental concepts.

It may be referred to as "the Infinite Narrative" or "the silence of Nature," but these are no more than linguistic signposts for something that cannot be spoken. The Infinite Narrative (which is also synonymous with the Tao) does not require egoic/willful intervention to "move things along," but serves as a paradigm through which to view the world like a sandbox to explore an infinite amount of philosophies and scientific discoveries without the telos-based drive for "Absolute Truth" or a unifying "theory of everything."

In this non-framework, one is free to explore the world with a sense of play and joy rather than seeking a single, all-encompassing truth to soothe an existential wound. It cannot be grasped in the conventional, conceptual sense, but it can be felt and experienced on a moment-to-moment basis. It is therefore malleable enough to stand up to any unanticipated natural phenomena that come from out of the blue (e.g., a pandemic, financial crash or major war).

To give the reader's mind something a bit more concrete than saying "exploring infinite possibilities" is the framework that supersedes science, the author offered a philosophical framework that says, "Life is designed to challenge the individual from one's subjective point of view and catalyze growth." This growth refers to the awakening of Unconditioned Consciousness to its own freedom and imperturbable peace. This is the inevitable evolution of humanity: Not more information-based intelligence, but a form of wisdom that can use thought and language as a tool for creative manifestation rather than being trapped in the illusion that thought-forms are one's identity—(most of which are isolating, fear-provoking and antagonistic to one's wellbeing).

Yes, spirituality is the term often associated with this talk of "Unconditioned Consciousness," but such a label is likely to turn off both the science-minded and religion-minded thinker who have both been conditioned by different, but equally definitive, explanatory frameworks for the silence of Nature. Therefore, it is best to consider this truth—of being aware of natural phenomena *without* language (i.e., resting on the foundation of not knowing)—as something that can encompass all of the aspects of the egoic self (including one's beliefs regarding science and religion) and more.

It is akin to becoming aware that one is the entirety of the ocean whilst embodying a single wave.

If categorizing this essay as too religious or spiritual (in the disregarding sense of the word) for one's taste is inevitable; if one cannot disidentify from their thoughts long enough to be aware of the spacious emptiness from which all language arises and judgements are formed; then it is best to cling to one's beliefs as tightly as possible. The truth of what is being written can be verified through enough suffering (i.e., self-induced stress) coupled with awareness of the link between said suffering and one's own thought patterns. Said another way, **once the ego is severely bruised by its own faults, then it becomes possible to return to Awareness Now.**

The peace and aliveness felt upon coming into presence can happen in a more intentional way than merely waiting for a bout of intense mental suffering, but this, of course, cannot be forced.

Once Unconditioned Consciousness is realized in the individual, whilst one will not dissolve in a flash of light, the conditioned, egoic personality subsides (or opts to humble itself in light of the Witness Consciousness) and the human being can become a conscious participant in this miraculous mystery. It is a mystery that the five senses know only the surface of and conceptual thought knows only the shadow of.

It is only here. It is only Now.

THE POETRY

When power leads man toward arrogance, poetry reminds him of his limitations. When power narrows the area of man's concern, poetry reminds him of the richness and diversity of existence. When power corrupts, poetry cleanses.

— John F. Kennedy

PITTER patters on the tin roof,
Made a tune. I couldn't help
But dance too.
The rains of June.
I was just a boy.
The summer went,
My boyhood spent,
The winter came and stayed.

Dark nights
That last
For days.

Somewhere and somehow
The boy I once was
Fell into a well:
Black and bottomless.
I was scared when I first
Stared eye-to-eye
With the—
But falling long
        My fear faded,
        My eyes adjusted,
        And my heart beat on.

THE BOY,
Introduction

All along,

I think

I thought

Someone would pull me up.

But with age

I grew wings,

And found that I could float,

Then found that I could fly.

When I made it to the sky,

The sun was rising too.

… Such a lovely golden hue.

163

BOY WONDER

A YOUNG boy wonder,
Born with the gifts of a violinist.
A winter bug's a-lingerin' in the air.
The boy plays on to fight the sickness.

When the days are short,
The nights are long.
The window's frosty,
The boy's alone.

Until spring comes again,
He'll play his old symphonic tune.
Not a soul to hear a string of sound,
Except that old face on the moon.

The bell tolls.
The snow melts.
Our spirits lift,
A spring is felt.

Hear the cheers from melancholy people?
"Spring is coming, Spring is coming, Spring is here!"
Spring up with the bright pink tulips,
Spring up—your crowd is near.

"Play us many good songs, Boy Wonder,
Play long past the sun's ablazing light.
Sing for us, if your voice is strong,
Sing us into that sweet goodnight.

"Play us some old melodies,
Sing us some old songs.
For old is gold, Boy Wonder,
And new is too quickly gone."

A man sat in the back,
In the place the boy has played,
Walks over at the show's end,
A silver tooth, a jacket suede:

"Do you know who I am, young man?
I'm the one who'll make you rich.
This is power you've yet to imagine,
In that speck in your eye I see the itch."

Some months later,
In a theatre tall and wide,
Boy Wonder sits alone,
Blue suited, bow tied.

The same ol' violin,
He played those winter nights.
'Cept now the nights feel lonelier—
No face to find in that cold stage light.

"Bravo, Boy Wonder!"
The show goes well.
An ovation from the darkness.
How swell. So swell …

Boy Wonder wants to punch his mirror,
Though he can't say exactly why.
You've made it big time, young gun.
Yet this is where the gifted go to die.

Palpable longing from nameless faces,
People who prosper when the spotlight points away.
These—the greedy, gluttonous connoisseurs
Of sophisticated music and ballet.

What do you seek, you cowardly nobodies?

The music or the man?
The man or the show?
The show or its memory?
The memory or the stories from which they flow?

"Hear my voice, when not in song,"
Says Boy Wonder, whose gift
Has made him dumb to the masses.
"From the culture we must sift…

"The art from the status,
  The stillness from the words,
  The joy from the winters,
  The souls from the herds."

The man responds,
  On his neck—protruding veins.
  His silver tooth's been replaced by gold,
  In his eyes, the boy sees flames:

"Play that damn music!
  Speak not when not in song.
  Your gift is the music, Boy Wonder,
  Your opinions won't keep you here long."

Boy Wonder quits the gig;
  He plays only for himself now.
  That same ol' beat-up violin,
  But with no more obligation to bow.

The snow is back,
  Who could have guessed?
  The boy reflects,
  Which time was best?

The lonely nights, still rich in possibility?
  The stages played for just a chosen few?
  Or the sellout shows, of unpinchable dreams,
  Where crowd becomes homogeneous slew.

Let me ask that man on the moon,
  Who listened when I was young.
"Which is best? Which is joyous?"
  Speak loud with that rocky tongue.

"Perhaps," says the wise old moon,
  "It is *I* who ought to be asking *you*."

BUGGING ME

THE pollen in the wind,
Made my vision blur.
It was spring time. I had
Let my life defer ...

But it is summer now, nearly,
When the heat is a short-lived boon.
I watch the bugs as they buzz,
How assured! as they fall for false moons.

Yet I am not much smarter.
Even with crystalline eyes—
A false light and a true light
Will wear each one's disguise.

So choose well,
Choose wisely.

THE BLUE BALLOON

THERE is a boy—with a blue balloon,
He stands alone on an empty coastline.
The sky is gray, like a lackluster moon,
The ocean looks harsh and curls like spilled wine.

The boy lets go of his pale, blue balloon,
He watches, as it floats into the haze.
It's almost swallowed, by a great typhoon,
Until it and a passing seagull cross ways.

The popped balloon, like a small piece of gum,
Strangles the bird and contorts her light grace.
She falls from the air, all tranquil and dumb,
She falls to the ocean—all but erased.

The boy looks solemn; the tide has come in.
He looks towards the sky. Oh, what could have been.

BIG TALL TREE

I CAN see you,
From so far away,
In the land behind the eyes.

You make me sad.
The last of them.
The Big Tall Tree,
Who stands strong,
    And stoic,
      And foolishly alone.

And me,
Among the many,
Another blade of dry grass.
    I cower to the wind.

Tell me,
What is your secret?

Tell me or else I will cut you down.
    I will burn all your wood.
    I will grind all your leaves to dust.
    I will dig up your roots and sink them in the ocean.

Tell me and tell me now.
    How is it you stand so steady against the wind?

Speak or I will kill you.

RAGE/TIMIDNESS

      I

WE, the men of no faith.
We, the timid and enraged.
We, who fear ourselves and our brothers.
We, the cultured and caged.

A rage boils and floods in my veins,
And I cannot say quite why.
I wish to scream until my voice is strained,
But I fear for whom sits nearby.

II

A current that loops, back into itself,
Warms, then sparks, then explodes.
For the timid and enraged, are one soul the same:
Two ends down one crossroad.

We have evolved! Say the People.
So masculinity is an inherent offence.
Make room for all others! Say the People.
So we deconstruct our moral sense.

I am not blind the history of inequalities!
Do not write this off as some proud man's self-defense.
But the problem of the purposeless young man
Is barred by the culture's postmodern fence.

III

To the young man who reads these words,
See to it that you let go of your enemies.
Your rage could serve a higher purpose;
Don't lose that energy in vengeful entropy.

And to the timid man,
Who I admit knew too well.
Inspiration never strikes the stagnant man.
Find some. Make some. Wait on no one else.

For the timid and enraged
Are one soul the same.
Take the Middle Path forward;
Walk on—without pride or shame.

THE BOY WHO PICKED THE SUN

A BOY, with eyes glossed over,
And a perpetually scowling face,
Lives inside—a cold, dark cellar;
    A reflection of his own headspace.

Affixed to false blue lights,
His mind grows faster than his age.
He smiles like a cardboard man,
    And his heart pumps only bloody rage.

Look! The sun outside your window;
It speaks in tongues of silent light.
It demands nothing, seeks nothing,
    And fears not even the night.

Though the boy, who has seen the sun before,
Looks out for only a moment.
Numb to the real thing!
    In his mind, nature is just one more opponent.

This trap, arising from perpetual stimulation,
Says that once something is seen,
To the conquering mind, it need not be seen again.
    (You see, this mind was mine. This boy was me).

Is there hope for the hollow-hearted boy?
Let my words be a show of proof.
To choose the Sun over false blue lights,
    Requires self-confession of not truly knowing Truth.

To the youth,
Who grow old faster than their age.
To the young,
    Who have become parrots of social outrage.

Pick the sun.
Pick the sun.
Please, pick the sun.
    It's there outside your window.

A BIRD FELL

A BIRD fell from the nest today.
His wings were featherless,
Almost furry.
> Fly, baby bird.
> Please fly.
He couldn't hear me.
I was afraid
To touch him—
> You'll be okay, baby bird.
> It's okay.
He kept on getting up,
And limping around.
I wanted to cry.
I was rooting for him.
Fly, little bird.
Please fly, for me.
He couldn't hear.
I watched him move
With all his heart.
Too weak to chirp,
But he tried.
I waited with him;
Waiting for his mother to come home.
> She'll be back, little birdy.
> She'll be back soon.
She never came.
Not even a short goodbye.
Not even a quiet chirp from somewhere far away.
> I'm still here, little birdy.
> I'm still here.

FONTANINI, THE FROG

THERE once was a frog named Fontanini.
He hopped from thing to thing,
Never erring, never caring,
About pretty much anything.

Then one day, all at once,
His parents made a ribbit.
About how he always sat around,
And how he'd have to make a pivot.

"Grow up, Fontanini,
And find a job that pays the bills.
Live every day with tomorrow in mind
'Cause soon you'll raise a frog with gills."

"But Mama, but Pops," said Fontanini, the Frog.
"I'd rather not go that way.
I'm not looking for a lily pad made of cement.
I'm looking for something with sway."

"I want a life full of hopping," he went on to add.
'I want fleas and a belly full of flies.
I will work for my meals, cause I have to,
but I'd rather not limit my prize."

"Fontanini, Fontanini, you sound like a fool.
I only wish you could see it through.
Frogs are meant for a quiet sort of life.
Oh, how I wish you knew."

Beaten and broken by barreling voices,
Fontanini receded in his pompous.
He hopped less and worked more,
And found a quiet place to encompass.

For a while the frog imbibed in the comfort;
Perhaps there was truth in security.
There's nothing wrong with a quiet sort of life.
Nothing wrong with a bit of maturity.

But comfort is a kettle.
And one that's bound to whistle.
Except when the water boils,
Most stay past dismissal.

Most frogs take to warming water
Like a blanket to their skin,
'Cause no one ever taught them
That comfort's got a trade-in.

But maybe the price is worth it.
Most frogs never know they'll pay.
But 40 frog years down the line,
They'll wake up, like yesterday—

But something will feel off,
Something that's hard to describe.
They'll feel all light and airy,
With a ribbit they can't ascribe.

For comfort is a kettle.
And one that's bound to smoke.
So when a frog stays in too long,
Don't be surprised when he finally croaks.

And what about Fontanini, the Frog?
The protagonist of our story.
Well, a frog that hops is a frog that hops,
So his comfort was transitory …

   "Fontanini, Fontanini,
    We need a moral quickly.
    You sounded morbid, and very sordid,
    So lay it out quite thickly."

   "Okay, okay. I'll try my best,"
    He said in a quiet ribbit.
   "One frog's fulfillment is another frog's failure,
    So I beg you, quit trying to inhibit."

   "An arrow shot twice does no one any good;
    Most frogs know their standing.
    So if you're old and wise, for a frog that is,
    Then I recommend you stop commanding."

   For a frog that hops is a frog that hops,
   Not tethered by setbacks, nor tethered by flops.

BARBARIAN

Don't lick the plate,
Sit up with your back straight.
Quite making a racket,
Or I'll throw you in a straight jacket.
Don't make a mess.
Take ten deep breaths.
No, slower than that,
And take off your hat.
Don't speak while you chew,
The audacity of you!
Get your feet off the table,
You'll kill yourself if that thing is unstable.
Don't interrupt,
Sit still and shut up.
Use your words, not your hands.
I'm tossing out these Silly Bandz.
Don't invent games that exclude,
Or I'll make a mockery of you.
Don't use the word "dude,"
I find it quite lewd.
Don't run off before I say,
Or you'll have to stay inside today.
Curb your impulsiveness.
Your instincts will lead to repulsiveness.
Stuff all that stuff deep and away.
Don't talk when you're in the hallway.
Say "may" and not "can,"
Don't speak before raising your hand.

Alright, now let's review—
        …
Wait until I call on you.
        …
Yes, young man?
        …
You may go after my lesson plan.
        …
Well, you should've gone before we began.
        …
Oh please. Quite crying, be a man.

TAMED BARBARIAN

WHO once stood the loudest & foulest,
Now sits in meager silence ...

Here, ye! Here, ye!
We have succeeded—
Look at the tamed one,
How quiet! How obedient!

Cage him and praise him
For stifling himself.
The king of the wild things,
Has become proof of the homogenized self.

(At the unveiling ceremony,
The teachers and librarians
Fill bleacher seats and cheer
For the well-behaved barbarian.

The tamed one gets a drink from the hall.
An old woman stops him—full of educated gall).

"Young man?"
        "Yes, ma'am?"
"Congrats."
        "On what?"
"You're almost one of us."
        "Who?"
"The culturally-approved."
        "Woo-who."
"I detest sarcasm."
        "Detest?"
"It means hate."
        "I 'test' sarcasm."
"Test?"
        "It means love."
"I still sense an attitude on you."
        "Boo-who, ma'am. *Boo-who."*

RELEASED BARBARIAN

THE key turns—*click!*
The cage opens—*skreek.*
The barbarian walks out—*clunk. clunk.*
The sun hits his eyes—he cannot see a thing.

Blind and stumbling around the big, blue planet;
The barbarian seeks his true origin.

His mind still spins—*this! that!*
His feet still walk—*crunch. crunch.*
His heart still beats—*thump. thump.*
Yet, he is lost—full of doubt toward common sense.

These contrived morals, taught by the tamed ones,
Clogged the nozzle from which the barbarian's spirit flows.

On a stool, at a bar, he drinks alone—*gulp. gulp. gulp.*
On a walk, at midnight, he wanders home—*clomp. crunch. shuffle.*
On a step, at a door, he knocks on—*rap. rap. rap.*
No one wakes for him—in a blur, he finds the key.

In his bed, in the night, under clouds which cover the moon,
The barbarian closes his eyes and feels the spinning feeling.

In a dream, he hears—who are you?
In a dream, he hears—who am I?
In a dream, he hears—another voice of the empty wind.
Awake, he hears the wind beyond the window—*shurr. shurr.*

The wind, as it is, as it can be nothing else;
All the honeysuckle branches in the yard dance with it.

This is the way the world is—
This is the way the world is—
This is the way the world is—
Dance with the wind, barbarian—it can be nothing else.

KNIGHT ME

I KNELT before you,
With a sword presented
And a choice to make:
    Knight me or kill me.

You chose the third—
Dropped the sword,
And walked out the castle for good.
    I still hear the metal clatter in my dreams.

Some say you've gone
Deep into the forest,
Feasting with Artemis & her merry women.
    I've considered our next encounter:

    I would present the choice again.
    I would call you a coward.
    I would leave you no alternatives.
        What would you tell me then?

        You are the cowardly one,
        Who seeks validation to the point of death.

        And if I knighted thee here,
        What difference would it make?

Your majesty, with all due respect,
I live by the code and feel myself worthy,

        Then you are knighted by thine own words,
        Now go and fight the noble fight.

FATHER TO SON

RIDE off into the sun, Vincent.
I can't say you'll find the grass any greener.
Maybe a bit different,
More glossy, a bit cleaner.

But it'll fade soon, son.
Unless the Earth quits spinnin'
The new can't always keep the same,
The gamblin' man can't always keep on winnin'.

Chin up, kid.
Toughness is how you show it.
Cut some slack to everyone else,
But takin' some—it costs a price, and every man must owe it.

The world may laze around you,
Don't let that rub off on you,
Folks tend to stop swingin' just 'fore strikin' gold,
And start drinking 'fore their work is due.

The God-fearing coot—
What you must think of me.
Call me the last of the cactus kind,
'Cause this world is a desert full of thirstin' trees.

We'll miss you, Vincent.
Move fast and write to us plenty.
Advice like this is cheap to give,
But, with luck, you'll hold it like a heads-up penny.

OLD MAN & THE YOUNG TRAVELER

OM: HARK! Young traveler, what is your name?
YT: You have called me the traveler, and I go by the same.

OM: You know that I knew that—that's not what I meant.
OM: I ask what you do and why you look spent?

YT: I wander the world and walk 'til my feet ache.
OM: So you have stopped at my inn and will leave by daybreak?

...

OM: Have you any coins?
YT: I will work or tell story.

OM: Leave now, you bum. You mooch. You bright piece of scum.
YT: I will do all your chores and teach songs you can hum.

...

YT: I see not a soul, so I know there is room.
YT: So I ask you again, may I work for my room?

OM: Charity sees not the self-serving as deserving.
YT: And what of the man who lords his charitable serving?

OM: You think you are clever, and wise, and well-versed; but I
    smell a liar.
YT: I too caught a smell of the room, but I am wise to call a
    misfire a misfire.

OM: Wise is to use the tongue with less arrogance.
YT: Nay! The traveling life requires a tongue with irreverence.

...

OM: You think your irreverence will gift you my favor?
YT: I know every answer, until fully examined, is open to waver.

YT: If I may speak out of turn, I've felt your rage since I've arrived.
YT: This instant! you may choose to live a life uncontrived.

...

OM: Let me ask you one thing ... before I kick you away for good.
OM: What draws you to the unknown? For this I've never understood.

  YT: I am not deluded by idyllic visions of distant lands. I know no
      grass out greens the next.
  YT: But I find my life more interesting, when I cannot say what's next.

    ...

OM: Take room two.
OM: Be gone by noon.

I HIT the end of the road
And saw only the void.
Panicked, I turned around,
But from where I came
There was no ground.
On my little patch of land,
I was alone—the last of man.
We, the humans, all righteous
And grand.
We speak to deities for comfort;
And paint Nature
With a set of invisible hands ...

What is left without the metaphors?
What lies behind these symbols?
What exists beyond the myth?

I demand nothing but—
The wholly—
Purely—

THE VOID,
Introduction

A GHOST FROM THE VOID

DON'T play coy,
Great ghost from the void.
I see you there—
Clear as the sky is bare.

You speak in sensation,
Belittle my prideful temptations.
I thank you for your service.
Now take me below your opaque surface.

I am sick of the mysteries,
Of hazed and virtual histories.
I fear too much message is lost in translation,
Take me, directly, to that place of elation.

What is it I have to do?
Take off my shoes and bow to you?
Solemnly swear to never share
The Truth behind all known truths; the barest of all things bare.

Or perhaps it is for my own protection,
To see the eternal only in nature's reflection.
I see hints that other people might know you,
As a hustler knows a conman; as a monk knows a guru.

But this is yet another level of abstraction!
All these proud and social labels—another form of distraction!
I call it pure trickery when David is the villain,
And Goliath only speaks when there is emptiness not filled-in.

I know that you hear me, great and faceless ghost,
I know that you supersede all a man could possibly boast.
I know that personifications from a poet are impossible to avoid,
And I know that the ghost is my grasping at the great empty Void.

THE GREAT BIG STUMP

My remorse knows no words.
The birds, singing in a melancholy procession,
They sing for me too.
In your fractured center I see the scars of wood rot.
Was it I who caused this great decay?
In your flat remains, I can see
All the years you ever lived.
All the scars, all the droughts,
But the thick and lively years too.
I sit upon you and consider,
Had you any tongue for language,
What you might lament in your final breath.
I suppose, in your stoic nobility,
You would choose not to speak at all …

Now, as the fungi encases
What is left of your bark, and
Termites feed on your insides,
My mind turns to new life:

What flowers will blossom around your base?
What insects will find security in your fissure?
What lovers will sit upon you and treasure the view?
What youth will stand upon you and call themselves explorers?

No, I will not resist the heaviness in my heart
When death strikes down too soon,
But Nature has taught me to keep
A keen ear for the ever-longer tune.

"SEAN PATRICK GREENE" EXPLAINS ENLIGHTENMENT

WHAT did you expect
    Enlightenment would be?

A bunch of bells and whistles
    All sprouting from the trees?

As if Nature had another trick up her sleeve!
As if those enlightened are the only ones to see!

In my small mind,
    Upon the Grand Revelation,
        All things would bow to me ...

The wind would whistle
    And paint the air with fallen leaves ...

The birds would turn
    And serenade me in chirping harmony ...

The clouds would drift away
    And make way for a light
        That would wash away the sun ...

Delusions of grandeur.
    Complexions of superiority.
        My mind tried to blot away the thoughts
            With the ink of scientific superiority.

These grand-sounding thoughts,
    Overtook me on a walk to the park.
        This went on so long that by the time I reached
        The trees, my mind had gone dumb.

Suddenly,
    In the utter silence to my latent call,
        The mask behind these eyes began to fall.

Detached by measureless space,
    From a view that was All,
        I saw arrogance within himself
            As his inescapable fettering flaw.

Tell me, Sean Patrick Greene,
    What did you see?
        When your mind was as clear as the sky is blue,
        What on Earth did you see?

The same; sat in the shadow of a slouching tree.
    No apples conked my head
        As a show of serendipity.

I simply saw; all these eyes could see,
    No stupefying visions,
        Only thoughtless equanimity.

Sean Patrick Greene—who the 'I' calls 'me':
    The grandeur in my words
        Is never what it seems.

And too I forget,
    The plainness of nature
        Is never what it seems.

Miraculous, magnificent,
    The way the smallest acorn
        Becomes the tallest tree?

Don't you see?
    In the still mind, with no thought to think,
        There still exists—not I or you,
            But something old,
                And eternally new.

We need not get lost in this unthinkable thought;
Know that existence becomes a gift when we see what we are not.

THE MEANING OF LIFE

I

In the hunt for the meaning of life,
You will go hungry.
 Savor the taste without the food.

In the search for the meaning of life,
You will get lost.
 Savor your place without pursuit.

Frankl found meaning
In his explorations
Of meaning itself.
 A mirror cracked and held to itself.
And for myself,
I sought the same,
Another cracked mirror in search of his reflection.
 I saw nothing but nothing.
Desperate and afraid,
I turned the mirrors away.
But suddenly (in a length of time I can't recall),
The fear, once felt, transformed to awe:
 The land, the trees, the water, the falls,
 The snow, the sand, the sea, the gulls.
Specific and rich,
Nature had no need to hitch
Its purpose onto the coattails of language.
 It is self-designing & self-aspiring.
 It is self-refining & self-retiring.

II

Abstractions fizzle out,
Like popped champagne,
When we savor the natural
Without disdain.
 Say nothing,
 Say nothing more.

Though the question is asked,
No words need speak it,
Where, on Earth, is my natural place,
When I am told not to seek it?
    Say nothing,
    Say nothing more.

Quiet as the ocean waves
From far away,
The moon has a pull
On you too.
    What scares you?
    Tell me, what scares you?

In the rage that makes our hearts stiffen,
In the bliss that makes our smiles glisten,
In the sad that makes our stomachs weigh,
In the fear that makes our body shake,
    Our duty is clarified by these
    Sensations which concern us.

III

Follow the fear,
    It will lead to the den of the dragon.
Slay the dragon,
    Beyond him there is treasure.
Carry all the gold you can,
    There is enough to last a while.
Tomorrow, expect vengeance from his brother,
    These battles may last a while.

MENTAL NOISE

I

THIS city's always
    Buzzing like bee,
    Roaring like a lion,
    Itching like a flea.
So the people tune to another noise,
    Blunted to deafness by their own animal mind.
So the inner is always a reflection of the outer,
    Or do I speak out of order?
Always an order
Always an arrow
Always a beginning, middle and end—
    And when does it end?
    And how will it end?
In a bang or a whimper?
In a flash of light or a cold dark night?
    We ask on behalf of the universe,
    So we may find solace right here and now.
Asking for another attachment,
Asking for another abstraction,
Asking, as the fool asks the psychic,
    To read aloud—the lines from his hand.

II

Feeding from
The palm of his own hand,
The hungry ghost craves an ever larger self,
    Give him evermore experience,
    So he may feed for all eternity.
Yet eternity, I see, sparks fear in the unexamined mind,
    For a life lived forever is as frightful as death,
So the mind aims at enoughness.
    So it may feast after famishness.
    So it may sleep after tiredness.
    So it may remember after ignorance.
And to remember is to realize; beyond rationale,
    The mind spins itself—

To invent concepts and point out distinctions
   Is the nature of the mind;
      As a tree sprouts leaves,
         Or a bird spreads wings,
            Or a fire puffs smoke.
And to accept the unstoppability of this mental noise,
Makes space for the stillness behind it.

And distinctions of inner and outer dissolve into—
And patterns and cycles dissolve into—
And no thing, one thing and ten-thousand things dissolve into—

And where does that leave me and you?
If it all dissolves into the so-called "Unspeakable World,"
Does that mean I will fade away too?

Ask not, but watch and see,
The leap to know is hidden
Between the cracks of your so-called "identity."

KILL THE WOLF

LET the serendipitous events of life
Take us down the unknowable road.
   Across the river and through the woods,
   To grandmother's house we go.

Kill the wolf if you see him;
For there's not enough food for two.
   And if he eats you, as he's born to do,
   Then who does that make you?

      The tail-eating serpent.
      The chicken-eating cock.
         The self-cannibalizing among us;
         Gorge on their entrails with no means to stop.

Though this must be a metaphor?
Poets bake symbol from truth.
   Speak only in answers!
   We care not to sleuth!

This is the tale of the ungraspable;
The word salad cloaked in mystique.
    See not the words for what they are,
    See only your mind's critique.

I don't see the purpose.
I don't understand.
    This one is a poem of pure nonsense—
    The closed fist of an empty hand.

Give us the answer!
Give us the key!
    There is no great secret... or I would tell thee,
    I only wish to point out how hungry the mind can be.

    FIRE

      I

FIRE.
For the furnace of man.
What else could make the first heart beat?

My Promethean eyes,
Stole the fire from my heart,
And left my body cold to the touch.

      Ambitious in sight.
      Gluttonous in taste.
      Greedy in mind.

      I felt only the shadow,
         Only the surface,
         Only the shallowest things.

      II

Our purpose,
Built on foundations of sand.
Nature needs only the empty wind
    To knock down our house of bricks.

But can we rebel?
But should we rebel?
When death is assured at the end,
    Our stoic nobility is our only allowance.

In the fanged clutch of a viper's bite,
We may cry out in pain.
We may fight as an animal.
    But let us not ask "why me?"

You were not picked for pain,
You were not chosen to die,
You were not made as Nature's enemy,
    You are but a set of fiery eyes.

What could you possibly know?
Until the fire is returned to the Heart,
What could you possibly know?
    Your eyes see only the surface of things.

DEATH

THE people love to wallow in death,
Like hogs in the mud of despair.
In every cycle, every era and every shifting season,
The changes of Nature ignore our lust for reason.

Though it is there!
Reserved for those aware.
Not discovered by logic—this eternal law.
The Tao, the Way, the Churning—thus leads springtime to fall.

These leaves, that which we are, that which we see,
Origins from the formless—an ancient, immortal tree.
Though our Western impulse is to shun all mentions
Of death as the rest point between two lives of tension.

Fear not,
Wish not,
Aim not—toward or away.
Tomorrow's death will feel like yesterday's.

MEDIOCRE INDIVIDUAL

WHAT happened to your dreams, Jack?
You promised me you'd keep them.
But now, to me,
I only see
Another hungry ghost—
    Forever starving,
    Forever empty.

THICK GREEN FOG

CAUTIOUS, curious, coughing,
Coughing, coughing, coughing,
Longing, lighting, laughing,
Laughing, laughing, laughing.
Infatuated, inordinate, inflating,
Inflating, inflating, inflating,
Drunk-feeling, dreamless, dimming,
Dimming, dimming, dimming,
Mediocrity, malaise, monotony,
Monotony, monotony, monotony,
Excusing, enervating, exhausting,
Exhausting, exhausting, exhausting,
Fearing, fogging, forgetting,
Forgetting, forgetting, forgetting,
Refraining, reframing, repeating,
Repeating, repeating, repeating,
Shrouding, shielding, seeing,
Seeing, seeing, seeing,
Abounding, attentive, awakening,
Awakening, awakening, awakening,
Cognizant, cycling, calming,
Calming, calming, calming.
Realizing, resetting, releasing,
Releasing, releasing, releasing.

Let the fool persist in his folly,
So he may become wise in his ways.

#27*

THE bridge creaked
From the weight of my feet.
I could see the other island.
Still hazed from the fog,
It was there,
In shape
But nothing else.
How picturesque to see it from afar.
I stood
For a long while
Paralyzed in admiration.

Halfway there, halfway done.
I fear I'm getting sleepy
In the poppy field.

To move any closer
To see any clearer
I would have to push on.
Push on.
Push on.
Halfway means nothing
If you never make it to the end.

*The title refers to the 27th poem written for the book. This stands as the literal halfway point of all the included poetry. The reference to the "poppy field" alludes to the halfway point in Dorothy's journey to meet the Wizard of Oz.

THE THINKER

Go back to any time in history
And you will find me;
Behind the aims of victory.

I behead all kings,
Make rhyme and sing;
Does my joy, to you, seem puzzling?

The silence behind all thoughts.
The teacher to all untaught.
The actor & acted upon all onslaught.

I play the infinite game,
Go by many a name.
Know me and we become selfsame.

I see you—going around the circle 'til sickness,
Your eyes can't seem to follow the quickness,
But look forward, be still, and you will bear witness.

What do you see?
Nothing? Same as me.
Breathe deep and smell the irony.

THAT FAMILIAR THING

I AWOKE.
Forever and always.

I wish to bark,
Like a kenneled dog
Who caught scent of that familiar thing.

I am awestruck,
Like the young boy who sees the first flash
Of silent lightning over empty fields on a warm June night.

I wish to sing,
Like a bird aware of all songs to ever be sung,
Singing full-heartedly and unceasingly, yet never attached to one.

I am astounded.
I am.

I WALKED along
The rusted tracks.
In search of fellow feeling.
A vibration started—
The last train departed.
The last of the station's
From where I had started.

    I had no ticket to board.

When people passed,
Some people laughed,
But most left me ignored.

    I had become the lowly outcast.

When the last cart passed,
An arm was cast,
Steady where I stood, I yelled out,
    I am content on my feet.
She poked her head out the threshold,
Her eyes, I saw, were fiercely gold.
From there, she waved a sweet goodbye
Then mouthed the words,
    See you on the other side.

THE MAN,
Introduction

THE JESTER'S MANY KINGS

A JESTER awoke;
   Another beheading.
Another new king,
   Another refretting.

Clean up your act,
   And tighten your jokes,
This new one likes props,
   So sharpen your spokes.

'Tis the life of a jester—
   How pitiful the ridicule.
'Tis survival of the humorist,
   But have dignity—even as the public fool!

Ignore the harshest censure.
   Keep your dreams alive of ruling.
For a jester who's lived so long,
   By now, ought to know what he is doing.

Many masks,
   Many hats,
Many jokes,
   Many laughs.

News flash—another beheading,
   But this time by the People.
The masses have spoken,
   We need be lead by an equal!

The soft sound of bells jingled,
   The jester's thrown in his hat.
The people laugh, and then suppose …
   How nice! A king to be snickered at.

The jester's crowned king!
   Long live the noble joker.
The peasants throw parades,
   Though they act like king-provokers.

Tell us a joke, great King!
    Make us, the People, laugh.
A crown but no authority,
    He orders silence on all the riffraff.

Ignored. He demands that violators be hung.
    No jokes are told anymore.
The people fear their unrespected king:
    The jester, once loved, is now deplored.

The jester-king is awoken,
    In the cold dark of night.
A few men at his bedside,
    With a few torches for light.

They drag the poor man,
    From his castle made of stone.
Another beheading!
    Who sits next on the throne?

WAR ON RELIGION

I

HERE ye! Fear me!

The Catholic
Regime
Fell well
Before my birth.
Though it lingers on,
Like wine on the breath.
Already, in the eyes of a few,
I've sealed my life after death.
But I was religious,
[Once removed],
In my youth.
    I feared the hereafter,
    Prayed against disaster,
    Believed in thine omnipotent master.

Though I knew
  No hymns,
  Nor covenants,
  Nor fettered freedoms.

Off with this heretic's head!

I always felt the foolish
In the house of God.
In truth, I always felt
It was an odd
Sort of
Social club
Where you were
Meant to bring
Your heaviest heart,
Your gravest smile,
And everlasting guilt.
All blessings seemed
To me
Like formalities
Spoken in
Shakespearean tongues;
Like a play
I wish
I understood,
But never could.

II

God is dead.

Nietzsche declared.
The Church was
Unprepared:
Shots fired from
The Western front.
A war broke out.
It's still alive—
Live and mediavised.

In the coldest war yet,
This quest for moral high ground
Astounds even the mountaineer.
The atheists touch the clouds, but
The Christians point to *paradiso.*
    This push and pull
    of faith and faithlessness,
    of reason and unreasonableness.
Together make a musical score
We are destined to perform
A modo espressivo.

MAN IN THE MIDDLE

I

No patience for the old man,
With eyes cloudy
And body weak.

Kick him to the curb,
Speak of his faults and frailties,
Spit on the idols made in his image.

No Gods here. The People rule themselves.
The People demand to be heard;
But they speak
All at once.
Different thoughts
Like white noise—something loud to lull us to sleep:

Die, Emmanuel Goldstein! Die!
    (In the name of justice, we seek the villain).
Die, Emmanuel Goldstein! Die!
    (In the name of virtue, we seek the villain).
Die, Emmanuel Goldstein! Die!
    (In the name of peace, we seek the villain).
Die, Emmanuel Goldstein! Die!
    (In the name of purpose, we seek the villain).

II

Crabs in a barrel,
Crabs in a barrel,
Civilians go feral
At the bottom of the barrel.

¡Viva la Revolución!
And God bless America.

Imputing revolution on
    Political retribution,
    & moralistic delusion.
Abstractions turned excuses,
For the purpose of weaponizing recluses:

    He's talking about Red.
    He's talking about Blue.

(The People go colorblind
At the sight of accusation)

    But we are the innocent!
    But we are the victims!

(Linguistic manipulation
Of the highest order)

    Says the baseless racist!
    Says the pandering pansy!

Are you deaf to your own tongue!
Are you blind to your own view?
My soul aches for you—
The Red and the Blue.

III

We, the wandering cattle,
Surrounded by
    Pointed spears,
    & branding iron:
How will you mark yourself?

We, the starved and thirsty mule,
Caught between
    Sordid hay,
    & tainted drink:
Which way will you walk?

We, the last tree standing,
Tangled in
    Siphoning ivy,
    & crown rot:
To whom will you fall?

Choose a side or die.

      IV

The new world order:
Love, justice, and equity.

    Behead the nonbelievers.

The new world order:
Right speech, right thought, right action.

    Kill the silent monk.

The new world order:
Unity, central truth, collectivism.

    All hail the party.

          Our civil enemies,
       Divided by a few degrees,
            How sad!

           Our civil allies,
       Unified only in hate,
          How pitiful!

V

In our blind fury,
We forget history:

Eternal themes,
Of thrown regimes,
& power-lusting.
The culture's rusting,
Declare the next crusade!
Distraction by noble display.
Infection begins in the intellect,
With well-worded cases for the individuals' neglect.
(I fear this talk of "collective consciousness" breeds
More ideology in the minds of unenlightened seeds).

In our blind victimhood,
We forget Nature:

No invisible set of hands
Control the sum of humanity's plans;
Or people's minds or money markets.
How long until these conspiracy theories are finally part with?
Yes, history spins and history rhymes,
But each moment is based on the people of the time.
There is the individual, and many of them.
Thus, only 'I's will approve! Only 'I's will condemn!
Too often collectives are blamed for the bad times to come;
Yet, the blame game accounts for more bad times to come.
In the cold, dark of winter, we forget about spring.
Dogmas will melt with the snow; the birds will come back to sing.
We may craft more theories to live and morals to guide,
But none will be enough to control humanity's vast tide.
If only we could see the bulb of Life has been always glowing;
Holding strong—well before we clouded it with "knowing."

NUMBERS GAME

How many lines?
How many rhymes?
How many awards?
How much, now, can you finally afford?

Ignored.

How many days of the stress?
How big is the mess?
How large is the spoil?
How long, now, until you're living rich and royal?

Unloyal.

How long will this take?
How much will you make?
How much are you worth?
How many ideas, now, have you profitably birthed?

A pregnant pause.

How costly was your degree?
How many fruits have grown from your tree?
How many fans read your tweets?
How many celebrities, now, have you happened to meet?

Retreat.

What is fame,
    But a number's game.
What is fortune,
    But a greedy man's distortion.

INTELLECTUALISM

I

Hung by the nape
  Of their blue collar.
Strung high like a pinata—
  Let us beat out their ignorance!
They scream out for mercy,
  But we are deaf to the unenlightened citizen.

These
Discrepancies,
Plague the human race
In ways too magnified to see.

Awash in
Intellectualism.
Awash in
Abstractionism.

Don't miss the message.
Don't miss the meaning.

Though
This meaning
Demands more than
    our reason.
More than
    our lofty minds.
More than
    our sophisticated language.

But the professor resists with fervor,
    "I will not regress back to the heuristic lifestyle of the ancients!"
So the poet translates with composure,
    "He says, 'I reject tradition.'"

II

These
Social scientists
Spark unfalsifiable beliefs
In whichever narrative we, the People, seek.
Though
I see no conspiracy
Only mistaken relief
In the equating of ideals
And practical truth.
In truth, they are the same
In the intellectual's mind,
Prompting pseudo-journalism
To follow suit behind.
Though, in practical terms
Every handicap
Brought to the light of practical means
Places another Other
In the shadows.

Let them fester in Tartarus!
They deserve no more light!

In the blindness of
The righteous intellectual
The cycle of power yearning &
Unquenchable resentments
Continue
Down history's white-water stream.

Merrily, merrily, merrily, merrily,
Life is but a dream.

III

In practical terms,
        (Can the poet speak in practical terms?)
We have monetized and commoditized
These ideas and ideals,
So the most outraged and outrageous
Are admired to the extent of their extremist appeals.

A fallacy now lingers in the air,
When status symbols speak louder than truth,
When the civil war is fought to centralize truth.
    God save the teachers!
    God save the youth!
Unsuspecting pawns
Of voters in the booth.

IV

Rallied and planned,
Somebody find someone
To terraform the [promised] land.
Utopian visions extend a war that can never be won;
    Like writing a song to never be sung.

We speak of the
"Status quo vs. Progress"
As if both sides were equally defended.
No.
The status quo is the straw man
Each side has crafted to renounce.
Given the chance
Both sides would pounce
And tear its throat made of hay
In a defiant display.
(For a good show of politics
Keeps the pundits at bay).

V

Have I deceived myself?
Has my defiance against abstraction
Blinded me to my own ideologies?
    In the sensations in this body,
    In the knowing of *anattā*,
    In the acceptance of all perceptions,
I feel the water in which I swim.
Swimming around in my own words,
I hear the bias and the pointed speech too.

And yet,
I live in a world beyond them.
So speech, and truth, and reason,
And love, and beauty,
Are hollow words.
Dead on arrival.
Fought for in vain
By the red & blue
Intellectuals.

In pursuit of the war that can never be won,
   We must remember the Sun.
It does not require some ceremonious bow,
   Just stand outside and feel it Now.

SCAPEGOAT

WILL you kill the goat with your own two hands?
   Coward.
   You are a coward.
Tie his legs and cover his eyes,
   You cowardly scum.
Muffle his mouth and cover your ears.
   You are honorless.
He was once a kid too. Now you
Keep loud machines between
   Him and you.
Have you run out of stones?
Has your mob grown tired?
   Kill the goat yourself.
Have you dignity?
Have you any respect?
   Kill him with your own two hands.

Or set him free.

NEWS CYCLE

In the minds of many,
Lay the thoughts of a few.

Extra! Extra! Read all about it!

This slew
Of noise
Confines
Our minds
To the minuscule.

The shot(s) heard about the world.

Everyday,
Another firing,
Inspiring nothing
But the worst.
(The flower business
Is booming I hear).
Nothing beats
Capital gained
From distant fear.

Yet, we sit
And we cheer
Against enemies
So near.
Civil in war,
Vulgar in fear—

These
        Dystopian visions
        Painted in words by each
        Side's great, profit-able seer

Make
        Loyalist divisions—
        Two grand, hypocritical speeches.
        Already foretold in the ears of King Lear.

We want you!

Sticky like
A burr,
This propaganda
Was designed
To make
The masses
Purr.

How robust!

This system built
On professional
Mistrust.
Yet some of us
Lust for the
Days of old.
When morals
Overstepped
And dogmas
Were a man's
Best friend.

There must be a new
Kind of view.
Behind (or beyond)
This media slew.
        As the animals lived
Before the zoo.
        As the two-sides talked
Before taboos.

So that we,
The people,
May find
Independence,
        Once again,
In independent thought.

So that we,
The human beings,
May find
Ourselves,
        Once again,
Through the subduing of this media onslaught.

MOB MENTALITY

BARED teeth—barring speech.
They come bearing speeches,
All hollow and thunderous,
Like a forest full of thin-trunked trees.

No, their trunks cannot withstand the wind,
But their leaves can block away the sun,
They leave only shadows below them;
And what's left of the undergrowth they will shun.

Though, in speech they are saviors.
Speaking words so true and false,
With cadence so painful and provoking,
And what did I ever learn, but all of society's faults?

Underwoven on their Members Only® coat
Of "We Who Stand for Truth,"
Is the smallest of labels which reads,
"Here in lies the ambitions of Youth."

Still not knowing who they are yet,
Still full of self in their good deed,
Still full of unprovoked confidence,
Still rooted in fear and moral greed.

Yet, they say, "Look! The villain is over there!"
Perched in the palace of the oppressor,
Hidden in the house of the idiot,
"No sacrifice shown upon their doors. Mark them all transgressors!"

We miss, in their blame, the projection of fear.
Like a dog, in the house, on a thundering night;
Or a bird, in his cage, wings clipped to stop flight;
These activists cry loud to drown out their fright.

But what is one to do when the mob comes for you?
Stand firm, and part ways with the compliant.
Stand strong, and separate truth from mere defiance.
Stand tough, and remember David vs. the giant.

For when the moon is full,
Lost people like to howl.
And when a tribe is sought in the dark,
Even noble souls will run afoul.

So I say, let their voices shout;
Shout until they strain.
So I say, let their voices strain;
Strain until nothing but stillness remains.

HEDONISTIC

I

HEDONISTIC impulse
Masked as simple living:
    The forever fantasy
    Of perpetual pleasure.

We ask,
In our daze,
    What was it that made us strain?
    That gave our necks protruding veins?

Our voices get lost in
The wind when it blows.
    These, the huddled masses,
    These, the forgotten souls.

Alone on the banks of the Sea of Death,
The moon had lost its pull on me.
    I stood, unguided by rock or star.
    I stood, and strained to know delight.

II

No treasures to be found in the sand.
Though we live, convinced,
The buried treasure
Is always
One foot below the hand.
    Digging, digging, digging,
        Another doorless room.
    Digging, digging, digging,
        Another sandy tomb.

These pleasurable sensations
    [found in the form of vice].
For a time, fulfill their promise—
A trip to [the fool's] paradise.

But in time,
These pleasurable sensations
Bring lopsided views
Of which of nature's hues
We feel most attached to.
All the while,
The color of nature's paint,
Begin to desaturate,
Nature's beauty begins to abate,
And we are left
At the bottom of our pit—
Cursed to be a self-appointed inmate.

Another lame cry from the plighted,
   "When will this long night end?"
Another lame cry from the plighted,
   "When will this long night end?"

III

The sun rose at dawn,
   As it always had.
Pulled by Apollo's chariot,
   As it always was.

          From below the sand I saw something
          In the eyes of his magnificent stallion.

Endued, not endured—
Their work, their greatest gift;
To deliver the Sun at the start of each shift.
   Deserving in praise,
      yet immortally ignored.
Theirs is a strain that rivals Atlas',
   Yet they remain
      Strong enough to soar.

ALL PRAISE THE SCIENCE

So many heretics in the building,
They've started burning preachers.

Shifting tides,
Call for shifting sides.

All praise the science,
    All praise the unpraiseable.
All praise the science.
    All praise the uncaring.
We bow to your method,
    We know not our true origin.
We bow to your method,
    We know not whom to believe.

So cold we've made the stars feel!
    Our souls have gone stale;
        Spoiled by the cold, dark vacuum of space.
Brutish in truths,
    Proven by abstractions.
The illusion of retrofitting reason upon Reality:
    So these thin strands,
    On our clocks'
    Ticking hands,
    Appear to
    Spin the Earth
    & rotate the Sun,
In the minds of the reasonable.

How inventive our minds!
    How far collective genius has carried us!
Though we forget who we are,
    Too often.
Thus, utopian ideals get redressed in fine robes,
    Revived by charismatic orators,
Then manipulated with the justifications
    Of modern scientism.

And, through it all, where lives the quiet monk?
    Alone at the mountain peak.
    With a back turned to beauty,
    And a mind onto itself.
    Aloof to the Science,
        Unshackled by the Word.

Why seeketh the quiet one?
    Her heart is the purist,
    Her mind is the clearest,
    Her soul knows the Truth that cannot be spoken.

So far from the poet,
And yet, we are of the same.

SELF-MASTERY

I

In the quiet part of
The roaring city,
The clouds hang low,
So low I can almost grab one.
In the quiet place of
The roaring mind,
Self-mastery wafts
Just above the rafters,
Of my glass-ceilinged soul.
    Reach out! Grasp it!
As distant as the moon,
I oft forget I cannot pinch it
And pull it down to me.
    Rise up! Rise up to it!
Subtle touches of ascetic style
Make me lighter than air.
I drift up.
Though there lingers on
The fear of floating forever—
    Cast away to oblivion.
        A virtuous star
           Deplored for his
               Self-effacing discipline.

Indulging in vice,
I touch ground again.
In a way, I prefer the view
From far away. The haze takes
Shape as the Vitruvian Man.
　　Though,
　　In a breath,
　　In the heart,
　　In the quiet part of night,
　　Doubt fills my chest like an off-beat palpitation.
Is this ... where the ... white ... flag waving ... starts?
Is ... this where ... the ... white flag ... waving starts?

　　　　II

In the eyes of every unenlightened woman and man,
There lives a mind with no master.
We call it the elephant of impulse,
We call ourselves the rider.
Thus, the thinker called "me"
Is always deceived by the bodily plea
For more of, and more of, and more of, and...
　　When will we flee? The clutches of vice seem unrelenting.

　　　We must think back and ask, at the time when we were free,
　　　　"What drew 'I' to the vice that now ensnares 'me'?"

One self, partitioned into two;
Divides more than past and present time;
Divides more than mastered and mastering self;
　　Divides more than impulsive elephant and steering rider.

　　　Our division of the ideal and the actual is the root of all cause.
　　　　This lust for self-mastery is the root of all flaws.

　　　　III

But if I don't aim above the actual,
　　If I give up all cause,
　　Won't I solidify my destiny,
　　Won't my life slowly pause?

Oh, I see you have not reached where the sidewalk ends.
  For without a target out there,
  Without a desire worth prayer,
  It is only the ignorant who fall for despair.

For even there, an ideal still keeps the knotted mind defective.
  "To seek to end seeking" reflects the ego's bright glare.
  Only as Witness to this mind-spinning affair
  Will the split-self dissolve. The mind will repair.

        IV

I find serenity there,
Beyond the future,
Behind the past,
It's all right here—Now,
No-self can last.
And yet one finds one still will act,
Moving forward
Without the future's hook
  Clipped upon one's cheek,
And so it was written,
  What is passed onto the meek.
This is true nature,
  To move unabated without the bait.
This is true nature,
  To live outside the snare of fate.

        V

Aim without effort—there is no need to try.
Let the arrow go—without a where or a why.
Find a target struck—call it the self-mastered bullseye.

THE MUSE,
Introduction

THE divine feminine,

Esoteric to the unenlightened.

Speak through me,

All-flowing water,

For the roots of my tree.

In glee (or in jest),

You've behest in me,

The need to be seen,

So I'm greedy and lean.

Where is the gift in that?

Call it ungrateful.

(Aren't we all—of our flaws?)

But I see fate is the river

That no man can dam.

And to paddle upstream

Is to judge yourself damned.

So I sit and I write,
Without any plan,
Letting natural thoughts
Run their natural span.
And, at times, I will bow
To you, the Muse.
Because I know
This work, which is
Superficially mine, is
The result of a spark
From something divine.

L'UOMO UNIVERSALE*

In
This
Digital age
Of unenlightenment.
I am the renaissance man.

Alone.
The last of them.
At the edge of the hearth, I sit.
With crossed-legs and closed-eyes, I sit.
The fire crackles and dances to a song of its own.

  Speak to me,
  Speak to me,
  Speak through me.

A
Lone
Piece of lead,
Kindled these flames,
And gave them golden hues.
This fire was lit by the alchemists of old; neglected by the new.

In
Their
Fruitless effort
To turn base to noble metal,
They missed where the true fruits had grown.
Through these closed eyes, the smallest glint of light is shown.

  Speak to me,
  Speak to me,
  Speak through me.

In
Time,
This heart of lead
Becomes a heart of Gold—
The alchemical transformation of one's own soul.
Though a change this grand calls for some externalized toll.

---

*The title translates to "The Universal Man," or "The Renaissance Man."

In
Time,
L'uomo universale
Grows hungry for more.
Blind, he stumbles back to his mind's atoll.
The water is calm and the lagoon is infinitely deep.
And there, what does he seek? All the things that he has yet to speak.

> *Speak to me,*
> *Speak to me,*
> *Speak through me.*

Ours
Is a generation
Drowning in a sea of past discoveries.
How hopeless! When it seems we are left with nothing new.
Even the starkest of headlines leave one numb to new breakthroughs.

So
We open
Old wounds
In search of better truths.
But in this blood-stained exploration
I see only strife and populist-driven damnations.

> *Speak to me,*
> *Speak to me,*
> *Speak through me.*

Now
As the artificial
Seeks to overrun the natural,
We must remember that this automation mad dash
Will strangle the spirit, if not kept in check, until all fires turn to ash.

We,
The minds,
The spirits, the souls,
Gli uomini e le donne universali.
We kindle the fires which keep us warm.
We choose the labor, we embrace the toils, we pay the tolls.
We were all born the Alchemist; purposed in turning all lead into Gold.

FIRE ABLAZE

Boil the tepidness
　　Out from your heart!
We are the antidote,
　　We are the art.
Fierce as a monsoon
　　Against metal roofs,
We are the stallions,
　　Loud in our hooves.

A hoarse-screaming, chest-beating
　　Dance around the flames.
This fire's ablaze from humanity's timber;
　　This fire's stoked by humanity's aims.
We are the tigers, we are the tulips,
　　We are the lions, we are the lilacs,
We are the senses, we are sensation,
　　We are the yearning, we are the abstract.

Across the road, across the room,
　　Across the chasm of skin and soul,
My face is pressed, 'gainst unbreakable glass,
　　In search of other souls.
I am the whole, says the I,
　　Aware of the eternal shtick.
Let the fire in my words be the spark
　　That ignites your eternal wick.

A tower, ten-thousand paces away,
　　Signals me in blazing flames.
We are alive, you and I. We are the Infinite,
　　Born and bound to simple frames.
Is this not a cause for celebration?
　　A festival each night until the end of ages?
If only, say the mystics. But this life is a theater,
　　And the darkest of curtains keep us 'ever bound to our stages.

Between the untenable void, between the spinning galaxies,
　　Between the sun and the moon,
There is us. There is I. There is You.
　　Small is our glint, rhythmic is our tune.
We are the loud. We are the quiet. We are the real.
　　Feel, in every porous sense, our true and mighty repose.
Untold, but always shown,
　　Indefatigable is the chant by which all life grows.

HER ROYAL MAJESTY

Her royal majesty
Watches me
From the height of a tower.
    Her eyes are snakish.

I spit on the grass
That is miles
From her window.
    I know she has seen it.

She lifts her chin;
So soft and lively.
Do you love her?
    No name.
    Call her no name.

Do you love her, no name?
Or crave something new?
Something bright
    And forbidden
    And exotic
    And free.

Take your eyes off
The woman in the window.
She is only a reflection of the thing
    You cannot say.

So get back to work!
Your day dreams are derivative.
And she is not flattered by fantasy
    Or words that produce no profit.

Kiss her goodbye now.
You will not see her for many years.
Goodbye, no name.
    Until I see you again.

JAZZ IN THE AIR

I

I HEAR jazz travel
Through
Cracks in the air.
Incredible and quick.
I'm possessed
By the unknowable.
It seems this
Sunday afternoon
Is cold and hollow,
Or warm and sweet;
Depending on
where you stand.
Dance!
Dance, great dancing man!
This Sunday's made for you!
Let this jazz
Hit your ears
And spark
Feeling
From the blue.
Let this music
Travel long
To the ears
Of cold and hollow souls.
Start slow:
Stiff fingers
Tap a tune—
Mister, play on
The glass trumpet.
And I'll play on
The silent bassoon.
It seems this
Invisible rhythm,
Stretches down
To the toes,
And makes us free,
Like unkempt trees,
In quiet groves …
So alive,
Alert,
Awaking,

Awoken—
This ghost town.
Remember it?
Once breathtaking,
Open and oaken,
It grew
Dry and decrepit
When we let our
True nature wither.
But winter's almost over,
And spring is bound to differ.

II

You, the icicle in flesh,
Warmed by music
Without lyric,
Enlivened by the invisible.
Unpossess yourself
From tongues
That speak only
In the abstract.
Keep on!
We're all still young.
Until the day is dark,
We've found it here—
The land with no heirach.
Unattached to opinion,
Sweet sound
And smooth rhythm.
It's all right here;
All we ever need.
It's all right here;
To be ourselves, fully freed.

III

A dream I once had,
Recounted from its echo.
A river flowed,
In roaring sound.
Blind in sight,
The world felt round.
I stood at the bank
Of the river less traveled.

Carried by boat,
I went with no paddle.
Pushed and pulled,
with no means to row,
I fell back and let
the water guide me ...
No thought,
It seemed,
Could enter my mind.
Only song, undefined,
Without place,
Without time.
Yet I understood,
The purpose there,
The magic 'midst
The sound of air.
The anything,
The everything,
Contained within,
The wellspring,
Encircling and
Worshiping,
The origins of
Fact and feeling ...
So people sing,
So people swing,
Bouncing 'round
Like coil springs.
There's something true
To nameless tunes.
I've already said
Too much
Too soon.

NATURE'S ORCHESTRA

WAKE up, the sun is bright,
The air is chilled,
And the grass here grows a morning dew.
    Stand away from the city skyline,
    Put your back to all the noise.
The birds! Do you hear the birds?
They chirp as nature's orchestra—
    A new piece in praise of the sun.
How could they do it?
    So un-self-consciously,
    So unencumbered and instinctual.
    They speak not in rhyme or verse,
But in sound,
And the sight of their silhouette blurs
That streak through the skies without a trace.
    But the fool hears one chirp out of the many,
    And strains to tune out the rest.
This symphony is not written for, or listened for, the One;
No note needs more attention than any other.

SHE IS ...

WRITE fast because she is faint.

She is the mark of water paint
Without the colored ink.
She is the smell of an evergreen forest
Hidden in the breeze.
She is the silence in the chorused quiet
In the rest's of every symphony.

She is the reflection you see
At the midnight pond
When the moon is new
And the world has gone to sleep.
She is the flower that blooms only once:
Who lives and dies without a peep.

Find her once and she hides anew.

THE HUNTER & THE DOE

I

THE hunter waits—
  Patience is a lost art,
  A gifted trait,
  A virtue too quickly out of fashion.

The forest is unpathed—
  Natural confusion,
  Unkempt for a reason,
  No one speaks here.

A big-eyed doe wanders into the clearing—
  How graceful,
  She must have forgotten her tiara.
  Admire her, then remember who you are.
The birds squawk and fly off—
  Only the man and the doe,
  The hunter and the hunted,
  They look upon each other; eye to fading eye.

II

You will honor me even when the soul has left my body?
  Aye.
You will feed your children with me, the killed?
  Aye.
You will keep some remorse in your heart, in respect of me?
  Aye.

This is true nature,
  A forest of no natural foes.
This is true nature,
  A forest of no natural paths.
This is true nature,
  A forest of no natural ambitions.

Let there be honor for the deed,
  The family must be fed.
Let there be honor for the doe,
  The doe must be hunted even so.
Let there be honor for the hunter,
  The hunter must play his role too.

THE SWAN

THE swan was right,
We all live in paradise.

I spotted her, in water, near cattails
At the bank of a crystal lake.

She was basking in the sun
Alone. I knew her all at once.

We had met before.
We'd meet again, I'm sure.

I dropped my fishing pole,
And sat close by on a grassy slope.

She bowed, head down into the opaque lake,
And came up with roots of a plant that were snaked.

I clapped, like a fool with brass hands,
She left with poise, unswayed by my praise.

In her trail, the water sliced, like silk from knife,
I sat, awestricken, would I ever float in this opaque paradise?

LAND LOCKED

I

I FEAR the ocean deeply,
I whispered to the pond,
   To my distorted reflection.

There is nothing to fear,
Something said, faint
   And in my head.

                Leave soon, the sun just rose
                  On the other side of the Earth.
              The crowd awaits a fresh new story.

On Missouri's river bank,
In a town with more history
Than potential, my cowardice is

     Revealed by the dust which
     Collects on my travel things ...

     Revealed by the worn-in grooves
     Of my daily and unchanging life ...

     Revealed by the lack of news
     I have to share with all who ...

                Leave now, the people are
                Already awaiting your return.
             Give them something to remember.

II

On flight, I catch sight of all the ant people,
And the patchwork corn fields past the city,
And the thin gray veins of the river's path.

Through the all-white clouds, in a breath
We've risen up to the bluest, birdless sky,
With the sharpest Sun I've ever seen.

Where on Earth would you like to go?
The gold-eyed pilot has come back to ask me.
I recognized her, though I could not say where from.

Surprise me, I say. We land the next day.
On the sands of a jungle, whose clouds hide its peak.
This is the island where myth meets man.

Quick-shifting trees, housing antlered monkeys;
Big, inflating butterflies float from tree-climbing octopi;
I can only explain it through analogy.

> *What proof do you have?*
> *What good is your word?*
> *What weight does this story hold?*

Perhaps you won't believe me,
This island has always been elusive.
It always hides in the place where the intellect is useless.

L'AMORE CHE NON DISTINGUE*

I

LOVE.
Love as you must,
Love as you might. Love.
Love as I see it—infinite.
Sweet on the tongue,
Light on the heart,
Modest on the mind—
... *But are you not infatuated with her?*
Infatuation is oil burned bright, brighter
Than the stars. Bright enough to
Wash away the moon. Brighter
Than all the lighthouses beamed together,
Too bright to lead a single boat to land.
Too bright for a pair of eyes to drink it in.
I say, passion is just a flash in the pan.
I could already see her before,
So clear and soft
And glowing steady,
But now there is something,

*The title translates to "The Love That Does Not Distinguish."

Outside of me,
From the mouths of the Other,
Demanding something more,
Something *something* love.
More than love—lovely love;
The loveliest love of all, which always
Speaks with a puffed out chest
And demands an ovation.
        ... But have you no poems for her?

                                Did you hear that Muse?
                        The question was asked to you.

Will these words, which are nothing I control,
Prove beyond proof that my love is true
And full-bodied
And long-lasting? Idyllic love, love
That paints a warm picture, out there—
Unfelt and seen only in
The mind's humble telescope
Pointed somewhere in the distance:

                                Two lovers,
                                Holding hands,
                                Holding gifts,
                                Saying I love you,
                        Saying I love you more,

                Somewhere at sunset
                From the pier of a quiet lake
"This water's stillness reflects your ever present beauty, my love."
                Somewhere at sunrise
                From the sands of a quiet beach,
"This water's unceasing waves reflect my unceasing love for you."
                The love of nature or the love of her?

Ten-thousand more metaphors,
        Spoken until blue in the face.
Ten-thousand more expressions,
        Spoken until hollow to the ear.

Come si dice 'l'amore egoistico'?
Something something love—Seeking proof until death do us part.

... E come si dice 'l'amore che non distingue'?
Unspeakable love—Unhaveable and unholdable.

II

This strange and unforgettable feeling,
So open and pointed and present.
Reverberations of — that recognizes —,
Mind to mind, heart to heart, soul to soul,
   A gong-feeling.
Her eyes, her smile, her face,
From your humble eyes.
Your eyes, your smile, your face,
From her humble eyes.

   In this, two sides of the coin
   Are known, and though we cannot see
   What lies on the other side,
   It is there before us; seeing us,
   Holding us, kissing us, loving us.

The love which recognizes itself,
The love which loves itself,
The love which needs no metaphor,
   The love which needs no thought at all.

BEGGAR

Your appetite deceives you, young man.

I had only asked for a crumb.
I was sat alone, praying without prayer,
Waiting for the fat hen to walk my way,
The wind kicked up dust from the dry roads,
I could hardly see a thing.

The woman, the fattest hen I had ever seen,
With jewels around her neck,
Around her fingers, around her wrists,
Dangling from her ears,
Spoke to me as her equal.
     No pity in her eyes.
     No pity for the beggar man.

In the pit of the lowest low, I thought
Dignity had left me,
I thought I could feel
No more shame.
But her words, so sharp and pointed,
Took the wind from my chest,
And marked me as a lame.

I had sought her pity,
Deep in my caved-in gut,
Deep in my withering heart, I had craved
The pity more than the coins.

Your appetite deceives you, young man.

I fell back, defeated beyond redemption.
I felt the cold cement press against my spine,
I felt the sun seeping through my eyelids,
I felt all the faces that had ever seen mine,
     All the faces that would ever see mine,
I felt the words of the fat hen,
     Echo and echo and echo again.

Your appetite deceives you, young man.

I understood it then.
Running to her, I felt strong in a way I had forgotten.
Standing before her, I felt humble in a way I had never known.

I am not hungry any longer, I told her.

She looked for truth in my eyes.
I knew not whether I had spoken a lie.

Take this bracelet of jewels, she told me.
It held fire opals with a milky hue.
Consider this a reminder, she told me,
To turn a deaf ear to the beggar in you.

JASMINE GREEN TEA

How strange—the nose,
And what smell will bring.
Memory always lingers in the air.
In a single breath we can feel the subtle sting.

What a gift! To spark the past from the now.
So that childish smells of childish things,
Brings the oddest old memories.
Of gym floors and swings.

So that roses and daisies,
Take on new meaning.
Not only from colors,
But also from feeling.

But there is also memory trapped
In what we have yet to smell.
Hold close and breath in.
There is poetry to be found in the inkwell.

And what is the soft, quiet feeling,
From the scent of jasmine tea?
A smell we knew so well;
From an old lifetime's memory.

Let all my senses fade, but leave me my smell.
For within it, I know, lies an infinite well.

BECOME WHAT YOU ARE

BEFORE and after,
Who was I?
I speak of a line cut through
    The film strip of time.

The boy, the void,
The man, the muse.
These stages of life—all fanciful divisions:
    The memories all mix like liquid ooze.

Although, through all that time,
I remained the "I",
Looking back, who'd I expect to find?
    A separate me with separate eyes?

Who am I?
Stripped of words that point the mind
To the mystic and divine,
    I am That: stripped of face and time.

The seeing eye and thinking mind,
Behind the two, there is— I cannot say.
Pale and hollow is that word divine;
    Though mythical rhyme may point the way.

Exalting language seems to make
Poetry from the easily seen,
Though the easily seen is truer than the poet's painted-on words;
    True as the colorless screen that reflects all film scenes.

It seems, in becoming what I am,
    A boy,
Petrified by the Void,
    A man,
Captivated by the Muse.

I know, unreasonably so,
I am nothing but—
The wholly—
Purely—

AFTERWORD

Reality: What a concept!

— *Robin Williams*

Having made it to the end of this book, I wish to take a moment to balance the pointed essays and poems with a spoonful of humility. I don't know. I really don't. There is a quote attributed to Socrates that is often paraphrased as "I know that I know nothing," and the longer I write, the more I see the wisdom in it.

Yet, despite a growing confidence in my utter not-knowing, I have written this book regardless. The essays read with confidence and the poems with exuberant certainty. *How could I be so hypocritical?* The thought arose in my mind more than once. In fact, such inklings of doubt of not *totally* knowing what I am writing about drove me deeper into the questions that I sought to "answer" throughout the essays.

As recently as yesterday, I was struck by how limited the thinking mind is. Not only in the contents of philosophical questions (i.e., asking, "Why is this so?" leads to a limitless chain of cause-and-effect answers that cannot have an absolute starting point), but also in the shaky relation between perception and language. Between the *actual* view and saying, "Wow, this is a beautiful view!"

I feel as though I have spent the time writing this book inside a small bubble—poking at its malleable, slippery, opaque shell in an attempt to make a hole for some light to seep in. I feel as though I've spent this time writing attempting to have my cake and eat it too: To know it all and *know* that I am the one who knows it all.

What I found, in that vainful attempt to understand who I am and *prove* it in the contents of these writings, is that the surrendered claim of "I know that I know nothing" is *it*. Not knowing is *it*. To hit the limits of what the rational mind can know (which is not a linear limit, but rather an awareness of how the thinking mind can only grasp what is in the bubble of its limitations) is the jumping off point.

In asking, "Who am I?" any verbalized answer is obviously bound to the limits of the thinking mind as well as the constructs of language. The thinking mind cannot know how it came to be: It cannot understand itself as an object. It would be like a tongue trying to taste itself or eyes trying to observe, in real time, their perception process. Thus, the craving to know what this whole thing is—reality, existence, all of it—through the filter of language and grammar is peanuts to the actual.

PEANUTS TO THE ACTUAL

I realize that most people do not give this much attention to the nature of consciousness, and from the corner of one's mental eye, it might look like a trivial pursuit. Throughout the book, I have repeatedly outlined the rebuttal that arises from the egoic mind when this realization of Self-knowledge is put into words: *What am I supposed to do with this? What's supposed to happen because I now know this information?*

Ultimately, it's not information. What has been shared in this book—or rather, what has been pointed to—is the direct experience of the formlessness that exists outside of what the mind can comprehend in the *contents* of thought. In a weak concession to language, it might be described as the Void, or Tao, or the Great Emptiness, or God, or Infinite Consciousness, or Pure Awareness, etc., though such terms are bound to be misinterpreted as either depressing or evidence of a white-bearded fellow watching from above. Anything that is said is a concession to the thinking mind. It's like using the moon to observe the light of the sun, which we cannot stare at directly: Not because it would blind us, but because we *are* the emanation of the sun!

As a visualization, imagine that this moment now—as it is being observed by the five senses (as well as all inner perceptions of emotion, thought and memory)—is a space similar to a toll booth on a highway. The majority of people would believe, in this analogy, that you, the reader who thinks "I am this and that," is in one of the cars, traveling from the past to the future, with a small, if not irritating, stop in between to "pay the toll" of the present moment. Time (i.e., the highway) appears as the fundamental thing.

The *shift* in this analogy is to identify with the entity in the toll booth.[1] The cars of the past filter through the booth and then funnel out into the future—but you remain ever-present. Even more fundamentally, it's not that you are *in* the present moment, but that you *are* the present moment. This may sound a bit absurd, but it's as if the whole highway was built for you, the observer in the toll booth. In this case, You, the Being aware of all passing cars, are the most fundamental thing.[2]

This analogy may trivialize the shift in consciousness, but at the core, it's a shift from the *illusion* of being an ever-moving car—driving away from the past and into the future—to being an ever-present observer while cars move *through* you in the present. (Cars represent passing thoughts, sense perceptions, emotions, memories, etc.).

This was expressed in "The Thinker" poem:

I see you—going around the circle 'til sickness,
Your eyes can't seem to follow the quickness,
But look forward, be still, and you will bear witness.

One's life appears stressful, overwhelming and full of threat when there is the compulsion to follow something from the past to its apparent ending in the future. The moment you "look forward," not metaphorically to the future, but literally—in this ever-present now—you can return to the stillness of allowing life situations (i.e., the cars) to pass through you.

It's important to clarify two obvious rebuttals to this paradigm shift. I have mentioned them throughout the book, but I wish to simplify the points:

---

1   This would not be a person in the traditional sense, but rather like an invisible observer, like one of those 360-degree cameras that can film everything *but* itself. That's not to say it's mechanical like a camera; it's merely an analogy. I can write about it all day, but ultimately it cannot be spoken and it must be verified by the reader's direct experience.
2   Do not confuse this with solipsism, which refers to a delusional philosophy whereby one *thinks* he is the center of everything—the dreamer of the dream—so that everyone else is merely a thought in his head. In truth, the person who thinks such a thing is just as much a piece of the supposed dream as all other external phenomena. As the joke goes, put a bunch of solipsists in a room and let them debate, "Who is the real one?"

1.   *What about time?*

By no means does this paradigm shift deny the reality of time (or the "laws" of physics, more generally). Clock time does not vanish, but it is no longer viewed as fundamental. It exists on the level of practical mental construction, alongside money and any other method of measuring the external world in small, proportional units.

The clock is one of the most practical inventions in history, but treating it as the foundation of existence creates massive amounts of suffering (e.g., measuring the present moment against the span of time to our death or to predict catastrophic events; or even measuring the amount of hours until going back to the office). It's not that people are obsessively staring at the clock all the time, but that it runs in the background as a subtle, static feeling of discontent. *I'm having a great time now, but in 10 hours I'll be miserable again at my desk job.*

At the most destructive level, when time precedes all else, one's thinking mind (as a predictive, protective machine) works against one's well-being. Thoughts of the future, as they occur in the present moment, create the illusion that a person can prepare for—and thereby defuse—a predicted-to-be negative or stressful future event before it occurs. In reality, those negative thoughts about the future impose the effects of stress on the body *now*. Even more ironic is that this form of naive rationalization—of trying to outthink the fear or stress—rarely (if ever) alters the stress experienced once the dreaded moment occurs.

I'm not saying that "being more present" is *good for your well-being*; I'm saying that the present moment is all you can ever be aware of! Thoughts of the past or the future occur *now*—always and only. The future can't be experienced except when it takes place in the present moment. When you are unconscious of this, the feeble attempts to pre-experience a negative future or re-experience a negative past create more stress in the body than it will ever dissolve.[3]

---

3   There is, of course, the person prone to anxiety who *knows* how destructive and fruitless these negative visualizations are, but can't seem to stop or control them. To that person I would say the moment you are *aware* of the negative thought-pattern spinning in the mind, turn your attention toward present-moment perceptions (e.g., focus on the breath, feel the weight of the body, etc.). Any shift of focus away from the stream of thought will allow the pattern to dissolve more quickly than trying to "get over it" with mental self-talk (which is the equivalent of fighting fire with fire).

2. *What about taking action?*

With regard to the second question, I presume it to be a common rebuttal in readers' minds against shifting one's identity from the ever-moving mode of ego to the ever-present mode of Unconditioned Awareness.

Even my own mind plays devil's advocate with a question like this. I believe it's a cultural assumption that being "spiritual," in the vague sense, means living like the hippies in the 1960s. It makes sense. What other reference do Americans have of someone "spiritual" except the flower children of that decade? People like Eckhart Tolle, author of *The Power of Now*, have begun to create a new reference of what being spiritual (or a spiritual being) can look like at a physical level. But in the age of near-infinite content, his message can reach only a small pocket of the population.

I digress. The question "What about taking action?" (as in, "Will my ambition dissolve if I have a shift in consciousness? Will I be able to set and achieve goals anymore?") is about you, the reader. From my own self-observation, a major chunk of my previous ambitions have faded because I see them as a weak guise for egoic significance.

The activities that have remained—besides the practical actions required to stay alive and maintain my current lifestyle—are actions stripped of future expectation.[4]

Writing is one such example. I write now because I enjoy it. It would be silly to expand on that. To ask, *why do I enjoy writing,* complicates what is a simple, intuitive truth. It's a knowing-feeling that requires no words. To get a bit esoteric, that feeling of enjoyment is beyond clock time: It is unconditioned by the past or future.

However, to clarify, it's not as if certain future goals I had set a long time ago don't still exist as thoughts in my mind. I would still like to write a fiction novel and be a writer-director of a feature film. I would like to live near the ocean. I would like to run a business based on teaching and online courses. These are goals that I may someday work toward, and I see no point in willfully blotting out those desires from the thinking mind. They don't carry a heavy burden on my shoulders anymore. There will not be a lifetime of regret if they are not achieved, even if regretful thoughts arise for a time.

---

4 I still get pulled into egoic thought patterns. I still have wants and desires. All I can do is accept these thoughts as they occur and return to the present moment once I realize I've been caught in an old pattern. It is easier said than done, but it is also the *only* thing to be done.

Thus, *the game of goal-achieving and creative manifestation can be played without the stakes of life or death.* When the buzzer sounds, win or lose, I remain "I." The tension felt on the way toward the achievement is self-selected, and therefore won't reach destructive, uncontrollable proportions (unless, of course, I forget who I am). It is in this way that one can be, say, a fierce activist or policymaker while maintaining a deep, underlying acceptance of the moral opposition. It's the respect a boxer has for his sparring partner in spite of the desire to, in a prime moment, knock him out cold.

THE SHIFT IN CONSCIOUSNESS

In summary, action does not need to cease because someone shifts from an ever-moving to an ever-present paradigm. What really occurs is a dropping of the actions based soley on future achievement or past conditioning. While I didn't mention the latter, it's merely the other side of the coin of action justified by the conditioning of time. (Think, the millionaire who earns her fortune because she wished to prove her parents wrong, or the student who goes to law school because his parents expected it of him).

There is, as I have alluded to, action based on enjoyment—action that can't be (and does not need to be) justified by language because it is based on an intuitive knowing-feeling. It has no relation to past or future and could therefore be called *unconditioned action.*[5] It may appear that there is the risk of hedonistic or self-destructive behaviors falling into this category. Playing devil's advocate, one might think, *Hell, I* enjoy *watching TV and drinking beer, so I can just do that all day?* It's important to follow this while being absolutely truthful and aware of the trade-offs:

> While watching TV and drinking beer can be enjoyable, we must include not merely the enjoyable part, but also everything else that occurs prior to a return to baseline. The hangover must be included. The body-ache from sitting on the couch too long must be included. The mental anguish of feeling that a greater life pur-

---

5   The neuroscientist may push back on this by saying that it is all the chemicals in the brain that drive someone to action or inaction, and those are based on input variables from the past. Yes, okay, and … ? Scientific explanation brings the actual into the confines of language, and then what?

pose is being suppressed or ignored must be included. The effects of social isolation must be included. So all that, plus the short-lived feeling of blissful drunkenness and distracting television: *Is the cycle enjoyable?*

Awareness of the cyclical effect of a certain behavior is wisdom. It allows one to distinguish a hedonistic behavior from a sustainable one, even though both may have moments that feel *pleasurable.*

I will admit that when writing, I drink a large amount of coffee. In the afternoon, when I put away the computer, it's not uncommon for a headache to arise or a feeling of sluggishness or apathy. It's part of the cycle. I am aware of it.

To clarify, when I say I *enjoy* writing, I am not equating the word with pleasure. What I'm referring to is something quite difficult to express in language. "Destiny" might be a word to embody the feeling, but specifically it is a knowing-feeling that I, as Sean Patrick Greene, (as in the collection of skills, experiences and conditioned personality traits) am a puzzle piece. In order to place myself into "the right slot on the puzzle," all I have to do is take the action that I intuitively desire to do from a state of non-attachment.[6] Already I can tell language falls short of describing it properly. It's not based on free will or a sense that life is predetermined, but spontaneous arising.

It makes it quite simple to discern conditioned action from unconditioned action.

WHY DOES IT MATTER?

Does knowing the nature of reality pay the bills? No.
What am I supposed to do with this information? Nothing.

---

6   It's important to emphasize "non-attachment" because these intuitive desires are (usually) devoid of satisfying sensory pleasures. That rules out violent or self-destructive behavior, which are always based on an ignorant attempt to satisfy one's egoic self at the expense of others (including one's future self). In simple terms, if I felt angry and punched someone, then that violent behavior is an unconscious attempt to relieve the anger—it is based in a selfish desire to dissolve the uncomfortable sensations of anger in the body. The arising of anger (from whatever scenario sparked it) *is the intuitive desire*, not the urge to punch someone. It sounds confusing unless one also uses common sense: Breaking the law for selfish purposes does *not* constitute *intuitive* desire, but merely egoic desire.

Who are you to claim to know something that's basically meaningless? No one.

I am not writing these things to sound smart or clever; only to point out what is (and always is). In this book, I have sought to show you through *your* own example just how limited and blind the rational mind can be. I did this in order to point to a spacious emptiness, which You are, which exists beyond, below or behind the illusory sense of self that is formed and conditioned by the bundle of thoughts arising in the mind.

I have some understanding that anyone set in their current foundational beliefs without any suffering arising *from* those beliefs will hardly have a reason to shift their paradigm. This book may even read like an attack on such beliefs. It's not. It's not an alternative belief system either, but rather a zooming out. I wish for this book to provide a certain level of perspective (even if it doesn't create a fundamental consciousness shift in the reader) that one's strongest held beliefs— moral, political, religious, etc.—exist in the same space, or on the same playing field, as people with opposite belief systems.

It is imperative to our evolution as human beings that we become aware of that shared space in which even the most opposite personalities and opinions can exist. This goes so much deeper than a cry for more civil political discourse; much deeper than finding one's career-based purpose in life; and much deeper than even the age-old "pursuit of happiness." This is about who you are and who I am—at a level deeper and more absolute than physical appearance, patterns of thoughts, or conditioned personality traits.

"Off with his head!" I say. Hers and yours too.

This is not a violent declaration, but a request to go under the hood; to peek behind the curtain; to look behind the smoke show of a judgmental, existentially-afraid ego (i.e., the conditioned, mind-made self) and to do so with an open, courageous heart. It can be done in this moment now—it requires only focused, alert presence.

What is there behind the thoughts? What is left? What remains?

Nothing but—
The wholly—
Purely—

NOTES

Almost all of the scientific research in the book is free to access, but not necessarily by using the "doi.org" url listed in the citations. I recommend typing the article title into a search engine and adding "pdf" to the end of the search. At least one of the top results will contain the full research article free of charge.

1. Abi-Jaoude, Elia, et al. "Smartphones, social media use and Youth Mental Health." *Canadian Medical Association Journal*, vol. 192, no. 6, 10 Feb. 2020, https://doi.org/10.1503/cmaj.190434.

2. Achter, Paul J. "McCarthyism." *Encyclopædia Britannica*, Encyclopædia Britannica, inc., 7 Nov. 2023, www.britannica.com/event/McCarthyism.

3. Belli, Brita. "National Survey: Students' Feelings about High School Are Mostly Negative." *Yale News*, Yale University, 30 Jan. 2020, news.yale.edu/2020/01/30/national-survey-students-feelings-about-high-school-are-mostly-negative.

4. *The Bhagavad Gita*. Translated by Easwaran Eknath, Nilgiri Press, 2019.

5. "Bible Gateway Passage: Matthew 7:3-5 - English Standard Version." *Bible Gateway*, biblegateway.com/passage/?-search=Matthew+7%3A3-5&version=ESV. Accessed 12 Dec. 2023.

6. Bouie, Jamelle. "How the Enlightenment Created Modern Race Thinking and Why We Should Confront It." *Slate*, Slate Magazine, 5 June 2018, slate.com/news-and-politics/2018/06/taking-the-enlightenment-seriously-requires-talking-about-race.html.

7. Bryant, Andrew, et al. "Ivermectin for prevention and treatment of COVID-19 infection: A systematic review, meta-analysis, and trial sequential analysis to inform clinical guidelines." *American Journal of Therapeutics*, vol. 28, no. 4, 21 June 2021, https://doi.org/10.1097/mjt.0000000000001402.

8. Busby, Eleanor, et al. "Mood disorders and gluten: It's not all in your mind! A systematic review with meta-analysis." *Nutrients*, vol. 10, no. 11, 8 Nov. 2018, p. 1708, https://doi.org/10.3390/nu10111708.

9. Carey, Jacqueline. "UIC Study Details How Today's High School Cliques Compare to Yesterday's." *UIC Today*, University of Illinois Chicago, 2019, today.uic.edu/uic-study-details-how-todays-high-school-cliques-compare-to-yesterdays/.

10. Carse, James P. *Finite and Infinite Games*. The Free Press, 2013.

11. "Charles Darwin Biography." *The Biography.Com Website*, A&E; Television Networks, 29 Mar. 2021, www.biography.com/scientists/charles-darwin.

12. Darcy, Oliver. "Right-Wing Media Pushed a Deworming Drug to Treat COVID-19 That the FDA Says Is Unsafe for Humans | CNN Business." *CNN*, Cable News Network, 23 Aug. 2021, www.cnn.com/2021/08/23/media/right-wing-media-ivermectin/index.html.

13. Diangelo, Robin. "Basic Tenets of Anti-Racist Education." *Robin DiAngela, PhD*, Robin DiAngelo LLC, 2016, www.robindiangelo.com/wp-content/uploads/2016/06/Anti-racism-handout-1-page-2016.pdf.

14. "Edwin Hubble Biography." *The Biography.Com Website, A&E;*, A&E; Television Networks, 20 May 2021, www. biography.com/scientists/edwin-hubble.

15. "Expanding Universe." *Encyclopædia Britannica*, Encyclopædia Britannica, inc., 2 Nov. 2023, www.britannica.com/ science/expanding-universe.

16. Foulkes, Lucy, and Jack L. Andrews. "Are mental health awareness efforts contributing to the rise in reported mental health problems? A call to test the prevalence inflation hypothesis." *New Ideas in Psychology*, vol. 69, Apr. 2023, https://doi.org/10.1016/j.newideapsych.2023.101010.

17. Friedman, Milton. *Milton Friedman Speaks: Myths That Conceal Reality*, YouTube, Uploaded by Freedom to Choose Network, 31 July 2012, https://youtu.be/xNc-xhH8kk-k?si=-ZjUILpAA72AFYQ_. Accessed 12 Dec. 2023.

18. Ghrouz, Amer K., et al. "Physical activity and sleep quality in relation to mental health among college students." *Sleep and Breathing*, vol. 23, no. 2, 26 Jan. 2019, pp. 627–634, https://doi.org/10.1007/s11325-019-01780-z.

19. Gibson-Smith, Deborah, et al. "Association of food groups with depression and anxiety disorders." *European Journal of Nutrition*, vol. 59, no. 2, 3 Apr. 2019, pp. 767–778, https:// doi.org/10.1007/s00394-019-01943-4.

20. Goodwin, Renee D., Andrea H. Weinberger, et al. "Trends in anxiety among adults in the United States, 2008–2018: Rapid increases among young adults." *Journal of Psychiatric Research*, vol. 130, 2020, pp. 441–446, https://doi. org/10.1016/j.jpsychires.2020.08.014.

While this study is based on self-reported nervousness rather than clinical diagnoses of anxiety, 40% of those in the anxious category reported seeking mental health treatment within that past year.

21. Goodwin, Renee D., Lisa C. Dierker, et al. "Trends in U.S. depression prevalence from 2015 to 2020: The widening treatment gap." *American Journal of Preventive Medicine*, vol. 63, no. 5, 2022, pp. 726–733, https://doi.org/10.1016/j.amepre.2022.05.014.

The 2020 results showed a further increase in depression rates in young people, but because the pandemic changed the survey methodology it was not mentioned in the essay.

22. Harding, Cheryl F., et al. "Mold inhalation causes innate immune activation, neural, cognitive and emotional dysfunction." *Brain, Behavior, and Immunity*, vol. 87, July 2020, pp. 218–228, https://doi.org/10.1016/j.bbi.2019.11.006.

23. Hayek, Friedrich A., and Bruce Caldwell. *The Road to Serfdom: Texts and Documents*. The University of Chicago Press, 2007.

24. Hayes, Scott M., et al. "An fmri study of episodic memory: Retrieval of object, spatial, and temporal information." *Behavioral Neuroscience*, vol. 118, no. 5, Oct. 2004, pp. 885–896, https://doi.org/10.1037/0735-7044.118.5.885.

25. Helden, Albert Van. "Galileo." *Encyclopædia Britannica*, Encyclopædia Britannica, inc., 25 Nov. 2023, www.britannica.com/biography/Galileo-Galilei.

26. Howlett, Jonathon R., et al. "Mental health consequences of traumatic brain injury." *Biological Psychiatry*, vol. 91, no. 5, 1 Mar. 2022, pp. 413–420, https://doi.org/10.1016/j.biopsych.2021.09.024.

27. Hughes, Coleman. "A Case for Color Blindness." *Ted: Ideas Worth Spreading*, TED, Apr. 2023, www.ted.com/talks/coleman_hughes_a_case_for_color_blindness.

28. "Isaac Newton's Achievements." *Encyclopædia Britannica*, Encyclopædia Britannica, inc., 23 Sept. 2020, www.britannica.com/summary/Isaac-Newtons-Achievements.

29. Jung, C. G. *The Undiscovered Self*. Signet, 2006.

30. Kravitz, Richard L., et al. "Influence of patients' requests
     for direct-to-consumer advertised antidepressants." *JAMA*,
     vol. 293, no. 16, 2005, p. 1995, https://doi.org/10.1001/
     jama.293.16.1995.

This request attempts to mimic the effect of direct-to-consumer advertising
of prescription drugs on patients. Can a patient be fully informed about the
risks, side effects and withdrawal effects from a 30-second ad?

31. Merckelbach, Harald, et al. "Misinformation increases
     symptom reporting: A test – retest study." *JRSM Short
     Reports*, vol. 2, no. 10, Oct. 2011, https://doi.org/10.1258/
     shorts.2011.011062.

32. Moeller, Julia, et al. "High school students' feelings: Discov-
     eries from a large national survey and an experience sam-
     pling study." *Learning and Instruction*, vol. 66, Apr. 2020,
     https://doi.org/10.1016/j.learninstruc.2019.101301.

33. Nuguru, Surya P, et al. "Hypothyroidism and depression:
     A narrative review." *Cureus*, 20 Aug. 2022, https://doi.
     org/10.7759/cureus.28201.

34. Pluckrose, Helen, and James Lindsay. *Cynical Theories:
     How Activist Scholarship Made Everything about Race,
     Gender, and Identity - and Why This Harms Everybody.*
     Pitchstone Publishing, 2020.

35. Riehm, Kira E., et al. "Associations between time spent
     using social media and internalizing and externalizing prob-
     lems among US youth." *JAMA Psychiatry*, vol. 76, no. 12, 1
     Dec. 2019, pp. 1266–1273, https://doi.org/10.1001/jamapsy-
     chiatry.2019.2325.

36. Schmitt, Glenn R, et al. "Demographic Differences in
     Sentencing: An Update to the 2012 Booker Report." *Unit-
     ed States Sentencing Commission*, Nov. 2017, www.ussc.
     gov/sites/default/files/pdf/research-and-publications/re-
     search-publications/2017/20171114_Demographics.pdf.

37. "Scopes Trial." *Encyclopædia Britannica*, Encyclopædia
     Britannica, inc., 19 Oct. 2023, www.britannica.com/event/
     Scopes-Trial.

38. Smith, Gregory A. "About Three-in-Ten U.S. Adults Are Now Religiously Unaffiliated." *Pew Research Center's Religion & Public Life Project*, Pew Research Center, 14 Dec. 2021, www.pewresearch.org/religion/2021/12/14/about-three-in-ten-u-s-adults-are-now-religiously-unaffiliated/.

Yes, religion is still dominant despite the statistical decline, but identifying as a certain religion does not assume one is devoutly religious. In addition to the decline in religious affiliation, the study found that only 25% of adults attended a religious service at least once a week (excluding weddings and funerals) in 2021.

39. Sowell, Thomas. *Intellectuals and Society: Revised and Enlarged Edition*. Basic Books, 2011.

40. Sowell, Thomas. *Social Justice Fallacies*. Basic Books, 2023.

41. Taleb, Nassim Nicholas.*The Black Swan: The Impact of the Highly Improbable*. Taylor and Francis, 2017.

42. Tromholt, Morten. "The Facebook Experiment: Quitting Facebook leads to higher levels of well-being." *Cyberpsychology, Behavior, and Social Networking*, vol. 19, no. 11, 11 Nov. 2016, pp. 661–666, https://doi.org/10.1089/cyber.2016.0259.

43. "United States Presidential Election Results." *Encyclopædia Britannica*, Encyclopædia Britannica, inc., 27 Aug. 2023, www.britannica.com/topic/United-States-Presidential-Election-Results-1788863.

44. Wallace, David Foster. "This Is Water." *James Clear*, 4 Nov. 2021, jamesclear.com/great-speeches/this-is-water-by-david-foster-wallace.

45. Watts, Alan. *If You Could Dream Any Dream You Wanted*, YouTube, Uploaded by Illneas, 25 Mar. 2020, https://youtu.be/abWBb1SxkXc?si=H_YFXSvSx7FX2cHt. Accessed 13 Dec. 2023.

46. Westman, Robert S. "Nicolaus Copernicus." *Encyclopædia Britannica*, Encyclopædia Britannica, inc., 11 Nov. 2023, www.britannica.com/biography/Nicolaus-Copernicus.

47. Wheeler, Jim. "Madison Grant and the dark side of the conservation movement." *The Public Historian*, vol. 45, no. 3, 2023, pp. 75–82, https://doi.org/10.1525/tph.2023.45.3.75.

48. Wong, Bonnie. "Social Media's Depression Jokes Severely Devalue and Normalize Mental Illness." *Study Breaks*, Study Breaks Magazine, 17 Feb. 2018, studybreaks.com/thoughts/depression-jokes/.

Made in the USA
Monee, IL
26 February 2024

53831967R00156